The

INNER GAME
—— *of* ——
CHESS

The
INNER GAME
—— *of* ——
CHESS

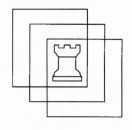

HOW TO CALCULATE AND WIN

Andrew Soltis

**DAVID M^cKAY
COMPANY, INC.**

Library of Congress Cataloging-in-Publication Data

Soltis, Andy
        The Inner game of chess: how to calculate and win / Andrew
Soltis.—1st ed.
p. cm.
Published simultaneously in Canada.
ISBN: 0-8129-2291-3
1. Chess—Psychological aspects. I Title.
GV1448.S65   1994
794.1'2—dc20   94-2784

Designed by Michael Mendelsohn of MM Design 2000, Inc.

Manufactured in the United States of America

9 8 7 6

First Edition

$\mathcal{C}$ontents

The

INNER GAME
—— *of* ——
CHESS

One

WHAT CALCULATION IS—AND ISN'T

"We think in generalities, we live in details."
—Alfred North Whitehead

L ike the rest of us, chess players think in generalities—the value of centralizing pieces, the way to exploit doubled pawns and bad bishops, the strength of a rook or knight. But they also live in the details of a game—the "if I move my bishop there, he plays knight takes pawn check" details.

Entire libraries have been devoted to teaching the generalities of chess. These books use specific examples, of course, to illustrate when files should be opened or passed pawns pushed or queens exchanged. But then, in a real game, when you have to apply several of those general principles to a very specific situation, you may find that they contradict each other. In a typical middlegame position there may be two or three solid principles recommending, say 23 Rc6, and a couple more endorsing 23 exf5, and still others that seem to urge you to play 23 Nf6+. And the *only* way to figure out which is best is to wade into the details.

Ask a master what he actually does during a game and, if truthful, he'll answer: "I calculate variations." He looks a few moves ahead and makes a judgment about the various possibilities at his disposal.

3

He knows the old saying that "Chess is 99 percent tactics," but he also knows it's inaccurate. Chess is really 99 percent *calculation*—the inner game of chess.

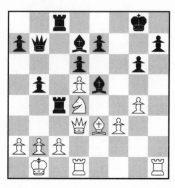

Piket–Sosonko, Dutch Championship 1993
White to play

An amateur looking at this position will recognize the basic elements: White is attacking on the kingside, Black on the queenside. There are potentially weak White pawns at f3 and d5 and Black ones at e7 and h7. White would love to occupy the holes at c6 and e6. Black is looking forward to the endgame where his two bishops and outside passed pawn (. . . h5!) will be trumps.

There is a lot to notice here. But the master notices quite a bit more than the amateur does. The master recognizes an idea for White—the attack on h7—and begins calculating variations. He sees quickly that 1 Rh2 and 2 Rdh1 is one method, but it involves the sacrifice 1 . . . Qxd5 and a Black capture on d4, with unclear results. He also sees another method of exploiting that idea, and quickly calculates the basic winning line:

1 Rxh7!!

The master knows this is what a winning combination "feels" like.

1 . . .	**Kxh7**
2 Rh1+	**Kg7**

Or 2 . . . Kg8 3 Qxg6+ and 4 Bh6+ with mate to follow.
3 Rh6!

The master will have also worked out the various side variations, such as 3 . . . Be8, 3 . . . Kf8, and 3 . . . Bf5!?, coming to a favorable conclusion after a few further moves of analysis. The actual game saw White emerge with a winning advantage after **3 . . . Rg8 4 Rxg6+ Kh7 5 Rh6+ Kg8 6 Ne6+! Bxe6 7 dxe6** and a decisive entrance of the queen.

Calculation may well be the most important skill a chess player can master. Yet more misinformation is circulated about calculating than about any other aspect of chess.

It is widely believed, for example, that you are born either with or without calculating ability, that it cannot be taught. Almost everyone agrees, furthermore, that computers calculate much better than humans. And it is stated with the utmost authority that there is one and only one correct method of counting out variations, which all masters follow rigorously.

None of these statements is true. Calculation is a skill that can be studied, learned, and sharpened. A player can calculate much more efficiently than any machine. And masters select moves and visualize and evaluate their consequences using a wide variety of methods.

We'll examine these claims in subsequent chapters, but right now let's consider a few more myths:

THE MYTH OF THE LONG VARIATIONS

A popular view among amateurs is that grandmasters are grandmasters because they routinely see 10 moves ahead. There are, of course, examples of this by GMs, but they are relatively rare.

Much more common is the kind of calculation that calls for seeing *not more than two moves* into the future. And most of the time these two-move variations lead only to minor improvements in the position. But these improvements can add up.

When Mikhail Botvinnik lost on first board during the 1955 Soviet–American match, the world champion explained the result simply: "It shows I need to perfect my play of two-move variations."

Let's see what Botvinnik meant:

Reshevsky–Botvinnik, U.S.–U.S.S.R. Match
Moscow 1955

1 d4 e6   2 c4 d5   3 Nc3 c6   4 e3 Nf6   5 Nf3 Nbd7
6 Bd3 dxc4   7 Bxc4 b5   8 Bd3 a6   9 e4 c5   10 e5
cxd4   11 Nxb5 Nxe5   12 Nxe5 axb5   13 Qf3 Qa5+
14 Ke2 Bd6   15 Qc6+ Ke7   16 Bd2 b4   17 Qxd6+!?
Kxd6   18 Nc4+ Kd7   19 Nxa5 Rxa5   20 Rhc1 Ba6
21 Bxa6 Rxa6   22 Rc4 Nd5   23 Rxd4 Rb8   24 Kd3
h5   25 Kc4 b3   26 a4 Rc6+   27 Kd3 Rc2   28 Rb1

Because it was played in the depths of the Cold War, this game drew enormous attention and the news accounts made much of White's queen sacrifice at move 17. Actually, it was just a three-move combination designed to trade down to an equal-material endgame.

What do we have now? White has a passed a-pawn, a somewhat better positioned king, and a minor piece, the bishop, with greater scope. But his pieces are temporarily tied to the defense of his second-rank pawns. Black's rooks and centralized knight should give him enough counterplay. Here, for example, Black has good winning chances with 28 . . . Rb6!, threatening 29 . . . Rd6, 30 . . . e5, and a powerful discovered check once the d4-rook moves.

       28 . . .   **Rbc8?**

Botvinnik saw 28 . . . Rb6 but talked himself out of it, thinking that 29 Rc4, threatening 30 Rxc2, was a strong reply. What he overlooked was 29 . . . Rc6! after which White's position is precarious (30 Rxc2 Rxc2 31 a5 Kc6 and White begins to run out of moves).

So Black prepares . . . Rbc8-c6-d6, stopping 29 Rc4 but costing himself a vital tempo. Black is not losing now, he's just not *winning*.

29 a5	**R8c6**
30 Ke2	**Rd6**
31 Ke1	

Now we see why the lost tempo is important. If White's pawn were still on a4, Black would be close to scoring with 31 . . . Nb6! 32 Rxd6+ Kxd6 33 a5 Nd5 followed eventually by . . . Kc5 and . . . Nb4.

31 . . .	**Nc7?**

A second miscalculation of a two-move variation. Botvinnik said he was in a rush to exchange rooks, overlooking that 31 . . . e5 32 Rd3 Nc7! reaches the same position as in the game but with an extra . . . e6-e5 thrown in (33 Rxb3 loses the d2-bishop).

32 Rxd6+	**Kxd6**
33 Bc3	

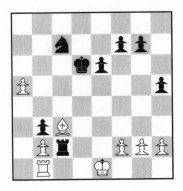

33 . . .   **f6?**

Strike three, and this one is fatal. Black wanted to play 33 . . . Nd5 but dismissed it because his g-pawn was hanging. Actually, 33 . . . Nd5 34 Bxg7 f6! should enable Black to draw easily because White's bishop is locked out and moves like 35 . . . Nf4 and 35 . . . Nd3+ are threatened. Another two-mover missed.

34 Ra1   **Na6**

No time for 34 . . . Nd5 now because of 35 a6.

35 Ra3!

And this is the fourth two-move variation the world champion overlooked. He saw that 34 Ra1 threatens to ram the a-pawn but didn't realize that 35 Ra3, winning the b-pawn, was also threatened.

The game was over as soon as Black sealed his 41st move: **35 ... Kc7 36 Rxb3 Nc5 37 Rb5 Na4 38 Bd4 e5 39 Kd1! Rc4 40 Be3 Kc6 41 Rb8 Kc7** and Black resigned this adjourned position.

Notice that the cost of each little slip by Black was minor: He didn't lose rooks or pawns but only an extra tempo (31 ... Nc7?) or a chance for improved coordination of his pieces (28 ... Rbc8? and 33 ... f6?).

"POSITIONAL PLAYERS DON'T CALCULATE"

From the last example you might conclude that positional players do nothing but calculate. Yet the image persists that strategists—such as Reshevsky and Botvinnik—choose their moves abstractly, using only general principles, while the attackers are the ones who announce "Mate in 27!"

But let's hear what a former world championship challenger has to say.

"Often a player who gravitates towards combinational solutions is automatically numbered among the calculating, logical brains," wrote David Bronstein. "In contrast," he added, "the one who is inclined towards positional play is said to possess an intuitive cast of mentality.

"Sometimes these characteristics are wrong by 180 percent, if only when one is talking about Capablanca or Tal."

By this Bronstein was suggesting that a positional-minded player could be a constant calculator—like José Capablanca. Or he could be a combinational player who relies to a great deal on intuition rather than long variations—like Mikhail Tal, another world champion. Of today's generation, we can speak of remarkable calculators as different in playing style as the "tactical" Viswanathan Anand and Alexey Shirov are from the "positional" Gata Kamsky and Boris Gelfand.

Or consider Aron Nimzovich, sometimes called the Father of Modern Chess. In his notes analyzing some of his original maneuvers, you find a remarkable number of long variations. And they are not necessarily forcing variations, as demonstrated by one of Nimzo's most famous "combinations."

Nimzovich–Marshall, New York 1927
White to play

Here White plays a move that is essentially positional but required considerable calculation. It threatens nothing but accomplishes everything.

1 Qb3!

The main benefit of this restraining move is that it sets up what Nimzovich used to call a "preventative combination." That is, he improves his chances by slightly increasing pressure on the enemy while also preventing his opponent from freeing his deteriorating position.

Black has no useful plan other than to take the d-pawn. If he tries to develop his queenside with 1 . . . Qc7 2 Rae1 Bd7, White plays 3 Bd2! and Bc3 with a considerable improvement over White's situation in the diagram (e.g., 3 . . . Re8 4 Rxe8+ Bxe8 5 Bc3 Ne4 6 Re1).

1 . . .   Rxd5

This enables Black to create a material imbalance so that he can sacrifice back the b-pawn with 2 . . . Bf5 or 2 . . . Be6. On 1 . . . Nxd5 White continues 2 Rae1, which restrains Black a bit further (2 . . . Be6 3 Bxc5! and 4 Rxe6).

2 f5!   gxf5

Or 2 . . . Bxf5 3 Bg5! and 4 Qxb7 with Black's defenses stretched over the board.

3 Bg5

And here Nimzovich's main point was that 3 . . . Be6 loses to 4 Qxb7 Rc8 5 Rae1! and Black's vulnerable e6-bishop and f6-knight will cost him material (5 . . . Qd7 6 Qxd7 Bxd7 7 Bxf6; 5 . . . Bf7 6 Bxf6 Qxf6 7 Qxc8+).

The game actually ended with a spectacular and purely "combinational" combination: **3 . . . Rd4 4 Nb6+ c4 5 Qc3 axb6 6 Qxd4 Kg7 7 Rae1 bxa5 8 Re8!! Qxe8 9 Qxf6+ Kg8 10 Bh6** and Black resigned in view of forced mate (10 . . . Qf7 11 Qd8+).

In fact, a primary use of calculation is to tactically justify a move you really would like to play for positional reasons:

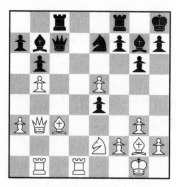

Murey–Volke, Podolsk 1991
White to play

White has no particularly forcing idea. But ask yourself this question: "If there is one piece I'd like to reposition on an ideal square, which piece and which square would it be?"

Most players would probably say, "I'd like to move my bishop to d6—but it's not legal to play 1 Bd6 here. Can I tactically justify 1 Bb4 and 2 Bd6?"

Through calculation, White can answer "Yes." After **1 Bb4!** the e-pawn is taboo (1 . . . Bxe5 2 Rbc1 Qb8 3 Bxe7 or 1 . . . Qxe5 2 Rd7 Bd5 3 Rxe7!).

So Black has to console himself with **1 . . . Rce8**. But after **2 Bd6! Qd7 3 Rbc1** White has transformed the slight positional edge in the diagram to a substantial advantage (3 . . . Qg4 4 Nd4 Bd5 5 Qb4! or 3 . . . Rc8 4 Rxc8 Rxc8 5 Qxf7).

"CALCULATION MEANS FINDING MATES AND SACRIFICES"

Most calculation is concerned with minor aspects of the game: Can I win a pawn here? What are the risks of repositioning my knight? Can I afford to trade rooks? How favorable is the approaching endgame?

When we say it is essential to calculate *major* decisions well, we don't necessarily mean combinations. A major decision may be a primarily positional one.

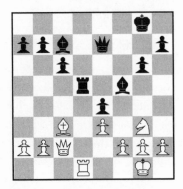

Seirawan–Tal, Montpellier 1986
Black to play

Black's active pieces, particularly his c7-bishop and rook, provide compensation for his slightly loose pawn structure and inferior bishop on f5. With 1 . . . Qd7 or 1 . . . Qd6 and then 2 Rxd5 Qxd5 he would have good chances. Instead, he decides to play for a draw:

    1 . . .   **Bxg3?**

This is a major decision because the bishop is such a strong piece. Tal concluded that after 2 hxg3 Rxd1+ 3 Qxd1 Qd7!

the invitation to an almost certainly drawn bishops-of-opposite-colors endgame could hardly be avoided; e.g., 4 Qe1 Bg4 and 5 . . . Qd1, or 4 Qb3+ Qd5 5 Qxb7 Qd1+ 6 Kh2 Qh5+ with perpetual check.

But this is all based on a faulty assumption.

    2 fxg3!   **Rxd1+**
    3 Qxd1   **Qd7**
    4 Qe1!

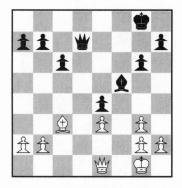

This retains queens (and winning chances) since 4 . . . Bg4 is met by 5 h3. Black finds he must now play a bishops-of-opposite-colors endgame but with the deadly addition of queens. The presence of the White queen creates severe threats to Black on the dark squares around his king and on the queenside.

This required some subtle foresight. But Tal would have seen that Black was probably lost after 2 fxg3 if he had bothered to calculate its consequences. The rest of the game saw him pay for this elementary miscalculation: **4 . . . Be6 5 b3 c5 6 h3 b5?! 7 Qf1 b4 8 Be5 Qd8 9 Qb5 Qc8 10 Kh2 Bd5 11 Bd6 a6 12 Qa5 Kf7 13 Bxc5**

Qc6   14 Qxb4   Be6   15 Bd4   h5   16 Qb8   Ke7
17 Qe5 Qd5   18 Qf6+ **resigns.**

Sometimes calculation means the simple visualization of a
plan. Instead of "I go here and he goes there and then I'll think
of something," it can be "I win by doing this, this, and that."

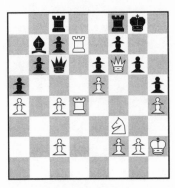

Short–Timman, Tilburg 1991
White to play

White's rooks are dominating and the Black kingside is
weak. But adding the one attacking piece that would lead to
a fast mate actually is a boomerang (1 Ng5?? Qxg2 mate).

    1 Kg3!   **Rce8**

    2 Kf4!

White had the rare opportunity in the diagram to calculate
"without an opponent"; that is, without having to concern
himself over Black's moves. He just had to visualize a winning
idea: Put the king(!) on h6 and play Qg7 mate.

In fact the game ended with:

    2 . . .   **Bc8**

    3 Kg5!   **resigns**

As we'll see, the more forceful the moves involved, the easier it usually is to calculate a series of moves. Yet even when a master uses mating ideas he is often seeking no more than a positional edge.

Polugayevsky–Wojtkiewicz, Haninge 1990
White to play

Tal once compared Lev Polugayevsky with another so-called "positional" master, Viktor Korchnoi: "Both move the pieces about feverishly, demonstrating a wide range of variations," he said. "These two are the most characteristic representatives of this class of calculators. To them, everything is very exact."

Here Polugayevsky holds a positional edge because of his rooks and excellent dark-squared bishop. But to realize an advantage he needed something concrete.

In chess, if you search you find. Polugayevsky found:

1 Bxe4	dxe4
2 Rc7!!	Rxc7
3 Qd8+	

A stunning idea, whose crucial point leads to 3 . . . Rxd8 4 Rxd8+ Kf7 5 Rf8 mate. But in its main line, which White had to consider in some detail, it leads only to a magnification of the positional plus that he held in the diagram.

3 . . .	Qe8
4 Qxc7	Bc6

The bishop is embarrassed (4 . . . Ba6 5 Rd7).

5 Rd6	Bb5
6 a4!	

And now after 6 . . . Rc8 the simplest win is 7 Qxa7.

THE JOYS OF CALCULATING

Calculation is an enormously valuable tool because it can compensate for a lot of other deficiencies. It can, for example, make up for a player's poor winning technique.

A case in point:

Barcza–Tal, Tallinn 1971

1 Nf3 g6 2 g3 Bg7 3 Bg2 d6 4 d3 e5 5 e4 Nc6
6 Nc3 Nge7 7 Be3 0-0 8 Qd2 Nd4 9 Ne2??

After this natural but tactically careless move White is lost.

9 . . .   Bh3!

Since the attacked bishop may not move (10 . . . Nxf3+!), and since castling loses the exchange to the same 10 . . . Nxf3+, White is forced into:

10 Nfxd4	Bxg2
11 Rg1	exd4!

Because this attacks the e3-bishop, Black now remains a piece ahead.

| 12 Nxd4 | c5 |
| 13 Nb5 | Bf3 |

White only has a pawn for the piece, and the rest of the game score could have been omitted with the comment "and Black won."

But what is remarkable is the way Black won. Instead of slowly exchanging off pieces and avoiding complications, Tal sought a knockout with his extra piece in the middlegame. This required a bit of enterprising calculation, particularly at move 18 below. But by making the effort, Tal insured that the game would be resignable by move 23, not 43.

14 g4	d5!
15 Bxc5	Rc8
16 Ba3	dxe4

Tal once cited the experience of another former world champion, Vassily Smyslov, in a difficult tournament, the 1967 Soviet Championship. Thanks to his general positional instincts and opening preparation, Smyslov had a clear edge in virtually every game by move 25. But by move 35 he was often lost, because he had to resolve the position by calculation, which was a problem for him.

Tal resolved his technical problems with:

| 17 dxe4 | Qb6! |
| 18 Bxe7 | Qxb5! |

19 Bxf8   Qxb2!

Black gives back much more material than he had gained. But he has calculated that even though he is down a pawn and the exchange his threats will be overwhelming.

20 Bxg7   Kxg7

21 Rc1   Rd8!

From here on the variations are short, like 22 Qxd8 Qxc1+ and Black mates.

22 Qe3   Qxc2!

And here both 23 Rxc2 Rd1 and 23 Rg3 Qd1+! 24 Rxd1 Rxd1 are mates.

23 Kf1   Rd1+

resigns

Understandable in view of 24 Rxd1 Qxd1+ 25 Qe1 Qd3+ and mates.

In this manner, Tal avoided having to play an endgame. But when you get into an ending, even a textbook one, calculation can be invaluable. It can be a substitute for "book knowledge" you never learned.

The subtle nature of endgame play often misleads improving players into believing that only memorizing a lot of similar positions—or having years of practical experience—will bring them mastery of basic endings.

Polugayevsky–Korchnoi, Candidates Match 1977
White to play

Here White makes a losing blunder just after resumption of an adjourned game. As it turned out, this virtually decided what might have been a close match leading to the world championship.

The moves White needed to find to achieve a draw were not difficult. They were based on the most elementary of endgame principles: 1 Kxf5! (eliminate as many of the enemy's pawns as possible) and then 1 . . . Rxb5 2 Ra8! (keep the rook flexibly distant from the enemy king so as to maximize the potential for checks).

After 2 Ra8! the game should have been quickly drawn—2 . . . d5 3 Ke5 and 4 Rc8+, or 2 . . . Kd4+ 3 Kf4 Rb1 4 Ra4+! Kd3 5 Ra3+ Kc4 6 Ke3.

What happened in the game is that White followed other basic principles—overlooking a simple but decisive reply.

    1 Rc8+??   **Kxb5**

    2 Kxf5

White has succeeded in eliminating one of the remaining Black pawns and, in contrast to the drawing line cited above, has pushed the Black king farther from the defense of his remaining pawn.

    2 . . .   **Re3!**

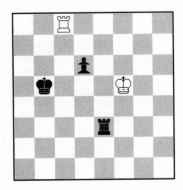

But he didn't visualize this stroke. It wasn't a matter of failing to evaluate this position correctly. As a grandmaster, Polugayevsky would know instantly that with the White king cut off from the e-file, Black can force the 400-year-old Lucena position, a simple win.

The rest of the game, although requiring many moves, took less than 20 minutes: **3 Kf4 Re1   4 Rd8 Kc5   5 Rc8+ Kd4   6 Kf3 d5   7 Kf2 Re5   8 Ra8 Kc3   9 Ra3+ Kb4   10 Ra1 d4   11 Rc1 d3   12 Rc8 d2   13 Rb8+ Kc3   14 Rc8+ Kd3   15 Rd8+ Kc2   16 Rc8+ Kd1**

White resigns (in view of the familiar "bridge-building" technique).

The point here is that Black didn't have to calculate very long to win, and White didn't have to see far to draw. White simply didn't visualize two somewhat obvious moves ahead.

LEARNING TO VISUALIZE

In the last example, White thought one minute each over 1 Rc8+ and 2 Kxf5 and then lost because he failed to visualize 2 . . . Re3. The power to consider positions that have yet to occur—and to recognize the possibilities in those positions— is essential to calculation.

Many newcomers to chess believe such visualization to be almost magical—so extraordinarily difficult that it's an ability you must be born with. Actually, it is a skill like any other chess skill.

In the pages that follow we'll consider the various components of good calculation: the selection of candidate moves, the role of force, the identification and evaluation of end-positions, and so on. But first let's do a bit of practice with our innate powers to visualize. This is an exercise to show what you are already capable of visualizing, and what you can develop into.

Let's visualize our way through an *entire game*. Don't use a chess set for the following. We are going to play through a grandmaster game in our minds.

This may sound impossible. But, with practice, it is quite within the range of most of the people who take chess seriously—provided you take your time. This will be the longest exercise in this book and should take you at least half an hour.

Piket–Anand, Amsterdam 1993

1 d4 d5   2 c4 c6   3 Nc3 Nf6   4 Nf3

Play through these moves, from a standard modern opening, in your head. Don't try to see the entire board. *Nobody* does that. By adding a move at a time to what you've already been able to see you should be able to walk through this 30-move game.

If the position isn't clear after 4 Nf3, close your eyes and ask the simple questions, beginning with: What does the pawn structure look like in the center? (Pawn structures are usually the most enduring aspects of the position, the landmarks of the middlegame.)

Only three pieces, all knights, have moved off the first rank so far and you should be able to see this position clearly.

Repeat this process after each move. Don't try to do more than a few at a time.

4 ... dxc4   5 a4 Bf5   6 e3 e6   7 Bxc4 Bb4   8 0-0 Nbd7

Now we have a change in the pawn structure. Where are the Black pawns? You should be able to see that they're all on their original squares except for three—the d-pawn has left the board and the c- and e-pawns have advanced one square. White's c-pawn is gone and his only advanced pawns are at e3, a4, and d4.

Then do the pieces. Where are the rooks? Try to see each one—they haven't moved except for White's KR, which is now at f1. Which minor pieces have been developed? You should be able to see the three White ones and the four Black ones.

Let's take another few moves.

9 Nh4 Bg6   10 h3 Bh5   11 Qb3 a5   12 f4 0-0

If necessary, refer to the last diagram. But you can train yourself to get through this entire game without it. If the position becomes blurry, it will help to try to examine a corner of the board. What does White's castled position look like? You can probably see the pawns advanced at f4 and h3 as well as the king at g1 and the rook next to it. The only piece that might escape your field of vision here is the knight at h4.

Then repeat the process for other sections of the board. Or simply review all the pieces: Where are the White rooks? His bishops? Does he still have two knights? And so on.

13 Nf3 Nb6   14 Be2 c5   15 Na2 Rc8   16 Nxb4 cxb4 17 Bd2

Which pieces have yet to move from their original squares? You should be able to see they are the a1-rook and Black's queen. And which file is open now? Yes, it's the c-file.

Even after such an unusual maneuver as . . . Bf5-g6-h5, you should be able to grasp the entire position by going piece by piece.

17 ... Ne4   18 g4 Bg6   19 Rfc1 Qd5   20 Bd1 Nc4
21 Be1 Ned6

The position is becoming more complex, with pieces crossing the fourth rank into enemy territory, and this will make visualization harder. Then again, the pawn structure hasn't changed since the 16th move and you should be able to describe it perfectly.

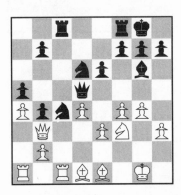

22 Be2 Rc7   23 Ne5 Rfc8   24 Nxc4 Be4!

Now the situation becomes even more difficult because of the material imbalance. What is the material situation anyway? Can you see that the knight on c4 is pinned two ways? Take some extra time for each move from now on.

25 Nxa5 Rxc1   26 Rxc1 Rxc1   27 Qxb4

Try to figure out what's left on the board. Notice: There's only one surviving rook. (The one that started at a1 has finally moved). Consider White's king position. All his pawns are advanced. And Black has some heavy wood (which?) trained on squares like g2 and h1.

27 ... g5   28 fxg5 Qxg5   29 Kf1 Qxe3   30 Qxd6 Rc2

Okay, let's do it one more time. There's still a rook left and you should know where it is. The pawn structure has changed quite a bit.

Which White pawns are left? Which Black ones? What's the material situation? Who's ahead? If you have worked out the placement of every surviving piece you should be able to see Black's threats. In fact, White resigned in this position.

This exercise should give you a good idea of how strong your visualization powers already are. If it proved too difficult, don't get discouraged. Practice with some shorter games, even with 10-move miniatures, until you can handle the longer ones.

Of course, in most situations you won't have to visualize more than three moves ahead. So let's turn our attention to what lies behind calculation: ideas that count.

Two

IDEAS

> *"The combination is born in the brain of a Chess-player. Many thoughts see the light there—true and false, strong and weak, sound and unsound. They are born, jostle one another, and one of them, transformed into a move on the board, bears away the victory over its rivals."*
>
> —*Emanuel Lasker*

Before a player can begin his calculations he needs something to calculate. It will probably come from a tactical or strategic pattern, perhaps from a particularly fortunate configuration of his pieces or weak spot in his opponent's position. In short, an idea.

Ideas inspire calculation. Without them we'd have to think like computers, searching through dozens of moves and evaluating hundreds of irrelevant positions. The absence of an idea is the most common cause of oversights. When we miss a two-move combination it's usually because we simply weren't aware of the *primary tactical idea* in the position. And usually this is because it didn't occur to us that there was one.

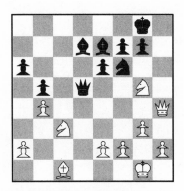

Alekhine–Euwe, Match 1937
Black to play

Here, in a world championship game, we witness a remarkable double oversight by the two best players of the day. Black moved his attacked queen with:

1 ...   Qe5??

If this position appeared in a magazine under the heading "White to play and win," most amateur tournament players would be able to find 2 Qh8+!. Certainly 99 out of 100 masters would find this elementary queen fork.

An amateur, however, might have some doubt about how good White's position is after 2 Qh8+ Kxh8 3 Nxf7+ Kh7 4 Nxe5. As we'll see in Chapter Five, it is the ability to properly *evaluate* a position at the end of a calculated sequence, rather than the ability to see 20 moves ahead, that most distinguishes the masters from the wanna-bes.

But here the amateur would surely conclude that the position after 4 Nxe5 is more favorable for White than the position in the diagram. (In fact it is close to a win.)

But there are no such magazine headings at the board when you're playing the game. So, without being aware that there was something important to find, Alexander Alekhine and Max Euwe both missed a primary tactical idea. Ideas are clues to the position and in this case, neither player had one.

2 Bb2??   Bc6??
3 a3??

And the game drifted on to a 65-move draw.

Of course, Alekhine and Euwe had other things to think about. They were thinking about general principles such as: Maximize the mobility of the minor pieces, centralize the queen, set priorities for the endgame, and so on. They weren't in the market for an idea as simple as a two-move combination.

More embarrassing was the following—another series of double oversights in which neither side realizes how close White is to mate. It ends when Black virtually forces White to see the mating idea.

Hort–Portisch, Madrid 1973
White to play

With plenty of time left on the grandmasters' clocks, there followed:

1 Qg5+?	Kh8
2 Qf6+	Kg8
3 Rfb1?	

Twice White has missed a forced checkmate (1 Rg4+! or, later, 3 Rg4+!).

| 3 ... | a5?? |

So Black, equally oblivious of the idea, directs his opponent's attention to the b4-rook, a piece White hasn't been thinking much about for the last few moves. Let's see, White asks himself, the rook is attacked: Where can I go with it?

4 Rg4+!	fxg4
5 Qg5+!	Kh8
6 Qh6	resigns

Because mate can be stopped on f8 or h7, but not both.

The first task of the calculator, then, is to be aware of the *possibility* of tactical ideas in the position he holds. Combinations like this are the simplest of all sequences to calculate because they are forcing (two of the three key moves were checks) and their final positions are the most clearcut to evaluate (it's mate). But the point to remember is that combinations are not invented, they are merely discovered.

Of course, not every position yields a combination. In most positions you can calculate only in the most general manner, usually only a move or two into the future. But because of the power of tactical ideas you must be able to recognize them quickly: pins, checks, double attacks, skewers, unprotected pieces, vulnerable last ranks, you name it.

Tactical ideas can arise suddenly:

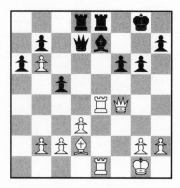

Larsen–Bednarski, Havana 1967
Black to play

Black faces some discomfort because of the doubled enemy rooks along the e-file. He would like to swap heavy pieces with a move such as 1 . . . Bf8. But a bit of calculation tells him that after the final recapture (3 . . . Qxe8) his f-pawn would be unprotected. Therefore, Black inserts a move which he believes will gain time (by attacking the e4-rook) and place the f-pawn on a safer square in preparation for the desirable 2 . . . Bf8.

1 . . .   f5?

Most ideas are hard to verbalize, but easier to visualize. When White saw 1 . . . f5 he may have been thinking, logically, "My rook is attacked, I must move it. Where can it go so that it attacks something?" But White's eyes are telling him something else: "Hmmm, aren't there an awful lot of vacant squares around his king, especially leading in along the long diagonals?"

Once the tactical idea is recognized ("Exploit those diagonals!"), the calculation process is streamlined. White looks for immediate methods of landing his queen on one of the key diagonals. He might start by considering 2 R4e2, with a threat of 3 Qc4+ and 4 Bc3+. But this packs no punch since Black has a free hand to defend with 2 . . . Bf6 and 3 . . . Kg7!.

This exercise leads White to examine a method of stopping the 2 . . . Bf6 defense, and he therefore turns his attention to 2 Re6. But another look at the position shows him that 2 Re6 Bf8 3 Qc4 is resolved unsatisfactorily for him by 3 . . . Rxe6 4 Rxe6 Qf7!.

So there is no obvious way of cashing in on the diagonals. But White can't get over how porous the Black king position is. As an experienced player he knows that positions like this often generate explosive sequences, and that such opportunities arise and disappear quickly. And this leads him to look for a more complicated (i.e., more forceful, riskier) sequence. And he finds it.

2 Bc3!!

It is natural to admire White's ability to work out a 15-move winning combination. It is all the more admirable because it leads not to a mate but to an endgame—a final position that must be correctly evaluated. *Yet for the experienced tournament player the counting out of variations, even 15-movers, is not as crucial to his success as finding the tactical ideas to begin with.*

2 . . .   fxe4

Black can keep the White queen off the dark-square diagonal with 2 . . . Bf8, but that permits 3 Rxe8 Rxe8 4 Qc4+!—exploit those diagonals!—and 5 Rxe8.

3 Qe5   Bf8

The bishop has to move to permit Black's queen to cover g7. Of no help is 3 . . . Bf6 4 Qxf6 because 5 Qh8+ cannot be stopped.

4	Qh8+	Kf7
5	Rf1+	Qf5

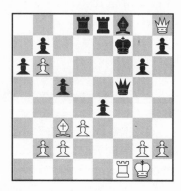

The alternative is 5 . . . Ke6 6 Qe5 mate. Notice that Black has had virtually no choice so far (it didn't really matter where he moved his bishop at move 3). Thus White did not have to juggle several different positions in his head. If White saw as far as 5 . . . Qf5 he knew he would win back his sacrificed material with interest. This may be a 15-move combination, but White had to see only the first four moves to feel confident about playing 2 Bc3!!.

The game continued **6 Rxf5+ gxf5 7 Qf6+ Kg8 8 Qg5+ Kf7 9 Qxf5+** (Why not pick off another one before forcing the king out into the open again?) **9 . . . Kg8 10 Qg5+ Kf7 11 Qf6+ Kg8 12 Qh8+ Kf7 13 Qxh7+ Ke6 14 Qxe4+ Kd6 15 Qxb7** and White won directly.

Few combinations are provoked in the manner of the last two examples. More often an opportunity arises because a player notices some subtle idea, such as an overworked or unprotected piece well inside the enemy ranks:

Timman–Short, Candidates Match 1993
Black to play

White has just moved a rook from d1 to d4, when it was better to put the knight on that square.

Black's position is somewhat freer but there doesn't seem to be anything immediate that he can do about it. Yet if we ask simple questions we can sometimes break down a complex position into its elements. A beginner's question here would be: Which enemy pieces are unprotected?

Once Black realizes that the c2-rook is not covered, he can begin figuring out ways to attack it, such as:

1 ...	Rxf3!
2 gxf3	Qg6+

The queen is now lined up against the rook (3 Kh1 Ng3+ 4 fxg3 Qxc2 with advantage, or 3 Kh2 Ng5! 4 Qd1 Nxf3+ 5 Qxf3 Qxc2). Black now has a draw, if that's what he wants. After **3 Bg2 Ng5! 4 Rc1** he repeated the position **(4 ...**

Nxf3+ 5 Kf1 Nh2+ 6 Kg1 Nf3+ 7 Kf1) but then clarified matters and clinched victory soon after **7 . . . Nxd4**.

Sometimes you have to visualize the simplest situations of the board, mentally stripping away all but two or three key pieces, in order to "get it."

Bielczyk–Slabek, Katowice 1992

1 e4 d5	2 exd5 Nf6	3 d4 Nxd5	4 c4 Nb6

1 e4 d5 2 exd5 Nf6 3 d4 Nxd5 4 c4 Nb6
5 Nc3 e5 6 d5 c6 7 Nf3 Bb4 8 Be3 cxd5 9 c5!
d4 10 Nxe5 dxc3 11 Qxd8+ Kxd8 12 0-0-0+ Ke7
13 cxb6 axb6 14 Bc4! cxb2+ 15 Kxb2 Ba3+
16 Ka1 f6

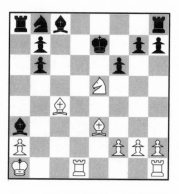

This looks like a complicated position. But it isn't. Strip away two pieces and the game is almost instantly over. Which pieces, you ask?

```
17 Ng6+!        hxg6
18 Bc5+!
```

With these two pieces gone, White's h1-rook will all but deliver mate on e1. After **18 ... Bxc5 19 Rhe1+** White mates on d8 after 19 . . . Kf8. The game actually ended with **19 ... Be6 20 Rxe6+ resigns**, in view of 20 . . . Kf7 21 Re2+.

These last diagrams offer graphic examples of rather simple tactical ideas—open diagonals, an unprotected rook, a vulnerable king in the center of the board. But on the other extreme, the "idea" often is something amorphous and difficult to quantify. It may have to do with indefinable feelings about the position. Consider this early game by Garry Kasparov:

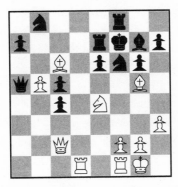

Kasparov–Lutikov, Minsk 1978
White to play

Black has managed to bring his king to relative safety and connect most of his pieces through mutual lines of support. White should be able to regain the two pawns he sacrificed earlier, but the time it takes to do that may enable Black to make his position whole again.

Yet here Kasparov makes a revealing comment. While searching the position for clues, "I suddenly noticed something wrong with the development of Black's rooks."

It is hard to imagine a computer using a concept as vague as "something wrong." But it led Kasparov to find the correct move, **1 Bf4!**. That threatens the 2 Bd6 skewer and exploits the absence of safe squares along the seventh rank for Black's e7–rook.

True, 1 Bf4 does not win by force as 2 Bc3 did in the Larsen–Bednarski example a few pages ago. But after the resulting **1 ...Nxc6 2 bxc6 Ne8 3 Rd7! Rxd7 4 cxd7 Nf6 5 Nd6+** Black's position was perceptibly unraveling. Although he managed to keep the game going for another 20 moves, the situation was beyond redemption after **5 ...Ke7 6 Nxc4 Qa6 7 Bd6+ Kxd7 8 Bxf8 Bxf8 9 Qd3+ Ke7 10 Rd1 Nd5 11 Qe4 Kf7 12 Ne5+ Kg8 13 Nd7** and so on.

As an exercise we'll offer this game:

Fischer–Ciocaltea, Varna 1962

1 e4 e5 2 Nf3 Nc6 3 Bb5 a6 4 Ba4 d6 5 c3 Bd7 6 d4 Nge7 7 Bb3 h6 8 Qe2 Ng6 9 Qc4 Qf6 10 d5 b5 11 Qe2 Na5 12 Bd1 Be7 13 g3 0-0 14 h4 Rfc8?

White noticed something funny about this position. What is it? The solution is at the end of the chapter.

Sometimes your opponent's position suggests an idea to you even though at first it doesn't appear that you have the pieces to exploit it. One example, by Kasparov's predecessor as world champion, illustrates this.

Karpov–Yusupov, Moscow 1983
White to play

Black has active pieces and enemy weaknesses on the light squares as compensation for his pawn minus. But something occurs to White: Black's knight has no moves. How do I go about exploiting that, he asks himself.

1 Kg3!

It requires nerves and good calculating ability to go piece-hunting this way. But here it is the fastest means of eliminating Black's counterplay.

The hard part of this was visualizing the game continuation: **1 ... fxg4 2 Kxh4 gxh3** (stopping the king from retreating the way it came) **3 f4 Qe6 4 Qh5 Qe7+ 5 Kxh3 Qf7** and now **6 Rh2!!** ended the threat of 6 ... Rg3+ and with it the game: **6 ... Qd7+ 7 f5 resigns**. But the easy part was coming up with the idea of Kg3xh4.

Sometimes ideas occur to you not because of obvious enemy weakness but because of the preponderance of your own fire power. If you ask yourself to find the weakest point in Black's armor in the next diagram, it is unlikely that you'll think first of f6 or g7. They seem very secure.

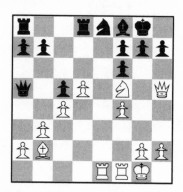

Khalifman–Seirawan, Wijk aan Zee 1991
White to play

Perhaps, you wonder, you should take aim at a more vulnerable point like f7, with 1 Ne7+ Bxe7 2 Rxe7.

But the most important feature in this position is simply that White has five excellent pieces available for attack. Even against an apparently solid kingside like Black's there are possibilities of a tactical breakthrough.

1 Rxe8!	Rxe8
2 Nh6+!	

Not particularly hard to find (2 ... Kh8 3 Qxf7 gxh6 4 Bxf6+ or 3 ... Be7 4 Qg8+! Rxg8 5 Nf7 mate). But most players would not have looked for such a combination if the idea hadn't occurred to them that White has so *many* attackers.

2 ...	gxh6
3 Qg4+	resigns

While we are focusing in these first pages on the creation of forcing lines that give us an advantage, we also must be aware of the flip side—anticipating your opponent's ideas and sequences. We'll call this *defensive* calculation.

This is a more difficult skill than you might think. Just because you're a great attacking player doesn't mean you won't overlook the simplest of tactics when the game turns against you.

Tal–Petrosian, Curaçao 1962
White to play

Here, Mikhail Tal, then the world's foremost calculator, was trying to defend his weak queenside and to reduce the scope of the terrible enemy bishops. He reasoned that the best way of protecting the queenside pawns as well as to meet the possibility of 1 . . . Bxf3 2 Qxf3 d3, attacking his a1-rook, was with:

1 Ra2??

Certainly if Tal had been sitting on the other side of the board he would have instantly spotted what's wrong with this move. But he wasn't.

1 . . .   Rxc4!

And White resigned in view of 2 Qxc4 Bd5, skewering queen and rook. Being able to anticipate enemy tactics like this is the hallmark of a great positional player.

MASTER VS. NOVICE

Throughout this book we will investigate why masters calculate better than novices. Most people who don't play chess—and many who do—believe the greatest difference lies in how far ahead a player can see. "The master can see 10 moves ahead, the amateur maybe only two," is a common attitude.

But a noted study by Adrianus de Groot, a Dutch psychologist and chess master, found that a key element is the master's ability to recognize patterns of pieces. A master can quickly memorize the placement of pieces in a particular position, breaking down the board into four or five chunks. Each chunk will have features that he remembers from other games and other positions. (We're talking about "normal" positions here. Masters show no superiority whatsoever in memorizing bizarre, problemlike positions. Such positions have no rational order, no "meaning" to them.)

Many familiar chunks, each having as few as five to as many as 16 squares, can be said to be "tactically neutral." Nothing much is happening in them. A typical example is a normal fianchettoed king position: king at g1, bishop at g2, knight at f3, and pawns at h2, g3, and f2.

But many chunks do have tactical ideas inherent in them, ideas that masters recognize much faster than amateurs. This is particularly true of weaknesses in an opponent's camp.

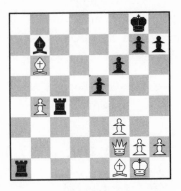

Pahtz–Fernandes, Albena 1989
White to play

An amateur might first note the balance of material on the board or whether one player is in check. A master, however, might be drawn to other features, particularly the diagonal leading to Black's king. As White, he immediately begins thinking of getting a checking piece—a bishop or queen—somewhere between a2 and e6. A pity, he thinks, that my bishop is pinned.

An amateur might miss that idea entirely. Or he might give up on exploiting it after a brief search of ways to unpin the bishop. But the master will be so struck by that long light-squared diagonal he will probably search and search until he finds the winning move. It's **1 Qa2!!** and once you spot it, the position seems easy.

According to De Groot and others, masters assimilate many more chunks than nonmasters; some claim that masters have 50,000-plus patterns in their heads.

How can you build up your storage of chunks? One obvious method is to play over many tactical games. David Bronstein, among other grandmasters, has suggested that most combinations are inspired by previous games that the calculator recalls. Some tactical themes, made famous by ancient brilliancies, are so familiar to modern masters that even a spectacular example like the following can be reduced to a matter of routine.

Kuzmin–Sveshnikov, Soviet Championship
Moscow 1973

1 e4 c5   2 Nf3 e6   3 d4 cxd4   4 Nxd4 Nc6   5 Nc3 a6   6 Be2 Qc7   7 0-0 Nf6   8 Be3 Bb4   9 Nxc6 bxc6   10 Na4 0-0   11 c4 Bd6   12 f4 Nxe4   13 c5 Be7   14 Bd3 Nf6   15 Bd4 Nd5?

A typical modern gambit has given White excellent piece activity and Black some obvious weaknesses. That in itself suggests a general notion: White should attack the enemy king position. And Black's last move, aimed at stopping

Nb6, should be a bright green light to White. It removes the only piece directly committed to the defense of Black's king.

From that general notion comes a specific tactical idea, the double-bishop sacrifice.

16 Nb6!	Nxb6?
17 Bxh7+	Kxh7
18 Qh5+	Kg8
19 Bxg7!	Kxg7

The Black kingside has lost virtually all natural protection and the game ended immediately: **20 Qg4+ Kh7   21 Rf3 Bxc5+   22 Kh1 resigns**.

If this is the first time you've seen such a combination, five forcing and sparkling moves long, it seems a work of genius. Actually it is merely a matter of good calculating technique. Some themes are so well-worn they may eventually be catalogued by numbers and letters like openings. This is one such theme, made famous by the following game.

Lasker–Bauer, Amsterdam 1889

1 f4 d5   2 e3 Nf6   3 b3 e6   4 Bb2 Be7   5 Bd3 b6
6 Nf3 Bb7   7 Nc3 Nbd7   8 0-0 0-0   9 Ne2 c5
10 Ng3 Qc7   11 Ne5 Nxe5   12 Bxe5 Qc6   13 Qe2
a6   14 Nh5 Nxh5

And now the same basic idea—**15 Bxh7+! Kxh7 16 Qxh5+ Kg8   17 Bxg7! Kxg7**—clears away the protective pawns for the heavy pieces: **18 Qg4+ Kh7   19 Rf3 e5 20 Rh3+ Qh6   21 Rxh6+ Kxh6   22 Qd7!**.

As we can see, the 1889 game was even more sophisticated than its 1973 imitator. In the modern game Black had no method of stopping mate. In 1889 Black did, and White had to foresee this final move of the combination (22 Qd7), winning more material, before he went into the sacrificial line. The rest is a mop-up: **22 ... Bf6   23 Qxb7 Kg7   24 Rf1 Rab8 25 Qd7 Rfd8   26 Qg4+ Kf8   27 fxe5 Bg7   28 e6 Rb7 29 Qg6 f6   30 Rxf6+ Bxf6   31 Qxf6+** and White won.

In fact, when Siegbert Tarrasch managed to play yet another version of the two-bishop sacrifice at St. Petersburg 1914, he failed to win the first brilliancy prize because the judges believed he was merely reworking the by-then-familiar idea of Lasker–Bauer. And the moves of Kuzmin–Sveshnikov were repeated *exactly* in another game, Barsegian–Garafutdinov, Tashkent 1989, until the very end when Black played 21 ... Bxc5+ 22 Kh1 Qxf4 23 Rxf4 f5 24 Qg5 before resigning.

As Tal once put it, to win a game you don't have to invent the bicycle. Great players do have great imaginations and that helps them play great combinations. But you are not required to invent anything to be able to calculate well. What you do need to do is *recognize*.

You should, for example, be able to recognize a more veiled and complex version of a single idea in the next three games, separated from one another by more than 75 years.

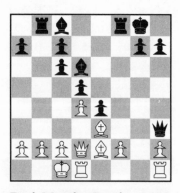

Bird–Morphy, London 1858
Black to play

Black has an extra pawn, and it appears that all the action is on the open kingside. But White is actually more vulnerable on the other side of the board, where he has fewer defenders.

Bogolyubov–Mieses, Baden Baden 1925
White to play

The pawn structure seems to deny the possibility of a sharp combination. And how can White's queen far off on a6 have anything to do with the rest of his pieces?

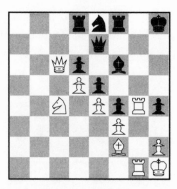

Lilienthal–Kan, Moscow 1935
White to play

One more White piece must be added to the kingside to break through. Which one?

The three positions seem to have nothing in common. But a careful study will reveal a similar idea: the offer of one or two pieces and the sweep of the queen laterally along the sixth rank and into the camp of the enemy king.

In the first example, Paul Morphy accomplished this with **1 ... Rxf2!   2 Bxf2 Qa3!**. The queen threatens mate, and since taking it allows mate in one (3 bxa3 Bxa3 mate), Black was able to capture next move on b2 or a2 with a powerful attack that eventually won.

In the second example, White forced a favorable liquidation with **1 Bxd5! exd5   2 Rxg7+! Kxg7   3 Qf6+ Kg8 4 Rg1+**. After **4 ... Qg4   5 Rxg4+ fxg4   6 f5!** and **7 e6** White emerged with a winning endgame.

And in the final example, the first step, **1 Bxh4!** set the table for the second: **1 ... Bxh4   2 Nxe5!**, with a further threat of 3 Ng6+. In this instance, the queen-sweep is confined to a footnote (if 2 . . . dxe5, then 3 Qh6+ and mate next), but it is still essential to the sequence.

Once you recognize such an idea it is your job to figure out whether, in fact, it works in the particular situation at hand. Calculating is not just a matter of playing moves that have been played before in similar positions.

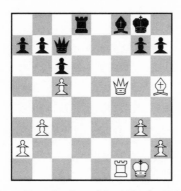

Reti–Bogolyubov, New York 1924
White to play

This position, from a brilliancy prize game, is familiar to every master. White wants to exploit the vulnerability of the enemy's last rank but only **1 Bf7+ Kh8 2 Be8!!** does it.

There is a danger of being carried away by ideas. Five years after the Reti game, one of the Czech master's rivals saw an opportunity to win another brilliancy prize with a Reti-like finish.

Saemisch–Vidmar, Karlsbad 1929
White to play

White can win simply and effortlessly with 1 Rxe7, and if
1 . . . Rd1+, then 2 Bf1. But he saw the chance for immortality and played:

1	Qxe7??		Qxc2
2	Be6+		Kh8
3	Bd5		

Very nice. By cutting the communication between the enemy rooks with that Reti-like bishop move, White threatens
a last-rank mate (4 Qe8+) as well as 4 Qxd8+.

3	. . .		h5??
4	Qxd8+		

And White was winning. But he shouldn't have been. If
Black had seen 3 . . . Rg8! he might have turned the tables.
Then 4 Bxg8 Rd2! threatens mate in three beginning with 5
. . . Rg2+ and forces 5 Qh4 Qc5+ 6 Kh1 Kxg8! when Black is
simply a pawn ahead.

There is a further irony to this ill-fated brilliancy. After
4 Qxd8+ Kh7 White could have won with either of the two

checks on g8. But instead he played the attractive **5 Be4+??**
and had to agree to a draw after **5 ... Qxe4!**. A classic example of bad calculation by both players.

LOOKING FOR THE WEAKNESS

A noted authority on composed endgames, C. M. Bent, once
explained that studies are created in two ways, one "warm and
spontaneous," the other "cold and efficient." The first is a matter of random exploration: A composer juggles the pieces,
adding and subtracting them on a board, until something occurs to him. In the latter method, which he called the scientific, the composer begins with an idea, often even away from
a board.

Competitive players don't have the luxury of random
exploration. And ideas don't often suggest themselves as
in Bent's "scientific" approach. But like a scientist, the
player can ask the right questions to make inspiration
easier.

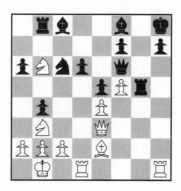

Short–Karpov, Match 1992
Black to play

To prevent Nd5, Black played:

| 1 ... | Ne7 |

Improving players know enough to ask themselves such questions as, "What does he threaten now?" and "What did he protect with his last move?" But they don't always ask, "What did he just leave *unprotected*?" You'll be surprised how often that question gives you an idea.

Here no ideas readily suggest themselves. But there is something a bit confused and uncoordinated about Black's position. What is it?

| 2 Nxc8? | Rxc8 |
| 3 Bxa6 | Rd8 |

And life went on. But had White spotted the problem with Black's heavy pieces he would surely have found the simple 2 Bxa6!, which would have won quickly (2 . . . Bxa6 3 Nd7).

Sometimes a weakness is well concealed. For example, would you detect the vulnerability of f8 in the diagram opposite?

White's position looks as fragile as Black's because his intended 1 Rxe7 is met by 1 . . . Rxc3, and if 2 Qxc3?? he's mated on f1. But a good calculator learns not to give up too early on a move he wants to play. As the Hungarian grandmaster Zoltan Ribli said, usually the first move you look at turns out to be the best.

| 1 Rxe7 | Rxc3 |
| 2 Qxf7+! | |

And Black was mated on his last rank, specifically on f8 (2 . . . Rxf7 3 Re8+).

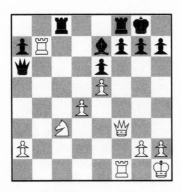

Lee–Sakharov, World Junior Championship 1963
White to play

PATTERNS

As you play over master games you will notice patterns, both tactical and strategic. A strategic pattern might be a favorable pawn structure or a thematic knight maneuver. A typical tactical pattern would be a formula for checkmate.

For example: A White bishop on c4 and rook on h1 facing a Black king on h8 and pawn on g7.

The basic elements here are the bishop's control of the g8-square, cutting off the king's escape, and the check by the rook along the h-file. There are minor variations on this theme. For example, the checking piece can be a queen, not a rook; and Black can be denied g8 because of a pawn (on f7) or a knight (on e7 or f6) instead of a bishop along the diagonal.

Once you become acquainted with this mate pattern you will find it easier to recognize when it's hidden in a position.

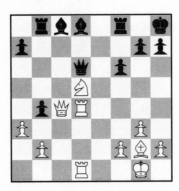

White to play

We can find the winning combination here in a variety of ways. We may recall similar past combinations. Or we could reason this way: Where is Black most vulnerable? Along the d-file, especially on d8, where there are latent last-rank weaknesses (1 N-moves Qc7 2 Rxd8! Rxd8 3 Qxc7 or 1 . . . Qe6 2 Rxd8! Qxc4 3 Rxf8+).

But there is also the glimmer of a weakness at h7, which has no defenders except the king, yet can be attacked by rooks, a queen, and a bishop.

Finally, however, there is the mating pattern we mentioned earlier. If we are familiar with such patterns, we should be able to find some way of reaching one of them. And then we find:

1 Nf4!   **resigns**

Because no matter where the queen retreats, it will allow 2 Ng6+! hxg6 3 Rh4 mate.

Once you recognize the basic elements of such a pattern, the addition of several irrelevant and distracting factors should not prevent you from identifying the winning idea. You should, for example, be able to see the same pattern in the following. The solution is at the end of the chapter.

Kaiszauri–Sznapik, Poland 1970
White to play

There are several basic mating patterns to be learned, including such elementary devices as Philidor's Legacy (the familiar combination that leads to a smothered mate) and last-rank mates with rooks and queens. Playing over master games is the easiest way to find and recognize them.

HINTS

Besides mating patterns a position will contain other hints. They include: (1) vulnerable (unprotected or otherwise exploitable) pieces, (2) "stretched" pieces, and (3) invasion squares.

(1) Vulnerable Pieces

Most calculated sequences involve, at least in part, the exploitation of hanging pieces. The more enemy pieces that are unprotected, the greater the chances that you can calculate something favorable.

Even in the early stages of a game, when few pieces venture beyond the fourth rank, those that do run a risk.

Portisch–Karpov, Moscow 1977

1 Nf3 Nf6   2 g3 b6   3 Bg2 Bb7   4 0-0 e6   5 d3 d5
6 Nbd2 Nbd7   7 Re1 Bc5   8 c4 0-0   9 cxd5 exd5
10 Nb3 Bb4   11 Bd2 a5   12 Nbd4 Re8   13 Rc1 c5
14 Nf5 Nf8   15 d4 Ne4

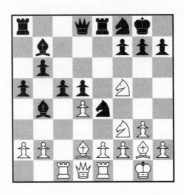

16 dxc5?

White assumes Black will now recapture on c5 to maintain material equality. He also assumes Black will not exchange off his well-placed knight on e4.

We'll explore the role of faulty assumption in Chapter Seven. Here the main reason Black forces a win is that White has one piece hanging at f5 and another that will soon be unprotected.

16 ...   Nxd2!
17 Nxd2   Qg5!

Even if White could safely retreat his knight to e3 he would stand poorly from a positional point of view. But it's worse for him from a tactical viewpoint since 18 Ne3 allows 18 . . . Rxe3! 19 fxe3 Qxe3+ and 20 . . . Bxd2 with a substantial material edge.

The game actually continued **18 Nd6 Bxd2 19 Nxb7** Bxc1 and White soon resigned.

Pieces need not be entirely unprotected to be exploitable—
just vulnerable, perhaps simply placed on high-risk squares.

Korchnoi–Balashov, Moscow 1971

1 d4 Nf6   2 c4 g6   3 Nc3 Bg7   4 e4 d6   5 f3 e5
6 Nge2 c6   7 Bg5 Qa5   8 Qd2 Nbd7   9 d5 cxd5
10 cxd5 h6   11 Be3 a6   12 Ng3 h5   13 Bd3 Nh7
14 0-0 0-0   15 a4 Nc5?

The first thing White notices after Black's last move may
depend on how optimistic or aggressive he is. A cautious player
will see the knight threatening 16 ... Nb3, forking heavy
pieces. He'll then notice that if he safeguards b3 with 16 Bc2
or 16 Ra3, Black can take greater control of queenside squares
with 16 ... Qb4.

But after he examines those positions for a bit, an idea occurs to him: The Black queen could get itself trapped after, say,
16 Bc2 Qb4 and now 17 a5. And once he gets that idea he
tries to find something more forceful than 16 Bc2.

On the other hand, a more aggressive player will immediately focus not on the ... Nb3 knight fork, but on the other
fork in the position, 16 b4. That gives him the idea, and all he
has to work out is a way of handling 16 ... Qxb4.

Both players may find the winning sequences but they'll
come about it in a different way. "Mr. Cautious" works on protecting against and then exploiting the queen. "Mr. Aggressive" focuses first on the b4-fork.

16 b4!   Qxb4
17 a5!

Now 18 Rfb1, trapping the queen, is threatened. Black can
interpolate 17 ... Nxd3 but after 18 Qxd3 the Black queen

still has no escape route. And the fork 17 . . . Nb3 no longer works because of 18 Qb2, followed by winning the pinned knight (19 Ra4).

In the game, Black actually tried **17 . . . Bh6?!** but resigned soon after **18 Bxh6** because of **18 . . . Qd4+ 19 Kh1 Qxd3 20 Qxd3** and **21 Bxf8.**

Often a strong player will walk straight into his opponent's crushing combination. "Didn't you see that coming?" he'll be asked afterwards. And he'll reply, "No, I saw his other threat but not the one he played."

This is what happens when we confuse variations with ideas. We see how an opponent can exploit a particular feature of the position, a pin or a double attack. But instead of countering the *idea* by getting out of the pin or protecting a potentially attacked piece, we convince ourselves that all we have to do is deal with one specific *variation*.

Sometimes that is sufficient. Other times it's not:

Ljubojevic–Stein, Las Palmas 1973

**1 b3 e5   2 Bb2 d6   3 e3 Nf6   4 c4 g6   5 d4 Bg7
6 Nf3 exd4   7 Qxd4 0-0   8 Nc3 Nbd7   9 Be2 Nc5**

The idea Black is trying to work with is the vulnerability of the White queen and, behind it, the c3-knight. The queen stands on a square that can be threatened by the fianchettoed bishop after any move of Black's f6-knight. After his last move, Black has the specific threat of 10 . . . Nfe4, and after the queen escapes to d1 or d5, White loses the knight.

10 Rd1?

White, an excellent calculator, disdained the precautionary 10 Qd2 in favor of the text, which allows him to meet the most dangerous-looking reply with a fine queen sacrifice (10 . . . Nfe4 11 Qxg7+! Kxg7 12 Nxe4+ f6 13 Nxc5 and if 13 . . . dxc5? then 14 Rxd8).

10 . . .   Ng4!

This wins because the queen has no safe square. After 11 Qf4 or 11 Qd5, it is too far away from the knight (11 Qf4 f5!

and 12 . . . Ne4!, or 11 Qd5 c6 12 Qxd6 Qxd6 13 Rxd6 Bxc3+ 14 Bxc3 Ne4).

11 Qd2   Nxf2!

And White is lost. The exploitation of the c3-knight is realized in the key variation 12 Kxf2 Bxc3! and 13 . . . Ne4+. The game actually continued **12 0-0(!) Nxd1** and White found a convenient spot in the middlegame to resign.

(2) "Stretched" Pieces

Related to unprotected pieces are ones we can call "stretched." These are pieces that are being overused—they are performing more functions than they are capable of. Knowing how to recognize such pieces sometimes requires a fine tactical nose.

Speelman–Plaskett, London 1986
White to play

Black has two pieces for a rook and pawn and seems to be doing OK. The first tactical element you might notice here is the pin along the b-file, but there doesn't seem to be a way to exploit it. The second thing you'll probably see is that there's only one unprotected Black piece. Can you exploit that situation? (Yes, with 1 Qa4.)

But there's something more subtle going on here. Black's pieces seem to be mutually protected but they are actually overworked. And with that in mind you can find the strongest continuation:

1	**Rxb5!**	**Qxb5**
2	**Qb6!**	**resigns**

The queen cannot both protect itself and prevent 3 Rxe8 mate. Its abilities were simply stretched too far.

Even when enemy pieces give the appearance of close coordination, they are often held together by light tethers:

Tarjan–Byrne, U.S. Championship 1981
White to play

Black has just defended against the possibility of Rh3 by attacking the queen (. . . g6!). After 1 Qh6 e5 Black beats back the attack.

But with the centralizing 1 Qe5!, preparing Bh6 and in some cases Qe4, White maintains his initiative. He preferred:

        1 Rg3?

This natural move has the drawbacks of (a) lacking force and (b) denying White the Rh3 resource because the rook is needed on g3 to pin the g-pawn. This last role of the rook also reveals how fragile the White attack force is.

        1 ...   **Bd6**

Now 2 Rg4 allows a strong 2 . . . e5.

        2 Rg5   **Bf4!**

Devastating. White can't take (3 Bxf4 Qxd4+ and 4 . . . Qxf4), so he has to begin a hasty and expensive retreat. He got nothing for his lost rook after **3 Qf3 Bxg5   4 Bxg5 Qxd4+   5 Kh1 Ra7.**

A more elaborate example of stretched pieces:

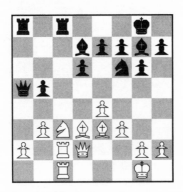

Portisch–Gheorghiu, Siegen 1970
White to play

White has exchanged pawns on b5 and is looking at the one obvious target in the position, the enemy b-pawn. At first it appears more than adequately defended. In fact, all of Black's pieces protect one another.

But White notices how fragile that protection is:

1 Nxb5!   Rxc2

On 1 . . . Qxd2 Black trades off a defender of b5, allowing White to keep his extra pawn with 2 Bxd2. And 1 . . . Bxb5 2 Qxa5! costs Black a rook.

2 Rxc2   Bxb5

Now it appears that Black's pieces will be stretched to the limit by 3 Qxa5 Rxa5 4 Bd2, e.g., 4 . . . Bxd3 5 Rc8+ and 6 Bxa5. However, Black improves his chances in this line with 4 . . . Rxa2! 5 Rxa2 Bxd3, with some compensation for the exchange.

3 Rc8+!

This breaks the connection of the stretched pieces. On 3 . . . Bf8 there follows 4 Rxa8 Qxd2 (or 4 . . . Qxa8 5 Bxb5 with an extra pawn and those great queenside passed pawns) 5 Bxd2 Bxd3 6 Bh6 Nd7 and Black is so tied up that 7 a4! followed by the advance of the a- and b-pawns will win.

3 . . .   Rxc8

Black recognizes that on 3 . . . Be8 4 Qxa5 Rxa5 5 a4!, the immediate threat of 6 Bb6 trapping the rook, as well as the longterm threat to promote a queenside pawn, will win.

4 Qxa5   Bxd3
5 b4

And even though Black does not stand badly from a material point of view, he has poor chances because his pieces lack coordination. He lost after **5 . . . Nd7   6 b5 d5   7 b6 d4 8 b7 Rb8   9 Bf4 e5   10 Qc7.**

(3) Invasion Squares

Often an unoccupied square is more important than any square with a piece on it. Noticing such a vulnerable point is the hard part.

Rhodes–Formanek, Whitby 1969

1 c4 e5   2 Nc3 d6   3 g3 Be7   4 Bg2 Nc6   5 e3 f5
6 Nge2   Nf6   7 0-0   0-0   8 d3   Qe8   9 Rb1   g5
10 f4 gxf4   11 gxf4 Kh8   12 Kh1 Rg8   13 Nd5 Qg6
14 Rg1?

Black's heavy pieces are massed against g2, and White felt compelled to defend with Kh1 and Rg1. But this creates a new danger because of a square that has become newly vulnerable and very harmful to White: f2.

14 ...   Ng4!
15 Qe1

White must stop the smothered mate . . . Nf2. Black now sees that another idea in the position, 15 . . . Nxh2 16 Kxh2 Qh5+, is not convincing after 17 Bh3. So he returns to the . . . Nf2 idea. Is there some way, he wonders, of drawing the queen away from the defense of f2?

15 ...	**Bh4!!**
16 Ng3	

The brilliant point of black's last move is 16 Qxh4 Qh5! and then either 17 Qxh5 or 17 Qe1 allows immediate mate (on f2 or h2). And the apparent protection of both squares by 17 Qg3 allows 17 ... Qxh2+! 18 Qxh2 Nf2 mate.

16 ...	**Nxh2!**

White resigns

The position is quite hopeless after 17 ... Bxg3 and a check on the h-file.

A more difficult case of the vulnerable square is the following. Black appears to be on the offensive—and also the defensive—on the king's wing.

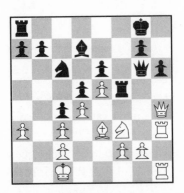

Mortensen–Karlsson, Esbjerg 1988
Black to play

Black would like to snap off the g-pawn, but 1 ... Qxg2?? 2 Rg3 costs him the queen. Moreover, he has to do something about White's threat of 2 Rg3 Q-moves 3 Qxh6.

But there is another way of looking at the position, and that is in terms of White's weaknesses. Where, Black asks, is White vulnerable? The g2-square is protected tactically, and he would have to overcome major transportation problems to get his pieces to a3. But there is one square that is not immediately attacked yet can be threatened by three different pieces very quickly. Take another look at the diagram and see if you can guess which one.

Time's up. The answer is revealed by Black's crushing sequence:

1 ...   **Rxf3!!**

This does two things. It eliminates the only piece that can come to the aid of the target square—c2—and it opens the queen's diagonal leading to it. Regardless of how White captures on f3, Black follows with 2 . . . Nb4! 3 axb4 Ba4 and wins (4 Kd1 Qxc2+ 5 Ke1 Qd1 mate or 4 Kb2 Qxc2+ 5 Ka1 Bb3 and 6 . . . Qa2 mate).

Ideas, as we've seen, are the building blocks of calculation. You simply can't start to analyze variations without them. In the pages that follow we move on from the inspirational side of calculation to the mechanical.

(Solutions: Fischer–Ciocaltea: Black's queen has no moves and can be trapped by 15 Bg5! hxg5 16 hxg5. Kaiszauri–Sznapik: 1 Ng6+! and 2 Qxh7+! followed by 3 Rh3+.)

Three

TREES AND HOW TO BUILD THEM

> *"Often at the chessboard we fail through simple ignorance rather than a lack of ideas, and on the verge of executing a magnificent combination we sit perplexed, at a loss how to realize it. Inexperience makes the most fertile imagination powerless."*
>
> —*Eugene Znosko-Borovsky*

Once you've identified the primary ideas in a position, your task is to work out the details of exploitation. Ultimately, these details will result in a calculated sequence, a series of moves that lead to a position about which you can form a judgment.

This is as true for a 10-move combination that results in mate as it is for two-move sequences of semi-forcing moves that just slightly improve your position. You are working with ideas in both.

Even many beginners will be able to spot the idea in the following . . .

White to play

. . . and also the two-move combination that takes advantage of it: **1 Re8+ Rxe8 2 Rxe8 mate**. The back-rank mating scenario is one of the oldest and most primitive in chess, and also one of the most common.

But consider the following:

Kr. Georgiev–Gulko, Saint John 1988
Black to play

Here again the idea is not greatly disguised: White's back rank is vulnerable. The immediate 1 . . . Rd1+ works in one variation (2 Nxd1?? e1Q+) but not in another (2 Rxd1 exd1Q+ 3 Nxd1 Qb1 4 Qd4).

So Black must work with the basic idea a bit.

> 1 . . .   Qc2!
>
> 2 Qb3

White's reply is forced since 2 . . . Rd1+ was threatened, and eliminating the pregnant pawn with 2 Qxe2 costs him a knight. After 2 Qb3 Black can force the win of that knight anyway with 2 . . . Qd2, preparing to promote the e-pawn. Then, following 3 Nxe2 Qxe2 4 h3 he should eventually be able to make his slight material edge count.

But a bit of inspiration will reveal a better use of the idea, a little combination, no more than three moves long, that is as decisive and pretty as it is hard to see.

> 2 . . .   Rd1+!
>
> 3 Rxd1

Naturally not 3 Nxd1 e1Q mate. But after 3 . . . exd1Q+ 4 Nxd1, where is the mate?

> 3 . . .   Qxc3!!
>
> **White resigns**

The best White can do to meet the threats of 4 . . . e1Q+ and of 4 . . . Qxb3 followed by 5 . . . exd1Q+ is the humble, and quite hopeless, 4 Qb1 exd1Q+ 5 Qxd1 Qxb4.

Aron Nimzovich made a distinction in his classic text, *My System*, between two means of executing a middlegame or endgame plan. One he called the evolutionary—the slow buildup. The other he called the revolutionary—the explosive, tactical method.

This distinction applies as well to calculated sequences:

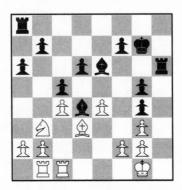

Cavellos–Mohring, Tel Aviv 1964
Black to play

Clearly, Black is on the attack and his primary route of invasion will be along the vulnerable h-file. The evolutionary means of exploiting this is 1 . . . Rah8, threatening mate in one move.

That would force 2 Kf1, after which 2 . . . Rh1+ 3 Ke2 Rxc1 4 Nxc1 is the most natural sequence (not 4 Rxc1 Bxb2), and Black is left with some means of improving his position but no obvious method of making major progress (4 . . . b5 5 b3).

But before dropping the idea of h-file attack, Black should consider the revolutionary method. If he does he will find:

1 . . .   Rh1+!
2 Kxh1   Bxf2

And White resigned in the face of 3 . . . Rh8 mate. The point here is not to assume that there is one and only one application of an idea. There may be two, three, or several.

A FAMILY OF IDEAS

When we speak of a tactical idea we may mean one specific combinational idea (Qh8+/Nxf7+ in the Alekhine–Euwe game of the last chapter) or a general concept (White's first rank in the Georgiev–Gulko example). It can also be a *family* of ideas bound together by the common use of certain pieces, such as Black's knights and queen in the following illustration.

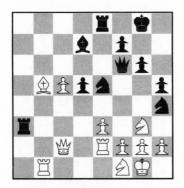

Andruet–Spassky, Coblenz 1988
Black to play

Black's attention is directed to the kingside, where he has more space as well as four potential attacking pieces. The experienced player develops a sense of where the tactics apply; here a master will smell something happening on f3 or g2.

How does he get the Black queen to one of those squares? He might examine 1 . . . Nef3+ (2 gxf3 Qxf3 and 3 . . . Qg2 mate) until he fails to find a followup to 2 Kh1!.

Then he may turn his attention to 1 . . . Nxg2 (2 Kxg2 Qf3+ and 3 . . . Bh3). But he will probably reject that once he sees 2 Bxd7!.

The vulnerability of f3 is so sharply defined to the master's eye that he doesn't stop there. Boris Spassky didn't. He played:

1 . . .   Qf3!!

White resigns

It's a forced mate: 2 gxf3 Nexf3+ 3 Kh1 Bh3 and 4 . . . Bg2 mate. Though it may seem difficult, almost anyone who works hard enough with an idea can find moves like 1 . . . Qf3.

As we've seen, there is often more than one idea at work in a position. Choosing between two or three ideas is taxing. But sometimes, as in the following example, you can use two ideas together.

Jones–Dueball, Nice 1974
Black to play

Black sees that if the White rook weren't where it is, . . . Nf2+ would fork king and queen. He also notices that if White's queen were not on the first rank, there would be a masked threat of . . . Qxf1 mate.

Neither idea in itself is enough. But mixed together . . .

    1 . . .   Re1!!

This wins the queen because of 2 Rxe1 Nf2+ (idea no. 1), while on 2 Bxe1 or 2 Nxe1 the reply 2 . . . Nb2! threatens both . . . Nxd1 and . . . Qxf1 (idea no. 2).

Actually, it's quite a simple combination. But looking back at the diagram, it would seem that the one square White has sufficiently protected, the one he doesn't have to worry about is: e1!

Vukic–Romanishin, Moscow 1977
White to play

In this example, we have two more ideas melding. One is the pawn fork at b4. White can threaten it, say by way of 1 a3, but it is easily parried (1 . . . Rc8; 1 . . . Qd8; 1 . . . Qc7).

The other idea is a last-rank mate. White begins to put one and one together and sees 1 b4 Qxb4 2 Rab1. But Black can then capture on c4 so that 3 Rb8+ allows 3 . . . Rc8.

At this point White can do one of two things: He can either give up on trying to make 1 b4 work and turn his attention to other moves, or he can look for a forcing continuation.

1 b4!	Qxb4
2 Rdb1	Qxc4
3 Be2!	resigns

White correctly kept looking and realized how stretched Black's pieces were after 2 . . . Qxc4. Black must move his attacked queen after 3 Be2 and must also avoid Rb8+. There could have followed 3 . . . Qc2 4 Bd3! Qc3 (the only move) 5 Rb8+ Rc8 6 Qxc3!.

Often when we miscalculate we overlook a single idea. That idea, perhaps a key move, may recur in several different lines:

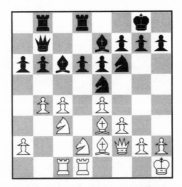

Psakhis–J. Polgar, Amsterdam 1989
Black to play

After lengthy maneuvering Black believes it is time for the liberating break in the center. What she overlooks is not apparent for four moves.

1 ...	d5?
2 cxd5	exd5
3 Bf4!	

This pins the knight and forces Black's reply. It won't be 3 ... Nfd7 because of 4 exd5 Bxd5 5 Bxa6! Qxa6 6 Nxd5.

3 ...	Bd6
4 exd5	Bxd5

Black would have preferred 4 ... Nxd5 5 Nxd5 Bxd5. But then comes 6 Ne4 Bxe4 7 Rxd6!!—the idea she overlooked. Then Black loses a piece in all variations (7 ... Rxd6 8 Bxe5 Rbd8 9 Bxd6 Rxd6 10 fxe4).

5 Nde4!	Bxe4

And here the same idea works against Black: 5 ... Nxe4 6 fxe4 Bxe4 7 Rxd6!!.

6 Rxd6!

And once more. Here at least Black could complicate matters with **6 ... Nd3!**, after which **7 Bxd3 Bxd3 8 Rd1? Rxd6 9 Bxd6 Rd8 10 Rxd3 Qc6** got a bit sticky (8 Qd4! would have won outright).

CANDIDATE MOVES

After you've had some experience calculating, or just playing chess, you develop a sense of what moves are likely to be best in a particular position. In one position you might recognize quickly that a single move absolutely looks correct, but in another there may be several "candidates." Each candidate move may involve its own tactical or strategic idea, or they may share a common idea.

The task of the calculator is to identify the candidates and determine which is best. Here is a position with considerable choice:

Khalifman–P. Nikolic, Moscow 1990
White to play

Black has just captured an enemy bishop (. . . cxd3). Because of the half-open g-file and the four White pieces attacking a king position defended by only a rook, White has reason to be optimistic. Some kind of tactical assault on g7 is likely to work, if not now (i.e., 1 Bxg7), then perhaps in a move or two. What are the candidate moves here?

First, there are the two most violent moves, 1 Bxg7 and 1 Qxf7+. Because they are the most forcing they are probably the easiest to calculate.

Second, there is the attempt to create a new threat, 1 Nh4, which intends 2 Nxf5 and then a capture on g7.

Third, there are the moves that bring up reinforcements, i.e., 1 0-0-0 or 1 Kd2, followed by the entrance of the other rook.

Finally, there is the least forcing move, 1 cxd3.

That makes a total of six candidates, a large number. But we can whittle them down quickly: As a practical rule of thumb, we start with the most *forceful*. We can always play 1 cxd3 if we find that the other five are faulty. But if we discover that 1 Qxf7+ wins outright, there is no need to calculate the others.

Actually, White can eventually win with 1 Kd2!, or with 1 Bxg7 Rxg7 2 Kd2 (followed by 3 Qh6, 3 exf6, or 3 Rxg7+), or even with 1 Qxf7+ Kxf7 2 Rxg7+ Ke6 3 Kd2 (e.g., 3 . . . Bd7 4 exf6 Kxf6 5 Rag1).

After some thought White settled on **1 Kd2** and won quickly: **1 . . . Be6   2 Bxg7   Rxg7   3 Rxg7+   Kxg7 4 Rg1+ resigns** (4 . . . Kh8 5 Nh4 and 6 Ng6+ or 4 . . . Kf8 5 Qxh7 Ke8 6 Rg7).

Being able to recognize candidate moves is an essential, time-saving skill. The principal difference between human players and many computers is that those machines cannot identify candidate moves and as a result cannot budget their time. They might consider all 35 legal moves in a position rather than the only two that make sense. Humans can budget their time, if they develop good instincts and intuition. These are qualities that may seem innate but can be trained.

Some young players consider too many moves in a position, and others not enough. Alexander Kotov, a Soviet-era player who taught a generation how to calculate, recalled how he tried to improve when he was a young master. Kotov discovered that he wasn't examining *enough* candidates, looking at only one or two "natural" moves when there were three or four.

Kotov provided unintended documentation of this in a series of lectures on the theme "How to Become a Grandmaster" (later issued as the book *Think Like a Grandmaster*). Kotov's very first example was:

White to play

According to Kotov, in this amateur game White decided he should sacrifice and began to consider three candidate moves: 1 Bxh6, 1 Nxg6, and 1 Ng4 (intending 2 Nxh6+). But his "faulty unsystematic thinking" undid him, Kotov said, because he considered 1 Nxg6, then gave up after a few moves of analysis and turned to 1 Bxh6, which he also gave up on. Then he analyzed 1 Ng4, found problems with it, and went back to 1 Bxh6 and 1 Nxg6 again.

In the end, White, thoroughly confused, ended up playing something completely different (1 Bc3?), which got him quickly crushed (1 . . . Nf4!).

It's a nice, instructive story, but there's a question that goes unanswered: Why, if White was looking to sack a piece, didn't he consider one of the most natural moves in the position?

After 1 Nxf7, it's easy to see that if the knight is taken, 2 Bxe6 wins. So the real calculation involves 1 ... Bxg3 and then 2 hxg3 or 2 Nxh6+ Kf8 (not 2 ... gxh6 3 Bxe6+ Kf8 4 Bxh6+) 3 hxg3. This appears to be at least as promising as the line endorsed by Kotov (1 Ng4 Qh4 2 Nxh6+ Kf8 3 Qxh4).

And why didn't Kotov mention it at all? Probably because candidate moves are a lot more personal than anyone likes to admit—and Kotov may have missed 1 Nxf7 himself. What Garry Kasparov considers "natural" may be something that would never occur to Viswanathan Anand or Gata Kamsky. But for each of the remaining diagrams in this book you should try to pick out the move that seems most natural *to you* and then find at least one other candidate.

When we calculate the ramifications of a particular move we'd like to play we look for our *opponent's* candidate moves. This is another form of defensive calculation.

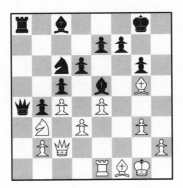

Bisguier–Fuderer, Goteborg 1955
White to play

White understands that 1 ... Nd4!, winning a piece, is threatened. He has passive defenses such as 1 Kg2 or 1 Re2. But he also notices that 1 Ra1 wins material. Should he pass, or grab?

White chose:

1 Ra1??

He mistakenly stopped looking for Black candidate moves after calculating 1 ... Qxa1? (2 Nxa1 Rxa1 3 Kg2).

1 ...   Qxb3!

White resigns

This, too, surrenders the queen, but what a difference: 2 Qxb3 Rxa1 with two devastating threats (3 ... Bh3 and 4 ... Rxf1 mate, and 3 ... Nd4, trapping the queen).

In more difficult positions, you may be required to find enemy candidates several moves into the future. Kotov himself cited the following example in a magazine article.

Eingorn–Malaniuk, Baku 1979
Black to play

Can Black's attacked rook take on a2? Black decided it can because he had calculated 1 ... **Rxa2** 2 **e5** as the most dangerous candidate move that White has in reply (2 ... Qc7 3 Rdc1 and the queen has no good retreat). But he saw that 2 ... **Qd5** 3 **Bb3 Qa5!** 4 Bxa2 Qxa2 gives Black excellent compensation for the exchange and pawn.

Yet, as Kotov pointed out, Black failed to look for candidate moves throughout the sequence. At the fourth move White need not take the rook. "If [Black] had added one candidate move, 4 d5!, he would have understood without difficulty that his position immediately becomes hopeless."

In fact, White did play 4 **d5!**—the second most forceful move in the position and one Black should not have missed. Black resigned not long after 4 ... **Bxd5** 5 **Bxd5 exd5** 6 **e6!** and then 6 ... Nf6 7 exf7+ Kxf7 8 Rbc1 and 9 Rc7+.

In Chapter Six we'll explore the matter of choosing between equally appealing candidates. But before you can make an educated choice you have to know there *is* a choice.

Speelman–Levitt, London 1992
White to play

In this example, White instinctively looks for a way to meet Black's last move (. . . f6) with a knight move. It doesn't take long for most players examining this position to see 1 Nd7, based on the idea that 2 Rxe8+ is threatened and that 1 . . . Rxe3?? allows mate on f8.

But before he examines that move further, it should occur to White that there's another candidate with the same idea: **1 Ng6!**.

Once he understands that a choice is available, White can weigh the two and see that 1 Nd7 Qc8! is not clear but that 1 Ng6 Qa8 2 Rxe8+ Qxe8 3 Qd5+! Qf7 4 Qd8+ is. In fact, there is a second successful defense to 1 Nd7 that fails against 1 Ng6, and that is 1 . . . Kf7 (which loses in the variation 1 Ng6 Kf7 2 Nh8+! Rxh8 3 Qe6+ and mates).

In the game White correctly chose 1 Ng6 and the game ended with **1 . . . Ra8   2 Ne7+ Kh8   3 Qe6!** and Black resigned in view of 4 Ng6+ hxg6 5 Rh3 mate (or 4 Qg8+! Rxg8 5 Ng6+, etc.).

It's tempting to consider all the forcing moves in a position as candidates. But we should remember that less forceful moves may have other benefits that mandate their consideration.

In the following position, there's obviously only one really forcing move, 1 exf6:

Kengis–Anastasian, Frunze 1989
White to play

But he should also consider alternatives, such as 1 Qf4.

In the game, White rejected 1 exf6 Bxd6 and then 2 Rxd6 Qxd6 3 e5 because of 3 . . . Qd2! 4 Bxc6 Qxc1+ 5 Rxc1 Rd2 6 Rb1 b5. He eventually chose **1 Qf4!** since Black's knight cannot move (2 Qxf7+) and therefore White will be able to play 2 exf6 with almost a free move thrown in.

The game went **1 Qf4! Bf8   2 exf6 Bxd6   3 Rxd6 Qxd6   4 e5 Qd2   5 Bxc6** and White won (5 . . . Qxb2 6 Qg5).

The result of this identification and evaluation of candidate moves is that construct we call the Tree of Analysis.

THE TREE OF ANALYSIS

So far we've talked a lot about calculating a sequence without considering its "shape." A calculated sequence resembles a tree; branches represent the subvariations, and the trunk represents the sequence's main line. Trees come in various shapes and sizes—some tall and thin, some short and fat, and some very difficult ones that are tall and fat.

The simplest trees to calculate are, not surprisingly, the short, thin ones:

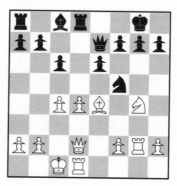

Krasenkov–Sveshnikov, Moscow 1992
White to play

Here White began a winning combination with **1 Bxf5!**. Black, with no forcing alternatives, naturally responded **1 ... exf5**. After **2 Nh6+** he had a choice of two king moves, but in either case White replies 3 Rxg7!. Again, Black's hand is relatively forced since 2 ... Kf8 3 Rxg7! Qf6 4 Rxf7+ loses the queen and 3 ... Be6 4 Rg8 is mate. Therefore he played **2 ... Kh8 3 Rxg7! Kxg7 4 Rg1+ Kh8** and after **5 Qe2!** he resigned (5 ... Qxe2 6 Nxf7 mate; 5 ... Be6 6 Nxf7+ and 7 Qe5+).

The resulting tree looks something like this:

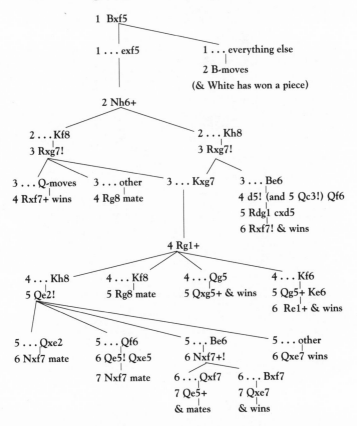

The branches look more impressive in size than they really are. Note how normally each variation branches off into two or more subvariations. But at one point, Black's third move, two subvariations merge to form the main line, 3 . . . Kxg7.

Now let's recall Bent Larsen's rook sacrifice from the last chapter.

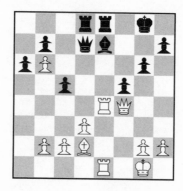

Here we get quite a different tree. Though there are a lot of branches at the top, all but one ends after a few moves because of simple refutations by White. That leaves one long main line:

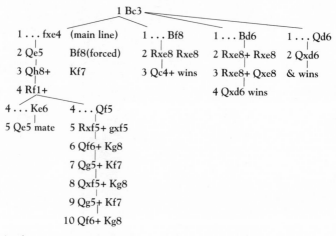

And so on until 15 Qxb7.

What aids our analysis of such long variations is the certainty of our conclusions. We don't have to calculate much into the side variations (1 . . . Bf8; 1 . . . Bd6, and 1 . . . Qd6) because we find a forced win of decisive material after three or four moves.

The *end-positions*, as we'll call them, of those lines are clear. Similarly, the 4 . . . Ke6 branch leads immediately to a mate. No doubt about evaluating that end-position.

As mentioned earlier, the length of a calculation tree is not as significant as the breadth of the variations. But there is another factor: The hardest move to find in the last example was at the very top of the tree. No difficult moves are required of White past the second move.

Trees have, in fact, three dimensions. We have considered length and breadth. But there is a third one that is not easily represented visually: difficulty.

Sometimes the hardest moves to find appear on the shortest branches.

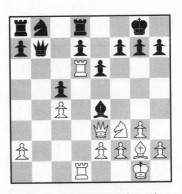

H. Olafsson–Levitt, Reykjavik 1990
White to play

The ideas to work with here include (a) Black's unprotected rook, (b) Black's potentially vulnerable first rank, and (c) the lineup of pieces on the g2-a8 diagonal.

White came up with this way of using the various elements: **1 Rxe6!** and then **1 ... fxe6   2 Ng5!**. In this tree the longest branches consist of 2 ... Nc6 3 Qxe4 g6 4 Qh4 h5 5 Ne4 "with a strong attack," or 2 ... h6! 3 Nxe4 Nc6 4 Nxc5 Qc7 5 Nxd7! Rac8! 6 Qxe6+ Kh8 7 Be4, etc.

But White need not calculate that far, and in fact can stop examining these trees after the third move. The hardest aspect of this calculation, in fact, is finding the answer to 2 ... Bxg2. It is the spectacular 3 Qxe6+!, which leads to mate in all lines (3 ... dxe6 4 Rxd8 mate; 3 ... Kh8 4 Nf7+).

(Incidentally, you should be able to figure out what is wrong with the similar move order 1 Ng5 and then 1 ... Bxg2 2 Rxe6. This transposes into the above example after 2 ... fxe6. So why didn't White play it? The answer is at the end of the chapter.)

A similar example from one of Bobby Fischer's earliest successes:

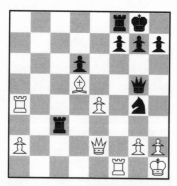

Fischer–Sherwin, U.S. Championship 1957–58
White to play

This tree is fairly short, only three moves long. But there are more branches and, perhaps most significantly, the most difficult move to see comes at the second level.

The first idea that probably occurred to White in the diagram was 1 Bxf7+ and if 1 . . . Rxf7? then 2 Ra8+ and mates. But after 1 . . . Kh8 White faces a number of pins and other tactical problems.

1 Rxf7!

Now there are three branches. The simplest and shortest runs 1 . . . Rxf7 2 Ra8+ and mates. The longest and most complex begins with 1 . . . h5! and runs into a variety of sub-branches after 2 Rxf8+ Kxf8 3 Qf1+, when 3 . . . Nf6 allows White a winning endgame (4 Rc4) and 3 . . . Qf6 retains a winning attack for him (4 Ra8+ Ke7 5 Ra7+ Kd8 6 Qb1!).

But clearly 1 . . . h5, while it may be the best move, is not the most dangerous. The key variation begins with:

1 . . .   Rc1+

What won this game for White was his realization that there were two branches here: the obvious 2 Rf1+, which gets White into severe difficulties after 2 . . . Kh8, and . . .

2 Qf1!!

A difficult move to find even though 2 . . . Rxf1+ 3 Rxf1+ results in a fairly short tree. There would be a branch for 3 . . . Kh8 4 Rxf8 mate; another for 3 . . . Rf7 4 Ra8+ Qd8 5 Rxd8 mate; and a third that begins with 3 . . . Qxd5!? and offers two sub-branches: 4 exd5?? Rxf1 mate, which wins for Black; and 4 Rxf8+! Kxf8 5 exd5, which wins for White.

In the actual game, Black played the desperate **2 . . . h5** and saw that after 3 Qxc1! Qxc1+ 4 Rf1+ and 5 Rxc1 that he would be lost. So he went off onto another limb with **2 . . . h5   3 Qxc1 Qh4** and resigned soon after **4 h3**.

HOW CHESSPLAYERS REALLY THINK

"When all hopeful attempts at solving the problem by traditional methods have been exhausted, thought runs around in circles . . . like rats in a cage."

—*Arthur Koestler*

Kotov, in *Think Like a Grandmaster*, argued that a player must approach the tree carefully. He must examine each branch once and only once. To jump from one to another is "an unforgiveable waste of time," something that no grandmaster would countenance, he claimed.

In reality, grandmasters think no more systematically than amateurs. They sometimes jump from branch to branch and back again. Or they calculate only a few moves deep into what should be a very large tree. As Mikhail Tal once put it, "To calculate sometimes all of the so-called 'tree of variations' is not simply difficult but impossible."

Tal spoke instead of a "zone of certainty" that allows a trained calculator to stop his calculation after a relatively brief testing of the various branches. There are many masters who follow Tal's example, calculating what end-positions they can see and then evaluating other branches on instinct.

In the late 1970s, the English master Simon Webb conducted a series of experiments, the results of which appeared in the magazine *Chess*. Webb gave players of different playing strengths a position to look at and had them describe how they'd go about choosing a move. None of the positions were forced wins.

His results were surprising for followers of Kotov. For example, the grandmaster in the test group jumped around from one idea to another and then back again. In another case, the two strongest players tested spent 10 minutes failing even to consider what was clearly the best candidate, and then selected moves they had considered for less than a minute.

What really distinguished the better players, Webb found, was that they could come to accurate conclusions faster, thought in terms of concrete variations, and were therefore more efficient calculators.

There is no perfect calculating method for all players, Kotov notwithstanding. We all think differently. In reality there is a strong element of serendipity in chess. When we look at one idea, we sometimes come up with another.

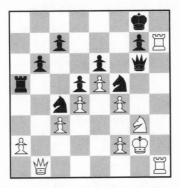

A. Rodriguez–Miles, Palma de Mallorca 1989
Black to play

Black studied the position in some detail, working down a tree that began with 1 . . . Nce3+ 2 Kg1 (not 2 fxe3 Qxg3+). He looked at one branch that had 2 . . . Qg4 as its key but gave up after he found that 3 Rh8+ Kf7 4 Rc8! sets up a strong checking threat. He turned to another branch that began 2 . . . Nh4 with the idea of 3 Qxg6 Nf3 mate. But he had to give up on it after he saw 3 Rh8+! and then 3 . . . Kf7 4 Qxg6+ or 3 . . . Kxh8 4 Rxh4+.

He examined other lines as well, and the main benefit of all this analysis was to tell him that Black's main problem was his king position. "If only it were somewhere safer," he thought. Therefore:

1 ...   **Kf7!!**

This winning idea would not have occurred to Black if he hadn't worked on a different tree. Now, for example, 2 Rh8 Ke7! 3 Rc8 allows one of the clever ideas of the first tree: 3 . . . Nce3+ 4 Kg1 Nh4! 5 Qxg6 Nf3 mate.

White eventually tried:

2	R7h5	Nce3+
3	Kg1	Qg4!
4	R1h2?!	Nxg3
5	fxg3	Qxg3+

And White resigned after several more moves.

In the real world, players get ideas from one branch that they suddenly realize belong in another.

Watson–Gutman, Brussels 1987

1 Nc3 c5   2 e4 d6   3 f4 a6   4 Nf3 e6   5 d4 cxd4 6 Nxd4 Nf6   7 Be2 Qc7   8 Be3 b5   9 Bf3 Bb7 10 e5 dxe5   11 Bxb7 Qxb7   12 fxe5 Nd7   13 0-0

At this point, while waiting for Black's reply White analyzed 13 . . . b4 and came up with the inspired attacking device 14 Qh5 g6 15 Qh3!, with the idea of meeting 15 . . . bxc3 with 16 Rxf7!.

Black did not play 13 . . . b4 but chose instead **13 . . . Nxe5**. White's compensation for the pawn was not clear until he found **14 Qh5 Ng6   15 Qh3!!**. He admitted afterward that it would have escaped him if he hadn't seen the queen maneuver to h3 in the previous variation. On h3 the queen supports sacrifices on e6 (e.g., 15 . . . Nc6 16 Nxe6 fxe6 17 Qxe6+) and f7.

In fact, the game went **15 . . . Be7   16 Rxf7!** and White had a winning attack, because 16 . . . Kxf7 17 Qxe6+ Ke8 18 Nf5 Qd7 19 Nxg7+ Kd8 20 Rd1 wins.

Finally, a revealing look inside a grandmaster's mind was provided by the winner of the following in his annotations of a brilliant win.

Nezhmetdinov–Chernikov, Rostov-on-Don 1962

1 e4 c5   2 Nf3 Nc6   3 d4 cxd4   4 Nxd4 g6   5 Nc3 Bg7   6 Be3 Nf6   7 Bc4 0-0   8 Bb3 Ng4   9 Qxg4 Nxd4   10 0-0 Qa5   11 Qh4 Bf6

White noticed that his attacked queen can't go to g3 or f4 because then 12 . . . Qxc3! and 13 . . . Ne2+ regains the queen in a favorable ending. But there were three other candidate moves.

First he saw that 12 Qh6 allows Black to repeat moves with 12 . . . Bg7 13 Qh4 Bf6. He also saw that 12 Qg4 or 12 Qh3 allows 12 . . . d5. He considered these lines before evaluating 12 Qg4 d5 13 Qd1! as slightly favorable to White.

Then he spotted the remarkable sacrifice 12 Qxf6!? exf6 13 Bxd4. Only two pieces for the queen—but they're terrific pieces after White gets to play Nd5.

He wondered what would happen if Black inserts 12 . . . Nxb3. He saw that 13 axb3! was playable—13 . . . Qxa1 14 Qxe7! and White has 15 Bh6 and 16 Nd5 coming up.

Then he found another way for Black to improve at move 12, with 12 . . . Ne2+! 13 Nxe2 exf6, after which it will take White an extra tempo to bring the knight to d5.

So he went back to 12 Qg4 and kept coming to the conclusion that his chances were nice but "can you really win with it?" Finally, after a thorough review of 12 Qxf6 Ne2+ 13 Nxe2 exf6 14 Nc3 he concluded that there was little Black could do to prevent him from continuing Bd4, Nd5, Rad1-d3-f3 with a winning position.

Finally, after much soul-searching and back-and-forth analysis he settled on the sacrifice and won a remarkably fine game: **12 Qxf6!! Ne2+ 13 Nxe2 exf6 14 Nc3 Re8 15 Nd5 Re6 16 Bd4 Kg7 17 Rad1 d6 18 Rd3 Bd7 19 Rf3 Bb5 20 Bc3 Qd8 21 Nxf6 Be2 22 Nxh7+! Kg8 23 Rh3 Re5 24 f4 Bxf1 25 Kxf1 Rc8 26 Bd4! b5 27 Ng5 Rc7 28 Bxf7+! Rxf7 29 Rh8+!** and White won.

Moral: Find the method of calculating variations that you are most comfortable with.

(Answer to Olafsson–Levitt: 1 Ng5 Bxg2 2 Rxe6 allows Black to answer the threat of 3 Re8+ with 2 . . . Na6 or 2 . . . Nc6. White should have played the more forceful idea, Ng5, after the less forceful—as we'll see in the next chapter.)

Four

FORCE

> *"Force and fraud are in war the two cardinal virtues."*
>
> —Thomas Hobbes

I f ideas provide the spark for a calculated sequence, forcing moves are the fuel that keeps it running. Moves that capture enemy pieces, check the king or, to a lesser degree, threaten such captures and checks, provide the dynamic element to a sequence.

Groszpeter–Radulov, Biel 1989

1 d4 d6 2 e4 Nf6 3 Nc3 c6 4 Nf3 Qa5 5 e5 Ne4 6 exd6 Nxc3 7 bxc3 exd6 8 Bd3 Be7 9 0-0 0-0 10 Re1 Be6 11 Rb1 b6 12 c4 Qh5 13 d5! cxd5 14 cxd5 Qxd5 15 Rb5 Qb7 16 Ng5 Bxg5 17 Rxg5 Nc6

Here White begins a combination that lasts eight moves in its longest tree limb. It is not only lengthy but requires definite risks, the sacrifices of a rook and a bishop. A mistake in calculation would be irreparable.

But don't let this scare you. It is actually a fairly routine combination and one that, with training, you should be able to visualize accurately to its end. Let's go one step at a time:

       18 Bxh7+!   **Kxh7**

Black has no real choice. On 18 . . . Kh8 19 Qh5, a discovered check by the bishop next move must lead to mate.

       19 Qh5+   **Kg8**

The only legal move.

       20 Rxg7+!   **Kxg7**

Again, obviously forced.

       21 Bh6+   **Kh7**

Black finally has a choice, albeit a slim one: On 21 . . . Kg8 White mates in two with 22 Qg5+ and 23 Qg7 mate.

22 Bg5+   **resigns**

If he had continued, Black would have had a choice between 22 . . . Kg8, which allows 23 Bf6 and 24 Qh8 mate, or 22 . . . Kg7, which lengthens the game by one move because of 23 Qh6+! Kg8 24 Bf6 and mate on h8 next move.

That's eight moves in all. But consider what a straight and narrow course the analysis took. At only three points did Black have any choice of replies. And none of those side variations extended more than two moves. This is a tree of analysis with a long stem but very few branches, and they are quite short.

Such trees are not found in remote forests. Garry Kasparov cited one in the notes to his game with Tigran Petrosian at Moscow 1982. The future world champion pointed out a better move for himself at one point, which in one key line called for a temporary queen and rook sacrifice. In another, a rook sacrifice was needed. And its main line demanded the offer of two pawns.

That last, main variation was *17 moves long.* But Kasparov went on to tell the reader that he shouldn't be surprised by that length. The forcing nature of the moves, almost all of them captures, checks, or mate threats, made the variation easier to digest.

On the other hand, much of the thinking you do during a game will involve very short trees. You won't be able to calculate more than perhaps two or three moves into the future, because there are few forcing moves in the position. This kind of calculation—the non-combinative kind—places a greater emphasis on evaluation.

Ivanchuk–Bareev, Linares 1993
White to play

In this relatively quiet position White saw nothing forcing and found instead a prophylactic, and very strong, move.

1 g3!

It is virtually impossible to calculate far in this position. But White was chiefly interested in the one line that could be examined in depth: He reasoned that if he held any advantage it lay in Black's inability to complete his development. After 1 g3 Black cannot bring his knight out to d7 because of 2 Bf4, after which the sacrificial 2 . . . Qf6 3 Bxd7 Bxf4 4 gxf4 Qxf4 5 Ne5 is unsound.

That was all White really needed to see. Black has various other moves after 1 g3, but none that trouble the position. After 1 . . . Nc6, for example, White continues to improve his position, such as with 2 Kg2 and 3 Rh1. He correctly saw that taking away Black's only good developing plan would leave White with a clear edge.

| 1 . . . | Ra7 |
| 2 Re1 | Nd7? |

After this mistake the game was virtually decided.

3	g5!	Rd8	
4	a4	Nb8	

Or 4 . . . Nf8 5 Qb3 and White brings the bishop decisively to f4 or a3.

5 Nh2!

And the knight went to f6 with crushing effect: **5 . . . Qf8 6 Ng4 Bd6 7 Kg2 Kh8 8 Rh1 Qg7 9 Nf6 h5 10 Qd1!**, and the threat of Rxh5+ led Black to resign.

To give a more elementary example, suppose you begin a game with 1 d4 and your opponent answers 1 . . . d5. One idea may occur to you: Black has weakened his defense of c7 because a White bishop on f4 or g3 cannot be blocked by . . . d7-d6.

Therefore, you might be inspired to develop this idea by way of Bf4 and Nc3-b5. But can you seriously calculate *anything* concrete after just 1 d4 d5 2 Nc3, with the idea of 3 Bf4 and 4 Nb5?

No, you are at least three moves away from threatening to capture on c7. We can say the position is just not forcing enough to generate specific calculated lines. All we can do is visualize a general course of events, say 2 . . . Nf6 3 Bf4 c6 4 e3, and evaluate this as best you can, either as equal or slightly better for White.

Players must be able to perform both kinds of calculation, the concrete forceful kind and the generalized kind. And in fact they often perform both during the course of a game. But the element of force must remain close to your attention because the consequences of missing a forceful move of your own or a forceful reply by the opponent are so severe.

LET THE FORCE . . .

The difference between forcing and nonforcing moves has been illustrated by some remarkable examples of grandmaster play:

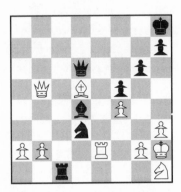

Huebner–Petrosian, Biel 1976
White to play

The winner of this game would almost certainly advance to the world championship elimination matches, and the loser would not. White had five minutes left to play four moves and reach the time control. He also had two healthy extra pawns. But more important, he had a mating attack.

White's search for candidate moves is relatively easy since he had only a few forcing moves (the two checks at e8 and the semi-forcing capture on d3). It is not particularly difficult to see that 1 Qe8+! is the best of the group. In fact, the only difficult task in selecting that move is to realize that after 1 . . . Kg7 2 Re7+ Kh6 White can play 3 Qf8+ because the rook on e7 shields f8 from the Black queen. After 3 Qf8+ Kh5 4 Rxh7 it is mate.

Aside from the minor visualization problem concerning f8, this is the kind of combination most amateurs can find. Black's only alternative moves are 1 . . . Qf8?? (which allows mate in one) and 2 . . . Qxe7, giving up his queen. In the diagram White has essentially a *forced mate in four*.

But White didn't find it. Reluctant to move his queen away from the defense of his bishop, and seeing the threat of 1 . . . Bg1+ 2 Kg3 Qxf4 mate, he played:

> **1 g3?**

And a desperate Black responded:

> **1 . . .   Nxf4!**

This renews the threat of 2 . . . Bg1+, only now it would be both check and mate. And the removal of the f4-pawn means Black's king has a flight square at g5.

Having missed a win when a forcing one was available, White misses a second one with 2 gxf4! Qxf4+ 3 Ng3. Worse, he plays forcing moves that lead to disaster:

> **2 Qe8+??   Kg7**
> **3 Re7+   Kh6**
> **4 Nf2**

A feeble attempt, but White is now lost.

> **4 . . .   Bxf2**
> **5 Rxh7+   Kg5!**

White resigned and his opponent took his place in the candidates matches.

The same principle of force applies to defensive calculation; that is, anticipating your opponent's tactics.

Shamkovich–Espig, Dubna 1973
Black to play

White has just played 1 Ng5!. With mate looming on h7 and 1 . . . fxg5 answerable by 2 Qg7 mate, Black appears to have nothing better than 1 . . . Qd7. Then 2 Re6! would be quite strong (2 . . . fxg5? 3 Rxg6+ hxg6 4 Qxg6+ mates). But Black found a better try:

    1 . . .   **Bxf2+!**
    2 Kxf2??

White is still winning after 2 Kh1! Qd7 3 Re6, the same winning plan mentioned above. The only significant difference is that here Black could complicate matters with 3 . . . Be3! (4 Rxe3 fxg5!), and White would have to come up with the stunning 4 h4! in order to score the point.

    2 . . .   **fxg5+**

White simply overlooked that this piece could be captured with the most forceful of all moves, a check.

    3 Kg1   **Nxb2**

And having lost two of his attacking pieces almost instantly, White played **4 Qxg5** and resigned after **4 . . . Nd3**.

During actual games, every time it's your turn to move begin your search for candidate moves by examining the most forceful moves available. And when considering any tree limb, make sure there are no enemy moves of any useful force in the end-position. If there are, it ain't the end.

FORCE VS. SPEED, FORCE VS. FORCE

As we've noted, people calculate differently from computers. One of the major differences is that humans tend to rely on the forcefulness of their moves, while machines concentrate on the fewest moves necessary to reach a conclusion.

In general, the most forceful line of play is usually the fastest way to reach a favorable conclusion. But not necessarily:

Sveshnikov–I. Ivanov, Minsk 1976
White to play

White found the most obvious idea in the position, the checks beginning with **1 Qd6+**. After he realized that **1 ...**

Kg8 **2 Ne7+ Kf8** sets up the opportunity for discovered checks and double checks, it wasn't hard to spot a second idea in the position, the smothered mate: **3 Nxg6+ Kg8 4 Qf8+! Rxf8 5 Ne7 mate**.

This is the easiest method for most humans to calculate *because it is the most forceful*. But if you give the diagrammed position to a competent chess computer, it will find 1 Qf6!, after which mate on g7, e7, or h8 can be delayed for only one move by a spite check. Thus, the "quiet" 1 Qf6 is two moves faster than the check on d6. Yet nine out of ten human players will tell you 1 Qd6+ is the easier to calculate.

On the other hand, there are bound to be times when long forcing variations are more difficult than simpler, short ones. Early in the twentieth century Emanuel Lasker pointed out this case:

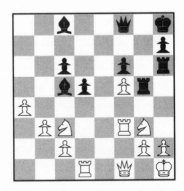

Lawrence–Fox, Anglo–American Cable Match 1911
Black to play

Here Black began to examine the ideas . . . Rxh2+ and . . . Rxg3. After considerable thought he worked out a combination that began with the diversionary **1 . . . Ba6** to draw the

White queen away from the kingside. After **2 Qxa6 Rxh2+!**
3 Kxh2 Qh6+ Black continued with 23 consecutive checks,
the final one delivering mate.

What amused Lasker was that even though the combination is sound (it won a gold medal), Black could have won
much faster with the less forcing 1 . . . Qd6!. Then 2 . . . Rxh2+
3 Kxh2 Rh5 mate is the main threat and White has no adequate defense (e.g., 2 Rf4 Be3).

Nevertheless, in the jungle of tournament tactics, it is
often the forceful who survive. The failure to recognize the
force of your own moves can be fatal. In a sense, it is sui-
cidal.

Mileika–Rosenfeld, Correspondence Match 1966
White to play

White appreciated the danger he was in. Black threatens a
mate in two by way of 1 . . . Re1+ or via the discovered check
1 . . . B-somewhere. White would like to play his own fairly
forceful defense 1 Rxh2, attacking the Black queen. But
Black's force is then greater than White's as he responds 1 . . .
Re1+ 2 Kg2 Qg5+ and mates. And the other obvious move of

force, 1 Qxd4+, is met by the counterforce 1 . . . Be5+! So . . .

1 White resigns??

A blunder. White could have won if he had looked for another forceful idea: 1 Rxh7+!. After 1 . . . Kxh7 2 Qf7+ White eliminates the rook or bishop *with check* next move and wins.

The move to worry about is 1 . . . Qxh7, but then 2 Rxh2 is strong, e.g., 2 . . . Re1+ 3 Kg2 and Black is out of ammunition.

Black's best is 2 . . . Bh3!, when 3 Qxd4+ begins a neat defensive maneuver to get the queen to the third rank with checks: 3 . . . Kg8 4 Qc4+ Kh8 5 Qc3+ Kg8 6 f4! Qb7+ (else 7 Rxh3) 7 Kg1 Rc8! 8 Qe3! Bf5 9 Nd6 and White is winning, not losing.

In its simplest form, therefore, calculation becomes a matter of weighing the force of one move against that of another. For example, a check is more forceful than a threat to capture something. An attack on a queen is more forceful than a threat to a knight. And so on.

Often when a player misevaluates a forcing situation it is because it never occurs to him that there is a reply to his last move that is at least as forceful.

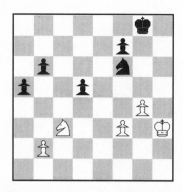

Bronstein–Bareev, Rome 1990
White to play

This is the beginning of the endgame, inasmuch as White has just forced an exchange of queens on f6. A draw is likely. Black is a pawn ahead but against the faster White king he cannot maintain any winning chances (1 Kg3 Kg7 2 Kf4 and 3 Ke5 or 1 . . . d4 2 Nb5 d3 3 Kf2 and 4 Ke3).

     1 g5??

This is a gross oversight, overlooking the compelling nature of Black's reply. White incorrectly assumed that, with so little material on the board, there could be nothing as forcing as the threat of 2 gxf6.

1 . . .	d4!
2 Nb5	d3

Only now does White realize that after 3 gxf6 d2 4 Nc3 (forced) b5!, Black wins with 5 . . . b4 6 Nd1 a4 and the advance of the a-pawn. In fact, White played **3 Kg3 d2** and then resigned in view of 4 Nc3 Nd5! 5 Nd1 Kg7 and the Black king invades.

Similarly, a threat to the enemy queen is very forceful—unless your opponent threatens to take your queen with check.

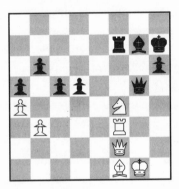

Aseyev–Hickl, Munich 1991–92
White to play

A piece down for three pawns, Black has excellent compensation. But, carried along by his calculations, he has just played . . . Qg5+, intending to meet 1 Bg2?? with 1 . . . Bd4. After White played the correct . . .

1 Kh1

. . . Black passed up an excellent, practical move of precaution (2 . . . Kg8, getting the king off a checking diagonal and protecting his rook).

1 ...   **Bd4??**

How can this be bad? After all, it's highly forcing.

　　2 Nh3!   **resigns**

But this is more forcing, as 3 Rxf7+ is threatened, and 2 ...
Bxf2 3 Nxg5+ hxg5 4 Rxf7+ clears the board.

Now we'll examine a slightly more elaborate example. It is not
just a case of "He threatens my queen, but I threaten mate in
two." The element of force is still present but it is of a long-
range nature.

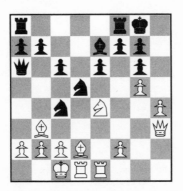

Fatalibekova–Ranniku, Soviet Women's Championship
1974
White to play

Black's centralized knights appear just as strong as White's
bishops—perhaps more so, when you realize that Black is
threatening 1 . . . Ba3 (2 bxa3? Qxa3+ and mates). But White
also has a strong plan involving the opening of the h-file. Only
through an accurate examination of the position will White
realize whose threats have greater force.

1 Rh1!	Ba3?

Better defensive chances are offered by 1 . . . Nxd2 so that . . . Nf4 can be played later. But Black saw that after 1 . . . Ba3 she cannot be stopped from a powerful capture on b2.

2 h5!	Nxb2

This certainly looks powerful. But force can often be deceptive.

3 hxg6!

She may also be winning with 3 h6!. As so often happens, Black has overestimated the power of a discovered check.

3 . . .	Nxd1+
4 Kxd1	fxg6
5 Qxe6+	Rf7
6 Qxg6	

And Black resigned after **6 . . . Rd8   7 Nf6+ Rxf6** (7 . . . Kf8 8 Rh8+ Ke7 9 Qe4+ Kd6 10 Rxd8+) **8 gxf6.** Black's threats were not illusions—they were forceful. But White's were more so.

Our final example helped decide a U.S. Championship:

Benjamin–Kamsky, U.S. Championship 1991

1 e4 e5   2 Nf3 Nc6   3 Bb5 a6   4 Bxc6 dxc6   5 0-0 Qd6   6 d3 Ne7   7 Be3 Ng6   8 Nbd2 c5?!   9 Nc4 Qe6   10 Ng5 Qf6   11 Qh5 Bd6

White now begins a powerful forcing sequence involving two pawn sacrifices.

12 f4!	exf4
13 e5!	Nxe5
14 Bxf4!	Nxc4

This appears to win a piece, but White has a surprise at the end. Now 15 Rae1+ isn't sufficiently forceful since Black can avoid immediate disaster with 15 . . . Kd7!.

15	Bxd6	Qd4+
16	Kh1	Nxd6

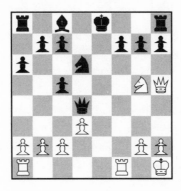

There is a strong temptation here to capture on f7 (17 Nxf7 Nxf7 18 Qxf7+ Kd8 19 Rae1 and against 20 Qe7 mate Black is lost; e.g., 19 . . . Qd6 20 Qxg7 Re8 21 Rxe8+ Kxe8 22 Rf7, or 19 . . . Qd7 20 Qf8+!).

But White saw that 17 Nxf7 has a curious flaw to it: 17 . . . 0-0 is a legal move! Not only is it legal, it eliminates all tactical dangers. So White played . . .

17 Rxf7??

. . . which threatens all sorts of murderous discovered checks of great force. But this spoiled his brilliancy because of . . .

17 . . .   Qg4!

White's discovered checks mean nothing now and he has nothing to show for his sacrificed material. He resigned on move 30.

Yet in the diagram there is a win, provided White recognizes the power of force. After 17 Rae1+! Black can lose quickly with 17 . . . Kd8 18 Nxf7+ (transposing to the 17 Nxf7 Nxf7 tree limb) or more slowly with 17 . . . Kd7 18 Nf3! and 19 Ne5+.

OPENING PANDORA'S BOX

Most middlegames are quiet. They become charged with energy only when one player makes a threat or two. His opponent counters with a greater threat and the two sides throw ideas at each other until they run out. Then the tactical energy spills off and a new period of calm is reached.

Therefore, provoking one of these showdowns of force is a high-risk enterprise. Saviely Tartakower alluded to this when he spoke of unleashing "the combinational genie." The possibility of a surprise you hadn't counted on increases dramatically.

Shamkovich–Botterill, Hastings 1977–78
Black to play

White has greater piece activity but also some weaknesses. Black can prepare an invasion of the vulnerable queenside or center with 1 . . . Rxd1+ or 1 . . . Rac8. Instead:

1 . . .   **Rd4?**

Black chose this precisely because it was more forceful. He foresaw what he called the "dreadful force" of the next series of moves.

2 Rxd4   exd4

3 e5!

Here we go. The knight on f6 is attacked, Qxa8+ is threatened, and Nd5 is looming. Black has one good reply.

3 . . .   **Rc8!**

Since 4 Bd2 Qxe5 favors Black, White's hand is also forced.

4 exf6   Rxc1+

5 Nf1   Qe1

Each of the moves since 2 Rxd4 was forced. But now Black pays for having made the position dynamic. Neither White's obvious threat (fxg7) nor Black's (. . . Qxf1+) is particularly devastating. But:

6 Rxa7!

Black said later he underestimated this move when he began the force-fight with 1 . . . Rd4, but he might have just overlooked it completely. Such an oversight is understandable in a sharp position. After **6 Rxa7** White threatens Qd5xf7+ or fxg7/Qxf7mate.

Black can delay matters with a few checks (6 . . . Qxf1+ 7 Kh2 Qg1+ 8 Kg3), but they are soon over and White then has all the threats (including 9 Ra8+ Bf8 10 Rxf8+ Kxf8 11 Qa8+ and mates).

In the game, Black went on the defensive with **6 . . . Bf8**
and lost directly: **7 Qd5 Qe6 8 Qxd4! Qe2 9 Ra8!**
(threat of Qd6 or Qb4) **9 . . . Rxf1+ 10 Kh2 Rxf2
11 Rxf8+!** (more forceful, of course, than a queen move)
11 . . . Kxf8 12 Qc5+! resigns, because of 12 . . . Ke8
or 12 . . . Kg8 13 Qc8+.

Of course, when a position is *already* dynamic, it seems to make
no sense to play quiet moves. But it would be a mistake to ex-
clusively look for the forcing candidates.

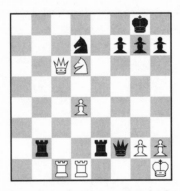

J. Polgar–Granda Zuniga, Madrid 1992
White to play

Black's knight can go to f8 to meet simple last-rank threats
and his own threat of . . . Qxg2+ prevents 1 Qxd7. Yet White
has a significant advantage, and the way to maximize it is simply 1 Rg1!, threatening the knight.

The knight cannot be protected and can only go to f8. Then
2 Rcf1 Qxd4 3 Rxf7 yields excellent winning chances (3 . . .

Rb8 4 Rgf1 Re6? 5 Rxf8+! Rxf8 6 Rxf8+ Kxf8 7 Qc8+ Ke7 8 Nf5+ Kf7 9 Qxe6+! and wins).

1 Rf1??

This is forceful, but opens up Pandora's Box. Both sides now have potentially vulnerable last ranks.

1 ...   Qxg2+??

A counter-blunder that led to a quick loss: **2 Qxg2 Rxg2 3 Rc8+ Nf8 4 Rxf7! Rxh2+ 5 Kg1 Rhg2+ 6 Kf1** and Black's defeat was assured. It was all the more embarrassing in that Black now had the advantage.

The way to exploit White's too-forcing move is 1 ... Rbc2!! because 2 Rxc2 Qxf1 is mate and 2 Rxf2 Rxc6! leaves White's rooks dangling. White's best, in fact, is 2 Qa8+ Nf8 3 h3, although it is Black who has the edge after 3 . . . Rxc1 4 Rxc1 Qxd4.

In the following example, White rejects a nonforcing defensive move, which he sees leads at best to a draw, in favor of an aggressive defense that appears to refute a sacrificial attack. But when you walk into such a forcing situation, where it is *possible* to calculate with a greater degree of accuracy, then you had better meet that standard of accuracy.

Alburt–Shirazi, U.S. Championship 1983

1 d4 c5 2 d5 Nf6 3 Nc3 g6 4 e4 d6 5 Nf3 Bg7 6 Be2 0-0 7 0-0 Na6 8 Nd2 Nc7 9 a4 e6 10 Nc4 exd5 11 exd5 b6 12 Bf4 Ba6 13 b3 Re8 14 Bf3 Nh5! 15 Bd2 Bxc4 16 bxc4 Qh4 17 Be2?! Be5

With his last two moves Black advertises his willingness to sacrifice pieces for mate.

18	g3	Nxg3
19	hxg3	Bxg3

Now White has a choice of defenses. First, he can capture on g3. This gives Black an immediate perpetual check as well as the possibility of a mate if he can get another piece to the kingside. The greatest demerit to 20 fxg3 is that it is passive, leaving Black with the opportunity to work out a winning continuation or grab a draw if he can't find one.

On the other hand, White can try 20 Kg2, threatening 21 fxg3 as well as 21 Rh1. This has the advantage of forcing matters.

20 Kg2??

As it turns out, this is a blunder because White, in his zeal to force matters, has overlooked . . .

20 ...		Qh2+
21 Kf3		Bxf2!

This move wins quickly. The bishop can't be taken (22 Rxf2 Qh3+ 23 Kf4 g5+ 24 Kxg5 Re5+, etc.). And the forcing defense of 22 Bf4 fails to 22 . . . Re3+! 23 Bxe3 Qg3+ and mate next.

22 Rg1   **Re5!**

And White resigned after **23 Bd3 Bxg1   24 Ne4 Rf5+**.

With 20 Kg2 he took the risk of allowing his king to be lured forward, thinking that by forcing matters he wouldn't allow Black time to add to his attacking army. (In fact, back at the diagram White chose 18 g3 over 18 h3 because he counted on 20 Kg2.)

Had he reviewed his thinking accurately at move 20 he would have found that 20 fxg3! Qxg3+ 21 Kh1 would have drawn since Black's other pieces are too far away to be of any immediate use.

THE LIMITS OF FORCE

Finally, it should be pointed out that "quiet" moves may also be forcing, and sometimes the apparently passive is better than the malevolently dynamic.

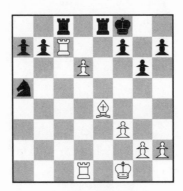

Lukacs–Luecke, Budapest 1991
White to play

White is a pawn down but has excellent compensation in light of his superior minor piece, advanced rook, and passed pawn. Instinct tells him he should look for a forcing idea, since quiet play is likely to neutralize his compensation and lead to a victory for Black's passed queenside pawns.

But when he looks for forceful lines he finds that 1 Ra1 (intending 1 . . . b6 2 Rxa7) leads nowhere after 1 . . . Rxc7 2 dxc7 b6 because 3 Rxa5? bxa5 4 Bb7 and 5 c8Q in fact loses to the distant a-pawn (4 . . . a4!).

The improved version of this, 1 Rd5 and then 1 . . . b6 2 Rxa7 or 1 . . . Rxc7 2 dxc7 b6 3 Rd8, also has a serious hole: 1 . . . Nc4 and then 2 Rxb7 Ne3+ or 2 Kf2 Nxd6!.

So White played . . .

     1 Kg1!?

. . . which, in fact, is forceful because now 2 Rd5 Nc4 3 Rxb7 is a winning line (no check with 3 . . . Ne3).

     1 . . .   **Rxc7?**

Black probably saw that his forcing 1 . . . f5? fails to 2 Rxh7, threatening 3 d7. On the best defense, 1 . . . Red8, White has only a minor edge.

     2 dxc7   **Ke7**
     3 Bxb7!   **resigns**

Because of 3 . . . Nxb7 4 Re1+ Kd7 5 Rxe8 Kxe8 6 c8Q+.

Sometimes you need to maneuver your thinking midway between the most forceful and the least. The following example helps demonstrate this:

Benko–Byrne, U.S. Open 1964

1 e4 e6 2 d3 d5 3 Nd2 Nf6 4 Ngf3 b6 5 e5
Nfd7 6 g3 c5 7 Bg2 Qc7 8 0-0 Nxe5? 9 Nxe5
Qxe5 10 c4 Qd6? 11 cxd5 exd5 12 Nc4! Qd8
13 Qh5 Bb7

White has just played four moves in a row of varying force
and is in the mood to push the action along. Now he has to
make a choice. With 14 Ne3 he will threaten a pawn, and in
fact must win it since 14 . . . d4?? loses to 15 Bxb7.

The alternative is a forcing move like 14 Re1+ or 14 Bg5.
White can mix the two ideas together with 14 Bg5 Be7 15 Rfe1
but has to find a good followup after 15 . . . Nc6.

After the game White explained that he gave up on this
last tree, and played the inferior **14 Ne3** instead, because
he examined only one continuation after 14 Bg5 Be7 15 Rfe1
Nc6, what he called the "Morphy style" 16 Rxe7+ Nxe7
17 Rfe1.

But then he saw that 17 . . . 0-0 18 Bxe7 could be met by
18 . . . Re8!, after which 19 Bxd8 Rxe1+ 20 Bf1 dxc4 is decidedly unclear.

White was correct to reject the violent "Morphy" line in
favor of 14 Ne3?!, which led to a solid advantage and, in
fact, to a win in another ten moves. But he missed the
best branch—the middle-of-the-road branch—which
would have won a piece immediately: 14 Bg5 Be7 15 Rfe1
Nc6 16 Ne5!.

FORCE IN ACTION

Finally, let's examine a full game that illustrates the dangers of misjudging force. The game shows how an obscure master missed an opportunity to mate a former world champion in less than 30 moves, then went on to lose because of a variety of calculation errors.

Tan–Smyslov, Petropolis 1973

1 e4 d6   2 d4 Nf6   3 Nc3 g6   4 Bc4 Bg7   5 Qe2 c6   6 e5 Nd5   7 Bd2 0-0   8 Bb3 a5   9 a4 dxe5 10 dxe5 Na6   11 Nf3 Nc5   12 Bxd5 cxd5   13 Be3 Ne4   14 Bd4 Nxc3   15 Bxc3 b6   16 Qd2 Ba6 17 h4! Qd7   18 h5 Qg4   19 0-0-0! Qxa4   20 Kb1 Rfc8   21 Rh4 Qe8   22 hxg6 hxg6   23 Rdh1 Rc4

White has sacrificed a pawn for a promising kingside attack. Black's last move, threatening to diminish the enemy army by a trade of rooks, compels White to weigh the various choices: He can block the fourth rank with 24 Bd4, 24 Nd4, or 24 g4. Or he can retreat his rook to h2 or h3. But these are all inferior because they lack force.

24 Rh7?!

Yes, this is superior to the moves just mentioned: It carries more power in the form of the threatened 25 Rxg7+ Kxg7 26 Qh6+ and mate next. But at the same time, White fails to consider the *most* forceful line, that is, moving the rook one square farther and giving check.

Once you spot 24 Rh8+! Bxh8 you have to examine 25 Qh6. This threatens mate on h8, but runs out of steam after 25 ... Bg7. Therefore, you should look for a more forceful second move, and find it in the form of 25 Rxh8+! Kxh8 26 Qh6+ Kg8.

Analysis variation after 26 ... Kg8

White is very close to delivering mate, and the final stage of calculation involves determining whether Ng5 and Qh7+ leads to that result. At first glance the double-rook sacrifice appears unsound because 27 Ng5 e6! 28 Qh7+ Kf8 29 Qh8+ Ke7 30 Qf6+ Kd7 and Black escapes, or 27 Ng5 e6 28 Nh7 Rf4!

But if you refine the sequence a bit with 27 e6! first, the game is over. After Black meets the threat of mate on h8 with 27 ... Rxc3 or 27 ... f6, White has the pretty and effective 28 Ng5!!. Mate is then unstoppable.

Meanwhile, back in the game, Black met the threat of 25 Rxg7+ with ...

24 ...   Qf8
25 e6

There is more than one idea for continuing the attack. With Black's queen now blocking the king's evacuation route, White can triple heavy pieces on the h-file, followed by Rh8+.

This has the drawback of calling for three "quiet" preparatory moves (e.g., 25 Rh2, 26 Qe1, and 27 Qh1, or perhaps the more accurate 25 Qg5 and Qg3-h2. But it's not obvious how Black can defend against this slow buildup (25 Qg5 d4 26 Qh4! f6 27 e6).

Instead, White opts for the more forceful idea, threatening 26 Rh8+ Bxh8 27 Rxh8 mate or 26 Rxg7+.

25 . . .	Rxc3

This can be called semi-forcing, since White must either capture on c3 or come up with a more forceful move of his own. Since there are checks and mate threats of various kinds in this position, the force-power of 25 . . . Rxc3 is relatively low.

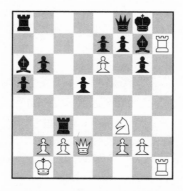

26 exf7+?

This is forceful but for only one move. White appears to have played this move without an idea in mind—a very dangerous policy. He could, of course, have simply played 26 bxc3. But that might have turned the initiative over to Black.

If he had looked a bit more deeply, White might have found 26 Ng5!, which threatens to win the queen with 27 exf7+. Then 26 . . . fxe6 is clearly unsatisfactory because of 27 Nxe6. So he would focus attention on 26 . . . f6, and then 27 Qxc3, preparing to win with 28 Qh3 and 29 Rh8+, looks good. But 26 . . . f6 27 Nf7! and 28 Rh8+ is better. It wins outright.

This is the second win White missed for failing to search for force.

> **26 . . .**   **Qxf7**
> **27 bxc3?**

White misses a third opportunity and plays instead a quiet recapture. What are the more forceful tries in the position? The chief candidates are the attacks on the queen (Ng5 and Ne5). The idea is to drive the queen away from the defense of two key squares, g7 and d5. Consider the consequences of 27 Ne5!:

(a) If Black abandons g7 with 27 . . . Qe6 he allows 28 Rxg7+! Kxg7 29 Qh6+ Kf6 (forced) 30 Qxg6+! Kxe5 31 Re1+ and wins.
(b) If Black abandons d5 with 27 . . . Qf6 or 27 . . . Qf5 he allows 28 Qxd5+ and 29 Qxa8+.
(c) If Black tries a desperado, meeting force with force, and tries 27 . . . Rxc2, then 28 Qxc2 Qf5! may kill the attack. But 28 Rxg7+! wins, since 28 . . . Kxg7 29 Qh6+ bags the queen, and 28 . . . Qxg7 29 Qxd5+ Kf8 allows 30 Rh8+ Qxh8 31 Qf7 mate.

> **27 . . .**   **Rd8**
> **28 Ne5**

One move late, now that d5 is covered.

> **28 . . .**   **Qf6**

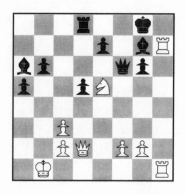

29 f4?

A final failure. White tries to consolidate with quiet moves, but the inadequacy of this policy is shown by the rest of the game: **29 ... d4! 30 g4 Bb7! 31 R1h3 Rd5 32 cxd4 Qd6 33 Qh2** (33 Rh8+ Bxh8 34 Rxh8+ Kg7! leads to nothing) **33 . . . Qb4+ 34 Ka2 Qa4+ 35 Ra3 Qxd4 36 Rxg7+ Kxg7** and as he played **37 Rh3**, White's flag fell.

What could he have done? The diagrammed position calls for force, and one likely policy is 29 Ng4!, forcing Black to choose between 29 ... Qd6 (30 Rxg7+! Kxg7 31 Qd4+ with unclear play) or 29 ... Qxc3 30 Qxc3 Bxc3 31 Rxe7 when White's rooks are suddenly very strong on the seventh rank (31 ... Bg7 32 Nh6+ Bxh6 33 Rxh6 Rd6 34 Rhh7).

With a healthy appreciation of force, the aspiring calculator is ready for the meat and potatoes of calculation—the counting out and evaluating of variations in the tree of analysis.

Five

COUNTING OUT

"Everyone complains of his memory, and no one complains of his judgment."

—La Rochefoucauld

Once we've examined the tactical and strategic ideas in a position and have assessed the forcing moves, we move into a different realm. This is the more familiar form of calculation, the mental processing of tree branches. The most important questions to ask in this process are:

(1) What is the final position in each sequence like? Is one more favorable than others? In short, how do we *evaluate* the branches of a tree?

(2) Am I sure they are the *final* positions? After my intended two-mover can I say "and wins"? In short, when can I stop calculating?

(3) Do I have the right move order? Can the idea be improved by a different sequence?

(4) Is there an escape route? If I begin a forcing sequence that runs four moves and suddenly realize after two moves have been played that I've made an oversight, can I bail out?

THE BOTTOM LINE

The most common misunderstanding about the powers of chessplaying computers—by experienced players as well as by novices—is that machines calculate more efficiently than humans. They don't.

They can't, because they lack a human's greater skills of intuition and evaluation. We can turn our attention to the most likely moves and responses and ignore the others. We don't have to work every variation out to mate.

"A master's strength is in the evaluation of a position," wrote Mikhail Botvinnik. You can have the Cray Blitz capacity to instantly analyze a candidate 15 moves deep. But if you conclude after those 15 moves that White is better when in fact Black has the edge, all your work is wasted.

In computer-only tournaments of the 1980s, much of the success of the champion program Deep Thought lay in its superior powers of evaluation. It won more than a few games from positions that its opponent had forced, considering them favorable, if not *winning*, when in fact they were unfavorable.

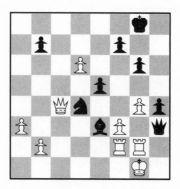

Ribli–Planinc, Portoroz/Ljubljana 1975
Black to play

White has the advantage of the double exchange (two rooks for Black's two minor pieces). But Black has what Bobby Fischer used to call "a juicy position." Black is the one with the threats, pins, and tactical ideas. Moreover, Black has just passed the time control so he can choose at his leisure between the various candidates (1 . . . Nxf3+, 1 . . . Bxf2+, 1 . . . Qxf3).

Instead, Black calculated one line out to the natural end-position, a position where the tactics are over and there seem no great issues left to be resolved. He quickly went into:

| 1 | ... | Nxf3+ |
| 2 | Kf1 | Nd2+ |

White's reply is forced and his rooks become disconnected.

| 3 | Rxd2 | Qh1+ |
| 4 | Ke2 | Bxd2 |

Here Black concluded that with 5 . . . Qe1+ and mate threatened, White must play 5 Kxd2, after which 5 . . . Qxg2+ puts Black a pawn ahead in a queen-and-pawn endgame.

All quite true. But Black is not better; in fact in the end-position he is worse. What he failed to remember is that the number of pawns in such an ending is often not as significant as how far they are advanced. In other words, he didn't evaluate the 5 . . . Qxg2+ end-position properly.

And the result was **5 Kxd2 Qxg2+ 6 Kc3 Qg3+ 7 Kb4 e4 8 Qd4!** and the powerful d-pawn decided the game quickly: **8 . . . Qe1+ 9 Ka4 b5+ 10 Kxb5 Qf1+ 11 Kb6 Qf4 12 Kc6 Qg5 13 d7 Qd8 14 Qb6 Qf6+ 15 Kb7 Qe7 16 Kc8! resigns**.

This was an important lesson for Black to learn, particularly since he can win from the diagram if he searches further and finds 1 . . . Bxf2+!. That requires a bit more computing time than 1 . . . Nxf3+ because the tree of analysis gets wider and longer: After the bishop's capture White has two ways of retaking on f2, and in each case the issue remains in doubt longer than the five moves that Black examined with 1 . . . Nxf3+.

But it would have paid off: 1 . . . Bxf2+ 2 Kxf2 Qxf3+ 3 Kg1 h3! 4 Rf2 Qxg4+ 5 Kh1 Qe4+ 6 Kh2 Nf3+ and wins, or 2 Rxf2 Nxf3+ 3 Rxf3 Qxf3 and the White king position makes this queen-and-pawn endgame a win for Black: 4 d7 Qd1+ or 4 Qc8+ Kg7 5 d7 h3! 6 Qc2 Qxg4+.

FIRST STEP: COUNT THE PIECES

In most evaluations, you'll be guided by the material situation. At the end of the main variation you will need to know who is ahead and by how much. The simplest way to do this is to count up what's left on the board at the end of the line.

Sound easy? Maybe so, but consider this example. Black not only misevaluates a variation materially, he doesn't even count the pieces on the board correctly when he resigns.

Verber (U.S.)–Mikenda (Austria), Haifa 1970
White to play

This comes from the last World Student Olympiad that was won by the United States. The Americans won by a single point—perhaps this one.

1 Ne4	Bxa1
2 Nxc5!?	

White appreciated that he has a poor game positionally because of the backward d-pawn and Black's ability to occupy d4. So, instead of the routine recapture (2 Rxa1 Nf5 and . . . Ncd4), he converts a slow strategic struggle into a dynamic, tactical one.

2 . . .	Qa8
3 Nxd7	Nd4!

After 3 . . . Bd4 Black has all the winning chances because White's knight is trapped on d7. The result of 4 Nxb6 axb6 is rough material equality (two pawns and a rook for two minor pieces), but the pieces would be much stronger than the rook. Black's choice, 3 . . . Nd4, is even better.

4 Qe4!?	Nxc2
5 Qxa8	Rxa8
6 c5	

This manages to free the knight at d7, and it also confuses Black. Somehow in the Austrian's calculations he convinced himself that he has *lost* material over the last five moves. He sees that he's minus a rook and remembers taking an enemy piece. But instead of realizing that he has won two pieces for the rook, he thinks he has lost the exchange. There followed:

6 ...	Ne3
7 Re1	Bd4
8 cxb6	axb6
9 Nxb6	Black resigns??

Of course, *we* know how to count the material on the board. But in a visualized position—a position not actually on the board—it is hardly easy. There are two basic ways of figuring out the status of material at the end of a mental variation:

The first, somewhat clumsy, method is to review the variation in your head, adding up the captured pieces by White and then the ones captured by Black along the way.

The alternative is to run through the sequence in your head until the end-position and then "see" the remaining pieces.

Let's consider how this works in practice. Even in a battle of world champions, one can mess it up.

Capablanca–Alekhine, Nottingham 1936
Black to play

| 1 ... | f4? |

"A miscalculation of a somewhat peculiar kind," wrote Alexander Alekhine. He thought he was winning two exchanges. Instead, he gives up three pieces for the rooks.

2 gxf4	Bf5
3 Qd2	Bxd3
4 exd3	

It was now time for Black to cut his losses by bailing out of his original combination. He should play 4 ... Na4 (after which 5 d4 gives White an excellent, but not yet won, position). However, Alekhine went on to lose the game because he failed to count accurately.

Had Alekhine employed the count-up method, either at this point or back when he was weighing the merits of 1 . . . f4, he might have sounded like this:

"Well, I will win one of his rooks for a bishop when I play 2 . . . Bf5. Then he'll give up his rook for the knight on c3, I'll recapture with the bishop on f6, and he'll make the last capture. Hmmm. I know it often turns out badly when your opponent makes the *last* capture.

"What's the score? I'll have taken both of his rooks and he'll have gotten my f-pawn, plus one, two . . . no!, three minor pieces. I know from experience that three pieces are almost always better than two rooks. So I have to play something else."

Had Alekhine employed the alternative method, visualizing the final position, he might have sounded like this:

"Let's see, after 1 . . . f4 2 gxf4 Bf5 3 Q-somewhere Bxd3 4 exd3, suppose I allow him to continue 5 Rxc3 Bxc3 6 Qxc3. What's left on the board?

"Well, we both have queens. And nothing has happened to my two rooks while both of his are gone. Hold on! I don't have any minor pieces left. How many does he have? He hasn't moved any of them. The bishop is still on e3, the bishop on g2, and the knight on f3. And I've also given up a pawn. The final score sounds even, but it must be bad for me."

Alekhine apparently used neither method. He played **4 . . . c5?**, and after **5 Rxc3 Bxc3 6 Qxc3 Qf6 7 Qxf6 gxf6 8 Nd2!** the true material picture was clear to everyone. The minor pieces swept into power with **8 . . . f5 9 b5 a5 10 Nf1 Kf7 11 Ng3** and Black resigned shortly.

Sometimes when a lot of material is traded off, or when your opponent is losing something heavy, such as his queen, we become blinded.

Onoprienko–Liberzon, Soviet Armed Forces Championship 1966

1 e4 c5   2 Nf3 e6   3 d4 cxd4   4 Nxd4 a6   5 Nc3 Qc7   6 Bd3 Nc6   7 Be3 Nf6   8 0-0 b5   9 Nxc6 Qxc6   10 Qf3 Bb7   11 a3 Bc5   12 Rfe1 d6   13 Bg5 Nd7   14 Qh3 Ne5   15 Rad1 0-0

Here White sees what appears to be a winning move:
16 Nd5
It threatens both a knight fork at e7 that wins the queen, and a check at f6 that leads to a very strong attack. "And, of course, on 16 ... exd5 White plays 17 exd5, attacking the queen and threatening mate on h7," White says to himself.

But this is not so simple.

16 ...	exd5!
17 exd5	Nxd3

Black's last move eliminates the mating bishop and forces White to continue:

18 dxc6	Nxf2

White had calculated this far: he's won the queen for two minor pieces and threatens a bishop. But his own queen is hanging and he will likely lose a rook by discovered check. There is nothing "of course" about the position.

19 Qf3	Bxc6!
20 Qxc6	Nxd1+
21 Kf1	Nxb2

Here is where the real calculation ends and the counting up begins. The score reads: White has won a queen for a knight, a rook, and a pawn. Material is roughly even.

But, as Botvinnik used to point out, the "evaluation function" is not just a matter of adding two plus two. Sometimes you're dealing with material apples and strategic oranges that can't be added. The reason is that evaluation has a material component, but also a positional one.

Here White has several problems. His a-pawn is weak, his king is insecure, and he has no natural defense to an assault along the c-file.

The game actually saw **22 Re4 Nc4   23 Qd5 Bxa3 24 Qd3 Bc5   25 Rh4 f5   26 Qh3 h6   27 Qf3 Rae8 28 Bc1 Re4!** and White fell apart in a few moves: **29 g3 Rxh4   30 gxh4 f4!   31 Kg2 Be3   32 Ba3 Nd2! 33 Qd5+ Rf7 White resigns**.

A more recent example shows how this kind of error can be made as early as the ninth move:

Taimanov–Zaichik, Leningrad 1989

1 Nf3 f5   2 d3 Nc6   3 e4 e5   4 Nc3 Nf6   5 exf5 d5
6 d4 exd4   7 Nxd4 Nxd4   8 Qxd4 Bxf5   9 Bg5 Bxc2?

This is an error. Black made it knowing that White could begin a dangerous sequence with 10 Rc1 and then 11 Bxf6 Qxf6 12
Qe3+ and Nxd5. But Black convinced himself that White
couldn't play it because of a surprise he intended at his 13th move.

10	Rc1!	Bg6
11	Bxf6	Qxf6
12	Qe3+	Kf7
13	Nxd5	Bb4+

Consistent with his last move. Black hopes to win the
queen with 14 . . . Rhe8. White promptly obliges.

14	Nxb4!	Rhe8
15	Bc4+	Kf8
16	0-0!	Rxe3
17	fxe3	Bf5
18	g4	

White's moves have been virtually forced since move 13.
But the final position of Black's combination must be greatly
in White's favor despite the loss of his queen.

The game, in fact, lasted only 10 more moves: **18 . . . g6
19 gxf5 Kg7   20 Nd5 Qe5   21 fxg6 hxg6   22 Rf3**
and White won.

Even in relatively simple positions, with no strange material
imbalances, a strong player can make horrible misevaluations.
This is particularly common in endgame transitions.

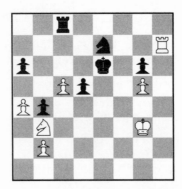

Ulibin–I. Gurevich, Santiago 1990
White to play

Let's evaluate: First, material is equal. Second, both sides have passed pawns but White's is a bit farther advanced. White's rook and knight are a bit more active than Black's, but Black has the more useful king.

Bottom line: Unclear. Normally, an "unclear" label is not a problem. Afterward, an annotator may decide to update his evaluation, changing from the equal sign at move 12 to the plus-over-equals, denoting a slight advantage to White, at move 20. But the players don't have to do this in the course of a game.

However, in this situation an evaluation is important because White has a relatively easy, forcing draw if he wants one: 1 Nd4+ Ke5 2 Nf3+. Black cannot avoid the repeat of the position without incurring problems; e.g., 2 . . . Ke6 3 Nd4+ Kd7 4 Nb3 Rf8 5 Nd4.

When you have the opportunity to force matters into a particular result, a win or draw, you should analyze the alternative with exceptional caution. However:

1 Nd4+	Ke5
2 Rxe7+??	Kxd4
3 Re6	

White saw this far and concluded he was better. In fact, he is probably already lost.

3 ...	Kc4
4 Rxg6	Kb3!
5 Rxa6	Kxb2

And with his king able to support both passed pawns—unlike White's—Black won easily: **6 Kf4 Kc3   7 Rh6 d4 8 g6 b3   9 g7 Rg8   10 Rg6 b2   11 Rg1 Rxg7** and White resigned shortly. White threw away this game because of gross misevaluation.

Finding the bottom line is not only part of processing variations. It can also play an inspirational role. When evaluating a seemingly forced line of play the position may reveal to us a superior alternative.

Azmaiparashvili–Yudasin, Soviet Championship 1986
Black to play

White has just retreated his attacked knight from c4 to d2, simultaneously threatening the enemy queen and Rxc8. He appears to be on the verge of winning:

1 ...   **Bd7**

At a moment like this, when a player is at the decisive point of the game and emotions are naturally peaking, we can understand how White might bang down 2 Qxf8+ and then 3 Nxb3.

But as students of calculation we cannot excuse him. Because after 2 . . . Kxf8 and 3 . . . axb3 White, although up the exchange, is not winning. He is not even better. In fact, he stands worse.

His rooks can dominate the only open file but lack significant targets (Rc7 is met by . . . Bc6). His bishop is locked in at g2 by Black's center pawns. Black, however, can attack a significant target—b2—while bringing his king toward the center to advance his pawns.

White understood this and so he looked for a better move than 1 Qxf8+. He realized that he needed a new idea. And, as so often happens in chess, when you look, you find.

2 Rc8!!   **resigns**

A hard move to spot, but working out the lines is easy (2 . . . Q-moves 3 Rxf8 mate; 2 . . . Rxc8 3 Rxc8+ Bxc8 4 Qxc8+ Kf7 5 Nxb3; 2 . . . Bxc8 3 Nxb3 and White has won a queen for a rook).

Many errors are made in evaluating positions with material equality, or what appears to be equality. Unless the two sides have exactly the same pieces left on the board, there is some difference in the value of their armies.

For example, the first book you read about chess told you that when you give up two pieces for a rook and a pawn (or two pawns), material is roughly even. This is rarely true in practice. Often the minor pieces are much better, particularly in an active middlegame. And sometimes the rook is winning, particularly in an ending with only a few pieces left or when there are passed pawns on both wings.

Evans–Rossolimo, U.S. Championship 1966
Black to play

Both of Black's rooks and his knight on h4 are under attack. But rather than begin defensive measures with 1 . . . Rxd1+, he found a combination—in fact, it helped win the best-played-game prize in this event. The idea of exploiting the last rank (1 . . . Rxc2) is not very difficult to find. Working out the combination to its end is much more of a challenge. This is because the main line is five moves long and requires finding an inspired "quiet" second move.

But many a strong master would have played something else even if they saw all five moves. They would have rejected the combination simply because they could not appreciate how well Black stood at the end.

Let's see:

      1 . . .   **Rxc2!**

So far, so good: 2 Rxc2 allows mate in one (2 . . . Rxd1) and 2 Rxd5 allows mate in two. The real question is what happens after 2 Qxh4.

      2 Qxh4   **Rd4!!**

A terrific move. Its strength is hard to foresee in the diagram but the variations are easy to work out at this point:

(a) Protecting the knight with 3 f3 allows 3 . . . Qxg2 mate.
(b) Taking either rook allows the same last-rank mates as after 1 . . . Rxc2.
(c) Any quiet move allows Black to play . . . Qxe4 and remain a pawn ahead; e.g., 3 h3 Rxc1 4 Rxc1 Qxe4 or 3 Ra1 Qxe4.

That leaves one "loud" move:

      3 Qd8+   **Rxd8**
      4 Rxd8+   **Kh7**
      5 Rxc2   **Qxe4**

Now examine what we have left:

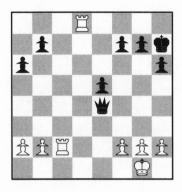

In terms of material, Black has won a queen and a pawn for two rooks. According to the primers, material is equal. There is a good reason for that judgment. If the White rooks were able to attack the same Black pawn and Black were forced to defend it with his queen and king, the result of a liquidation beginning with rook takes pawn and queen takes rook would be a dead-even material ending with just pawns and kings left.

But the position in the diagram is not even. The rooks are not coordinated, while both 6 . . . Qxc2 and 6 . . . Qe1 mate are threatened. That means 6 Rc1 is forced, and Black has time to begin mobilizing his extra pawn and king before White can double his rooks against a target. Eventually, the Black king can shepherd a passed pawn to a square on which White will have to begin the liquidating combination.

Black is the only one who can win such a position. This important realization—the evaluation of the end-position—is what crowned a prize-winning game.

It lasted some 40 more moves but the power of the queen was evident after **6 Rc1 Qe2   7 Rb1 f5!   8 Rdd1 e4 9 Re1 Qc4   10 a3 Qa2!   11 g3 Kg6   12 Kg2 Qb3 13 Kg1 Qa2   14 Kg2 Kf6   15 f3 Ke5   16 fxe4 fxe4**

17 h4 Qb3   18 Kh3 Qc2   19 Rec1 Qf2   20 Rf1 Qb6
21 Kg2 g6   22 Rf8 Qb5   23 Rf2 e3   24 Re1 Ke4
25 a4 Qc5   26 Kh3 b5!   27 axb5 axb5   28 Rf6 Qe5
29 Rf8 Qe7   30 Rf4+ Kd3   31 Rf3 Kd2.

When he saw this game published in a Soviet magazine, the great violinist David Oistrakh, a strong amateur player, explained, "On a violin I could not have played better."

WHAT IS COMPENSATION?

Before we leave the subject of evaluation, we must acknowledge that players often go into sequences that leave them decidedly behind in material, but with plenty of that vague commodity we call "compensation."

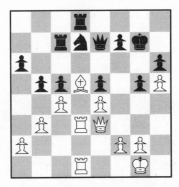

Yusupov–Karpov, Candidates Match 1989
White to play

Black's last two moves, . . . Rc7 and . . . Nd7, begin a transfer of the knight from b6 to the kingside, either to f6 or perhaps to f8-e6-d4. Then White's absolute control of the d-file will be somewhat reduced and his winning plans curtailed.

It is moments like this when temporary opportunities arise.

1 Bxf7!!

This sacrifice was universally praised. Now on 1 . . . Qxf7 White invades with heavy pieces by 2 Qh3 and 3 Rd6.

1 . . .   Kxf7

2 Qd2?!

But this was sharply criticized. When White decided to sacrifice he well understood that he would keep total control of the open file. But what else did he have in return for a bishop besides a single pawn?

It appears that even against a former world champion, White did not think he had to foresee a specific winning sequence in order to make such a sacrifice. What he saw was that Black couldn't extricate himself from the pin and achieve king safety.

Afterward, annotators found a number of improvements for White, such as 2 Rd6!, followed by the invasion of the queen to f5, via f3 or h3. Then 2 . . . Rcc8 3 Rxh6 Nf8 4 Rd5! or 2 . . . Rdc8 3 Qf3+ Ke8 4 Qf5 White is close to a winning position.

The game actually continued **2 . . . Ke8   3 Qa5 bxc4 4 bxc4** and now instead of 4 . . . Rc6 and 5 . . . Qe6 with a solid position, Black blundered with **4 . . . Rcc8? 5 Qa4! Rc7?   6 Qxa6 Rb8   7 Qg6+h Kf8?   8 Rf3+ resigns**.

Even though the attack and defense were both flawed, White's original decision was quite correct. He had compensation even though he did not specifically see how to use it.

A great master of evaluating such positions was the late Mikhail Tal:

Tal–Letelier, Havana 1963

1 e4 e5 2 Nf3 Nc6 3 Bb5 a6 4 Ba4 d6 5 c3 Bd7
6 d4 Nge7 7 Bb3 h6 8 Nh4 g5? 9 Qh5 Rh7
10 Bxg5 exd4 11 f4 Qc8 12 f5 dxc3 13 Nxc3 Ne5
14 Bf6 Ng8 15 Bxe5 dxe5

Many players of less than Tal-strength could have calculated the next three moves in advance. But few of them would
have forced the play as the former world champion does here.
His genius lay not in the length of his variations, but in the
evaluation of positions such as the one that occurs three moves
later, at 18 Nd5.

16 Ng6

This was more or less expected. There were only a few forcing moves to consider. One of them, 16 Bxf7+, doesn't quite
work, and another, 16 Qg4, permits what we will call an
attack-defense response, 16 . . . Nf6!, that halts White in his
tracks.

16 . . .   Bd6

Tal's threats were 17 Nxf8, to set up the king for attack, and
17 Nxe5. Clearly, 16 . . . fxg6 17 Qxg6+ was out of the question.

17 Bxf7+!	Kxf7

It isn't hard to spot 17 . . . Rxf7 18 Nh8!. After the king moves there are a number of discovered checks with the knight. Yet Tal played:

18 Nd5!

In reaching this position from the diagram Tal disregarded the material imbalance (a bishop for a pawn) and the absence of specific positional compensation, but regarded the White knights, supported by the heavy pieces following 19 0-0, as sufficient to engineer a mating attack.

It's impossible for humans to calculate much further than 18 Nd5 with any degree of certainty. Tal relied on general principles, his instincts, and the consideration of a few likely continuations. The most obvious defensive moves either fail outright (18 . . . Nf6? 19 Nxe5+ Kg7 20 Qg6+) or allow more attacking pieces to join in (18 . . . Kg7 19 0-0).

18 . . .	Kg7
19 0-0	Nf6
20 Nxf6	Kxf6
21 Nxe5!	

Now we again have a position that can be calculated with some certainty (21 . . . Bxe5 22 Qg6+; 21 . . . Kxe5 22 f6+). Tal's decision at moves 16–18 is soon proven correct.

Compensation, then, is in the eye of the beholder. Whereas some players would never consider the position after 18 Nd5 acceptable for White because there are no concrete variations that show White winning, Tal reasoned the other way: There are no concrete variations that show Black consolidating.

21 . . .	Qe8
22 Nxd7+	Rxd7
23 e5+!	Bxe5

And Black resigned after **24 Qxh6+ Kf7   25 Rae1 Rd5 26 Qh7+ Kf6   27 Re4! Bd4+   28 Kh1 resigns** (28 ... Qxe4 29 Qg6+ Ke7 30 f6+.)

IS IT OVER?

When an amateur allows his opponent to play a strong combination, chances are he either completely overlooked the possibility of a combination, or misevaluated the final position.

But when a master allows a strong combination, it isn't necessarily because he and his opponent disagree about the nature of the end-position. Rather, the two players may be considering two *different* end-positions because one player stopped calculating the key line too soon.

Timman–Karpov, Montreal 1979

1 c4 Nf6   2 Nc3 e5   3 Nf3 Nc6   4 e3 Be7   5 d4 exd4   6 Nxd4 0-0   7 Nxc6 bxc6   8 Be2 d5   9 0-0 Bd6   10 b3   Qe7   11 Bb2   dxc4!   12 bxc4   Rb8 13 Qc1 Ng4   14 g3 Re8   15 Nd1

White is now lost, though it doesn't look that way. In fact, it won't be clear for several moves. But he has made a series of minor errors (10 cxd5 and 11 b3 was more exact, and 15 Bf3 was also better than what was played).

Jan Timman's fatal error was allowing the following combination, which he realized was coming. White had calculated 15 . . . Nxh2 "to the end," but misjudged where that end was.

15 . . .   Nxh2

"Timman foresaw this move, of course," his opponent said later.

16 c5!

Timman saw the main line, which was not very original but would have been quite effective (16 Kxh2 Qh4+ 17 Kg2 Qh3+ 18 Kg1 Bxg3 19 fxg3 Qxg3+ 20 Kh1 and now 20 . . . Re4! wins; e.g., 21 Rf4 Bh3!).

But he concluded that Black could not play 15 . . . Nxh2 because of 16 c5!, which deflects the bishop. On 16 . . . Nxf1 White takes the bishop first and, next move, the trapped knight.

16 . . .   Nxf1

Unfortunately for Black, the bishop cannot be diverted (16 . . . Bxc5 17 Kxh2!).

Karpov might have tried the finesse 16 . . . Be5 17 Bxe5 Nxf1, since White, with a bishop attacked, doesn't have time to capture on f1. There could follow 18 Bf4 g5 19 Bxf1 gxf4 20 exf4 with unclear results. But he has better.

17 cxd6

White saw this far . . . and stopped. He had good reason: Black's queen and knight are both attacked, and one of them will be taken next move. White's kingside remains pretty much intact despite the loss of the h-pawn, and he has attacking ideas of his own, such as Qc3.

White probably figured he stood much better in this position. Did he miss something?

17 . . .   Nxg3!

Yes, he missed the only forcing move in the position (18 dxe7 Nxe2+ and 19 . . . Nxc1 puts him the exchange and a pawn down). Timman probably saw it coming after 16 . . . Nxf1, but by then it was too late.

18 fxg3   Qxd6

This is where the calculation begun at 15 . . . Nxh2 really ends. The difference is considerable from, say, the consequences of 17 . . . Qxd6 18 Bxf1. In this case, White's king defense is a mess and he has one pawn less than expected. Moreover, his pieces are too late in arriving at the kingside (19 Kg2 Qh6! 20 g4 Qg5) while Black's get there quickly (. . . Re6 and . . . Qh6).

Black saw this far, White did not. The rest of the game was anticlimax: 19 Kf2 Qh6   20 Bd4 Qh2+   21 Ke1 Qxg3+ 22 Kd2 Qg2   23 Nb2 Ba6   24 Nd3 Bxd3   25 Kxd3 Rbd8   26 Bf1 Qe4+   27 Kc3 c5!   28 Bxc5 Qc6 29 Kb3 Rb8+   30 Ka3 Re5   31 Bb4 Qb6 and White resigned.

The moral is that you must not only evaluate a position correctly—you must evaluate the *correct* position.

There should be two general guidelines to the question "How far is far enough?"

The first is to calculate as many moves ahead as it takes to *reach a conclusion*. The conclusion may be as definite as "and White wins." Or it could be as vague as "and I prefer my position," as Tal might have said in the earlier example in this chapter.

Second, you should calculate until the forcing moves are over.

Generally, the stronger a player's sense of what constitutes an advantage, the easier it is for him to calculate because he can reach a firmer conclusion and therefore stop after looking just a few moves ahead. Computers have to look much further.

Larsen–Portisch, Siegen 1970
Black to play

It's not hard to pinpoint the squares that will figure prominently in Black's calculations: f2 and e4. One is protected only by the White king, the other only by a knight. Out of this comes the idea of 1 . . . Rxf2!

| 1 . . . | Rxf2! |
| 2 Kxf2 | Ne4+ |

The game went on for two more moves, but it could have lasted at least five more if White had insisted. Yet Black did not really have to see any further than 2 . . . Ne4+ in order to decide upon 1 . . . Rxf2.

The reason is that judgment would tell him that 1 . . . Rxf2 *has* to be sound in such a position. The knight check guarantees Black that he will get his piece back. Therefore, he'll have approximate material equality at move three. In addition, he can see that there will be checks and threats after that point.

The judgment that comes with experience tells him that (a) he will have enough material compensation for the exchange and (b) he'll be considerably better off than in the diagram in terms of positional considerations.

Black *could*, of course, examine all those checks and threats, as well as possible White defense, to verify his evaluation of the 2 . . . Ne4+ position. The lines are relatively easy to work out: White cannot move his king to g2 (3 . . . Qxg3 mate) or e2 (3 . . . Nxg3+). That leaves e1, which invites a strong 3 . . . Qxg3+, and the only other legal move, which White played. By examining this far, Black would be able to conclude that he is not only well off after 1 . . . Rxf2, but winning.

The point, however, is that in practical terms, Black didn't have to see that much when he decided on his move in the diagram.

| 3 Kg1 | Qxg3+ |
| 4 Bg2 | Qxe3+ |

resigns

There are at least three winning moves now (5 . . . Nxc3, 5 . . . Bh6 and a check on f4, and 5 . . . Nf2).

A more elaborate version of the same principle is:

Reorl–Palme, Austrian Championship 1977

1 c4 c5   2 Nc3 Nc6   3 Nf3 e5   4 e3 d6   5 d4 Bg4
6 Be2 Nf6   7 0-0 cxd4   8 exd4 Be7   9 Be3 0-0
10 Rc1 Re8   11 h3 Bh5   12 dxe5 dxe5   13 Qb3?
Nd4!   14 Nxd4 exd4   15 Rfd1 Bc5   16 Bxh5 Nxh5
17 Ne2?

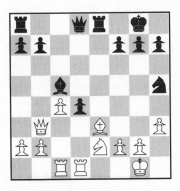

White is trying to exploit the pin on the d-pawn. He might have played 17 Bxd4 Bxd4 18 Nb5 but rejected that because of 18 . . . Bxf2+, and in the resulting equal-material position White has a vulnerable king.

Nevertheless, the move he preferred, 17 Ne2, is bad, particularly since it allows a queen sacrifice whose soundness does not require much calculation.

17 ...	dxe3!

We tend to label every queen sacrifice as "brilliant." This one is not.

The tactical idea is fairly simple. A novice can recognize that in the diagrammed position Black cannot defend his d-pawn. A better-than-novice would know to look for a tactical way out of the d-pawn problem. And a less-than-master would recognize that the only tactical way out is a sacrifice.

So once Black gets the idea, the rest is the processing of variations. The tree of analysis is a narrow one. But how tall it stands depends on how long Black wants to examine it.

18 Rxd8	exf2+

Now 19 Kf1 appears best in order to protect the knight. The alternative is 19 Kh2 Raxd8 20 Qf3 (20 N-moves invites a strong . . . Re1), after which there are several forcing methods but the simple 20 . . . g6 leaves White hard pressed to meet 21 . . . Rd2; e.g., 21 g4 Rxe2! 22 Qxe2 Bd6+ and a knight fork wins the queen.

19 Kf1	Raxd8

Should Black have looked this far? Should he have stopped when he saw that he had rook, bishop, and pawn for the queen and retained chances for attack with . . . Rd2 or . . . Rxe2?

20 Qf3	Nf6
21 Ng3	Rd2!

Or this far? That is, until he realized White could do little about his threats of doubling rooks on the second rank or on the d-file; e.g., 22 Rb1 Red8 and the threat of . . . Bd6xg3 followed by . . . Ne4 or . . . Rd1+ must win.

22 Qc3	Red8
23 b4	Rd1+
24 Rxd1	Rxd1+
25 Ke2	Ne4!
resigns	

Or did he figure it all out to the end?—26 Nxe4 f1Q mate or 26 Qe5 Re1+ 27 Kd3 Nxg3 and queens with check.

Any answer could be correct depending on the confidence and evaluation skill of the calculator. Many grandmasters would play 17 . . . dxe3 on instinct and stop looking after 19 . . . Raxd8, realizing that the position offers excellent compensation for the queen and would be better than any variation in which Black just loses the pinned d-pawn.

Other players do not trust such short-run evaluations, and would work out the variations at least as far as 21 . . . Rd2. (And there are still others who do not trust *long* variations because they feel there's bound to be a mistake.)

This example should be contrasted with others in which you must reach the end. The nature of such positions requires you to calculate a long series of thrusts, parries, and counterthrusts to the end—and be absolutely sure it *is* the end.

Barda–Keres, Moscow 1956

1 d4 Nf6   2 c4 e6   3 Nc3 Bb4   4 e3 b6   5 Bd3 Bb7   6 f3 c5   7 Ne2 cxd4   8 exd4 Nc6   9 Be3 d5 10 0-0 dxc4   11 Bxc4 0-0   12 Qd3 Qe7   13 a3 Bxc3   14 Nxc3 Rfd8   15 Rad1 Rac8   16 Rfe1?

White, realizing that Black's last move contains the threat of 16 . . . Ne5, calculates a forcing series of replies that appears to refute that knight move.

But Black has calculated further . . .

16 . . .	Ne5!
17 dxe5	Rxd3
18 exf6	

White counted on this when he took no precautions against 16 . . . Ne5. If Black now takes time to defend his queen, 19 Bxd3 will give White two pieces and a rook for his own queen.

18 . . .	Rxd1
19 fxe7	Rxe1+
20 Kf2	

White undoubtedly saw this far—five moves ahead—when he considered his 16th move. Almost certainly he assumed Black would now move the attacked rook (e.g., 20 . . . Rh1) to retain his material edge. But then 21 Bb5! queens the e-pawn.

Remember that there are two criteria for determining when a sequence is over. Often a player will consider one criterion (it's over when you can reach a clear conclusion, such as "White is winning after 20 ... Rh1 21 Bb5") and under-appreciate the other (it's over when the forcing moves are *absolutely* over).

20 ...   **Rxe3!**

This is what White missed. He stopped looking for forcing moves and permitted this final desperado twist. After **21 Kxe3 Re8** White recognized his material deficit, and realizing that this was the true end of the sequence begun by 16 ... Ne5, he resigned.

In both these examples the tree was tall and very thin. But decisive, game-winning combinations aren't the norm. The branches of most trees don't have to be analyzed in great detail. The following example illustrates why:

Anand–Ye Jiangchuan, Kuala Lumpur 1989

1 e4 c5   2 Nf3 e6   3 d4 cxd4   4 Nxd4 Nf6   5 Nc3 d6   6 g4 h6   7 Rg1 Nc6   8 h4 h5   9 gxh5 Nxh5 10 Bg5 Nf6   11 Be2 a6   12 h5 Bd7   13 Qd2 Be7 14 0-0-0 Qc7   15 h6 gxh6

Here White began a combination:

    16 Bxf6   **Bxf6**

    17 Nf5!

The tree unveiled by this yields at least five branches of consequence. Let's consider their sizes:

(a) 17 . . . "pass"—a nonviolent move, such as 17 . . . Rd8. All such moves are met by 18 Nxd6+, re-establishing material equality but with Black's king trapped in the center. After 18 . . . K-somewhere, Black threatens nothing, so White can confidently conclude that 19 f4, followed by 20 e5 will be good enough.

In other words, White need look no further than move 19, even though the end-positions are only relatively favorable.

(b) 17 . . . 0-0-0 at least removes the king from the center, but after White sees 18 Nxd6+ and 19 Nxf7 he knows that his advantage may even be greater than in (a) lines. Actually, he has to look one move further to see that 19 Nxf7 Bxc3 20 Qxc3?? Qf4+! wins for Black but that 20 bxc3 wins easily for White.

Here, White had to look to move 20 in the longest sub-variation, but it ends in a winning material edge.

(c) 17 . . . Bg5 is a natural counterattacking move since 18 Nxd6+?? loses to 18 . . . Qxd6! and White is pinned up. However, White meets the bishop move with 18 f4.

After 18 . . . exf5 19 fxg5 or 19 Nd5 followed by 20 fxg5, how much further does he have to calculate? It's a matter of taste, but many masters would see that White will, at worst, be a pawn down after 20 fxg5, and know that a knight on d5 is more than worth such a pawn. They would stop calculating as soon as they saw 18 f4.

(d) 17 . . . Be5 also looks reasonable. But by the same token as (c), White can stop looking past move 18 when he sees 18 f4.

(e) **17 . . . Be7** was the game continuation but it is again fairly easy to see that 18 Nxe7 gives White excellent prospects however Black retakes. If White wants to, he can work out ideas such as 18 . . . Kxe7 19 Rg3! followed by Qf4/Rf3 or Rd3xd6, or 18 . . . Nxe7 19 Rg7 or 19 Qxd6.

(f) Finally, there is 17 . . . exf5, after which 18 Nd5 is the natural continuation. Unless Black wants to return the piece immediately, 18 . . . Qd8 is the only response. This is the most important variation we have to calculate because it is the only one that leaves White a *significant amount of material behind*.

Yet, it turns out to be also one of the shortest limbs. Once White finds 19 Qxh6!! he need see only that 19 . . . Rxh6 20 Rg8 is mate and that anything else allows either 20 Nxf6+ or 20 Qxh8+! Bxh8 21 Rg8 mate.

The game actually continued **17 . . . Be7   18 Nxe7 Kxe7   19 Rg3 b5   20 Qf4 Rad8   21 Qh4+ Ke8** and White won soon after **22 Bxb5! Ne5   23 Be2 Qc5 24 Bh5 Rf8   25 f4 Nc6   26 e5 d5   27 Bxf7+! Rxf7 28 Rg8+**. (Q.E.D.)

The reverse side of missing an opponent's move after the apparent end of a sequence is missing your own strong move. That's just as embarrassing.

Many a winning combination is rejected by players when they find a surprising tactical response for their opponent. But often when your opponent has such a stunning move at his disposal, the position is so explosive that you have an equally stunning counter.

Short–Miles, Brighton 1984
White to play

White saw that 1 Nb6 forks heavy pieces and wins at least the exchange. But when he rechecked his variation he found a surprise answer—1 . . . Ne2!, which (a) threatens 2 . . . Rc1+ and mate, (b) threatens 2 . . . Qxd1 mate, and (c) allows him to meet 2 Bxe2 with a mixture of the first two ideas (2 . . . Qxd1+! 3 Bxd1 Rc1 mate).

Very pretty, and White might have counted himself lucky for noticing 1 . . . Ne2 in time. That's why he actually played **1 a3?**.

But after the game he must have felt differently when 1 Nb6 Ne2 2 Qf8+!! was pointed out: 2 . . . Kxf8 3 Nxd7+ and 4 Bxe2 wins a piece; 2 . . . Rxf8 3 Nxd7 attacks pieces at e2 and f8 and also wins material.

As a result of this failing, many calculated sequences never get started at all. A player gets a very good idea, then halts abruptly when he sees "the refutation."

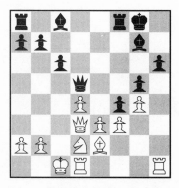

Kovacevic–Thipsay, Thessaloniki 1988
White to play

Here, for example, White has two tempting ideas. One is to get his bishop somehow on the b3-g8 diagonal, winning the pinned queen. The other idea is the opening of the h-file via Rxh6.

He first examines quiet methods of exploiting the first idea (1 Qc3) and rejects them as insufficient (1 . . . b5). Then he puts the two ideas together and sees 1 Rxh6 with the idea 1 . . . Bxh6 2 Qg6+ followed by Bc4 (2 . . . Bg7 3 Bc4; 2 . . . Kh8 3 Qxh6+ Kg8 4 Bc4).

But when he looks further and sees the reply 1 . . . Bf5, what happens then?

There is a strong temptation to drop the matter entirely and look for another move in the diagram. The sequence 1 Rxh6 Bf5 appears to be a perfect case of a mildly forcing move (1 Rxh6) being refuted by a more forceful counter. After 1 . . . Bf5 White loses his opportunity to play Qg6+. On 2 gxf5 Bxh6 or 2 e4 Bxh6 3 exd5? Bxd3 or 2 Qc3 b5 (3 Rxc6 Rac8!) White's original plan is in tatters.

Nevertheless:

1	**Rxh6!**	**Bf5!**
2	e4	Bxh6
3	**gxf5!**	

White correctly looked further after he noticed 1 . . . Bf5. He didn't search for a sparkling counter-refutation but merely kept his head and evaluated the position after 3 gxf5 as being strongly in his favor. In fact the game ran its natural course quickly. Now 3 . . . Qxa2 4 e5 followed by 5 Rh1 or 5 f6 decides the game.

3	. . .	Qd7
4	Nc4	Bg7
5	Ne5!	Bxe5
6	Qb3+	resigns

Because of 6 . . . Kg7 (6 . . . Qf7 7 Bc4; 6 . . . Rf7 7 dxe5 and 8 Bc4) 7 dxe5 Qc7 8 Qe6 followed by Rd7+ or Qg6+.

It should be stressed that it takes great skill to sense when a variation is over and when there is still a bit of life in it. The absence of forcing moves is a good key to the location of an end-position. But often there are devastating "quiet" moves that drastically alter matters.

Filger–Dubinin, Soviet Correspondence Championship 1975–77

1 d4 Nf6 2 c4 e6 3 Nf3 Bb4+ 4 Nbd2 b6 5 a3 Bxd2+ 6 Bxd2 Bb7 7 g3 Nc6 8 Be3 d5 9 Bg2 dxc4 10 Ne5 Nd5 11 Nxc4 Qd7 12 Bc1 0-0-0! 13 e3 h5 14 b4 e5 15 dxe5 b5 16 Na5 Nxa5 17 bxa5 Qf5 18 Qb3

Black almost certainly intended 18 . . . Nc3, attacking the queen, the unprotected g2-bishop, and the mating square d1 all at once. The knight move would also regain Black's lost pawn (19 e4 Qxe5).

After 18 Qb3, however, White can meet 18 . . . Qxe5 with 19 Bb2. Now 18 . . . Nc3 doesn't seem to work because after 19 Bxb7+ and 20 Qxc3 White can answer the terrible 20 . . . Qf3 simply by castling. Right?

18 ...   **Nc3!**

Wrong. Since this was a corresponding game, Black had the luxury of being able to simply set up the position after 21 Qxc3 on his board and search for a Black response, no matter how "quiet." A trained calculator should be able to do the same, since the first few moves are so forcing that the "false end-position" after 21 Qxc3 is relatively easy to visualize.

19	Bxb7+	Kxb7
20	a6+	Kc8
21	Qxc3	

There is no safety in 21 0-0 because of 21 . . . Ne2+ 22 Kg2 h4, threatening 23 . . . h3+ and mates.

21 ...   **Qf3!**

Here White played the meek **22 Bb2** and resigned a few moves after **22 ... Qxh1+ 23 Ke2 Qd5**. But why didn't White just castle at move 22, covering both d1 and h1?

Because Black, to his credit, realized that just because there are no captures, checks, or mate-in-one threats after 21 Qxc3, it is not the end of the action. After 22 . . . h4! there is no defense to 23 . . . h3 and 24 . . . Qg2 mate (23 Re1 hxg3 24 fxg3 Rxh2!). Even though White has an extra piece, a weakened enemy king position, and two free moves to do it, there is nothing to be done on the kingside or queenside.

MOVE ORDER

The other key element of variation processing is the order of moves. Suppose the tactical ideas you are working with include a pin of the queen and a knight fork. You can use one idea or both. But if both, which comes first?

After all, if you are working with forcing moves, you are often in a position to determine not only the matters being disputed at the board but also the *sequence* in which these matters come up for debate.

Let's begin with a simple tactical idea arising out of an old opening trap:

1 d4 d5 2 c4 c6 3 Nf3 Nf6 4 Nc3 e6 5 e3 Nbd7 6 Bd3 Bd6 7 e4 dxe4 8 Nxe4 Nxe4 9 Bxe4 0-0 10 0-0 e5? 11 dxe5 Nxe5 12 Nxe5 Bxe5

At first glance the position seems to defy a search for ideas. Everything of White's, except the c-pawn, is on an analogous square as Black's, but on the other side of the board. And everything of Black's, except the bishop on e5, is protected. How can anything be happening in such a quiet, symmetrical position?

The answer is that White has the only significant advantage here: It is his turn to move. Perhaps he can attack the bishop and also something else.

Asking yourself questions like that produces 1 Qh5. It threatens the bishop and also 2 Qxh7 mate. Is that decisive? No, because there is a defense that meets both threats, 1 . . . f5!.

White should look further. Not further into 1 Qh5 f5, and not for different ideas. He should look for a different way of using the Qh5 idea. There are only a few good ideas in a position, so you shouldn't reject them hastily.

Here White can revive the double attack on h7 and e5 by using a different order: 1 Bxh7+! Kxh7 2 Qh5+ Kg8 3 Qxe5. This order wins a pawn, not a piece as White hoped to do with 1 Qh5. But it has the advantage of being more forceful than the queen move. And that makes it work.

Now examine a slightly different version. Remove Black's f-pawn and put it on d4. We see that 1 Bxh7+ works here, too, but again only wins a pawn. The best move order now is 1 Qh5!, which wins (1 . . . Qf6 loses outright to 2 Bxh7+! Kh8 3 Bg6+ Kg8 4 Qh7 mate, and 1 . . . Re8 allows 2 Bxh7+ Kf8 3 Bg6 with decisive threats).

The difference between the right and the wrong order can be brutal as well as embarrassing:

Petursson–Korchnoi, Wijk aan Zee 1990
White to play

This occurred two moves before the time control, and if White had found the correct order, the game probably would not have lasted much longer. The two ideas in the position are the check on h8 and the advance of White's f-pawn (attacking the knight and cutting off the king's escape square). After 1 Qh8+ Ng8 2 f6 gxf6 3 gxf6 Black loses at least a piece. But in time pressure:

1 f6??   Ng6!

And white had nothing more than a draw (2 Qh7 gxf6 3 gxf6 Qc1, etc.).

Move order can be a minefield, but it can also be an ally in unlocking the tactical secrets of a position.

Keres–Spassky, Goteborg 1955
White to play

White has a wonderful game here, with two crisp bishops cutting through the air that leads to the kingside. The natural idea that suggests itself is an attack on g7, using the forcing nature of a mate threat. Black's minor pieces play no role in the defense of that square. Any move of the White knight would open the b2-g7 diagonal and threaten mate.

But each of those knight moves would also permit 1 . . . Qxg3, squelching the threats. White might be able to extract an endgame edge with the zwischenzug (in-between move) 1 Nxd7 Qxg3 2 Nf6+, but 2 . . . gxf6 3 hxg3 Bxc4 is not at all clear.

But White knew his position deserved more than an endgame edge. And he didn't need to find a new idea:

    1 Qxg7+!!   **resigns**

The main—in fact, the only real—variation is a nice one. It runs 1 . . . Kxg7 2 Nxd7+ Kg8 3 Nf6+ and 4 Nd5+, winning back the queen at the profit of a piece.

You can praise Paul Keres for his magnificent tactical vision, but, technically, all he did here was re-order his moves—Qxg7+ before Nxd7, not after.

Differences in move order may determine whether a combination works or fails. Or it may mean that the superior order leads to a decisive result rather than just a significant advantage.

Sometimes we shortchange ourselves by taking the wrong order:

Sokolov–Sturua, Soviet Young Masters Tournament 1984

1 e4 e5   2 Nf3 Nc6   3 Bb5 a6   4 Ba4 Nf6   5 0-0
Be7   6 Re1   b5   7 Bb3   d6   8 c3   0-0   9 h3   Nb8
10 d4 Nbd7   11 Nbd2 Bb7   12 Bc2 Re8   13 Nf1 d5
14 Nxe5 Nxe4?

Here White played **15 Nxf7 Kxf7   16 Rxe4**. Both of his moves were awarded exclamation points because of 16 . . . dxe4 17 Bb3+ Kf6 18 Qh5 g6 19 Qh6 and wins, or 17 . . . Kg6 18 Qg4+ Bg5 19 Ng3.

The problem with this bit of brilliance is that after **16 Rxe4** Black played **16 . . . Nf6** and was able to put up stiff resistance before eventually conceding. Is there a better way, something that leads to more than just a pawn-up middlegame?

What draws some of sting of White's combination is that White played his most forceful move first and Black could ignore the less forceful 16th. Suppose we change matters a bit: first 15 Rxe4 dxe4 (on 15 . . . Nxe5 16 Rxe5, White remains a knight ahead) and now 16 Nxf7.

Now the consequences of 16 . . . Kxf7 are exactly the same as in the line 15 Nxf7 Kxf7 16 Rxe4 dxe4 because we have transposed exactly. The difference is that the second sequence ends with 16 Nxf7, a move that attack's Black's queen. After a queen move, the addition of 17 Bb3 and a discovered check looks like it should be quickly decisive; e.g., 16 . . . Qc8 17 Bb3 Kf8 (else 18 Nd6+) 18 Qh5 Nf6 19 Ng5!!.

But when you change the order, you usually change the opportunities for *both* sides. Black should have certain chances in the second order that he doesn't get in the first. If we look further we'll find them: After 16 . . . Qb8! 17 Bb3 c5 White can regain his material but no more. For example, 18 Be6 Nf8; or 18 Ne5+ c4 19 Nxd7 Qc7; or 18 dxc5 Nxc5 19 Nd6+ Kh8!.

Conclusion? The order chosen by White was best.

Now let's examine a more sophisticated example, which further illustrates the double-edged sword of sequence. Here it spoils a golden opportunity for a little-known player to defeat a world champion.

Grigorian–Karpov, Soviet Championship 1976

1 d4 d5   2 c4 e6   3 Nc3 Be7   4 Nf3 Nf6   5 e3 0-0
6 b3 b6   7 Bb2 Bb7   8 Bd3 c5   9 0-0 cxd4
10 exd4 Nc6   11 Qe2 Nb4   12 Bb1 dxc4   13 bxc4
Bxf3   14 gxf3! Qxd4   15 Ne4 Qd8   16 Rd1 Qc7
17 Nxf6+ Bxf6

This position, arising out of a then-popular opening, had
been endorsed by theoreticians but not really tested over the
board. White has sacrificed one pawn, and the health of his
other pawns, for a kingside attack. The ideas in the position
include Bxh7+, Qe4, and Bxf6, and even some supplementary
help from Kh1 followed by Rg1+.

Okay, so much for the ideas. Time to start processing the
variations. We might look first at the lines involving Qe4.
Suppose we break up the kingside with 18 Bxf6 gxf6 19
Qe4, how does Black protect h7? The obvious answer is 19

. . . f5 and on 20 Qh4 he can stop the attack dead with 20 . . . f6.

But is there a better way of using the Qe4 idea—that is, a better move order? Yes, and it lies in the immediate 18 Qe4 since the . . . f7-f5 defense is now impossible and 18 . . . g6 allows 19 Bxf6 at a time when it wins the bishop.

Does this mean that 18 Qe4 wins outright? No, because a further examination shows that Black can just move his king rook, vacating f8 for his king. The position after 18 . . . Rfd8 19 Qxh7+ Kf8 is hard to evaluate: Material is now even, but White's pawns are still a mess and it's not clear whose king is in greater jeopardy.

White turns instead to a familiar idea. Remember Lasker–Bauer and Kuzmin–Sveshnikov from Chapter Two? Well, a relative of the two-bishop sacrifice lurks under the facade of this position. White played:

> **18 Bxf6   gxf6**
> **19 Bxh7+**

Very nice. Now 19 . . . Kxh7 20 Qe4+ Kg7 21 Qg4+ and 22 Kh1! give White a crushing attack (e.g., 21 . . . Kh8 22 Kh1 Qc5 23 Qh4+ and 24 Rg1+). And on 19 . . . Kh8 White plays 20 Be4 Rad8 21 Kh1 with a very strong game.

> **19 . . .   Kg7!**

This is what White overlooked. When he examined the position of the diagram he failed to see that the g7- square would be available. He continued the game desultorily with **20 Rd4 Rh8 21 Rg4+ Kf8 22 Qb2 Rxh7 23 Qxb4+ Qc5 24 Qd2 Rc8** and lost not only his golden opportunity to upset a world champion, but the game as well.

We might say that this was an error of visualization, like those we'll consider in Chapter Eight. But here it was mainly a mistake of move order, because White could have avoided the . . . Kg7 defense had he played the right sequence: 18 Bxh7+! and if 18 . . . Kxh7 then 19 Qe4+ and 20 Bxf6 (with Qg4+ and Kh1 as he had planned). Black would have to avoid this with the unpleasant 18 . . . Kh8 or some other in-different defense, leaving him with doubtful chances of survival.

SERENDIPITY AND SEQUENCE

The juggling of move orders is a fine example of the serendip-ity at work that we saw in Chapter Three.

Vyzhmanavin–Novikov, U.S.S.R. Championship 1990
White to play

White toys with a few ideas in this position (1 Nxf6+ Bxf6 2 Qxh6 and 1 Rc7 Rxc7) and finds that neither seems to get anywhere. But what about 1 Qxf7+, he wonders.

Then on 1 . . . Qxf7 2 Bxf7+ Kxf7 White has 3 Rc7+ Rxc7 4 dxc7 R-moves 5 Nd6+! and wins.

Unfortunately, there are several holes in this sequence. For one, Black need not capture on move three but can play 3 . . .

Rd7!. Furthermore, he can refute the combination very simply with 2 . . . Rxf7!.

But the idea doesn't go away and White wonders about a different order. Try 1 Qxf7+ and 2 Rc7. Then 2 . . . Rxc7 is answered by 3 dxc7 R-moves 4 Bxf7+ Kxf7 5 Nd6+ or 3 . . . Qxb3 4 cxd8Q.

Ah, but there's another flaw: 2 . . . Qxb3!, leaving Black a queen for a rook ahead.

One last try and three is a charm: **1 Rc7!!** and now 1 . . . Rxc7 2 Qxf7+! Qxf7 3 dxc7 transposes into the most favorable of the previous lines.

In fact, after **1 Rc7** Black resigned. Another Soviet grandmaster later told the winner, "I looked at the position for ten minutes and couldn't understand what happens on 1 . . . Rxc7."

Sometimes, of course, it doesn't matter whether you play A before B or B before A. But perhaps three times out of four you will find there is a significant difference. Here's another example of how juggling ideas and sequences allows a player to be brilliant.

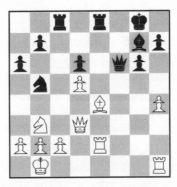

Honfi–Barczay, Kecskemet 1977
White to play

White can defend against 1 . . . Qxb2 mate by advancing his c-pawn one square. But he preferred to push it two: **1 c4** is more forceful.

For the same reason, most masters shown Black's position would look first at 1 . . . Na3+. It meets the threat to the knight with a gain of time. The only problem is that 2 bxa3! is a simple refutation (because 2 . . . Qa1+ allows 3 Nxa1!).

So Black tries to find a method of using the . . . Na3+ and . . . Qxb2 ideas. And there it is: **1 . . . Rxc4! 2 Qxc4 Qxb2+!!** and wins (3 Rxb2 Na3+ 4 K-moves Bxb2+ 5 Kxb2 Nxc4+ and 6 . . . Rxe4).

ORDERS AND OPTIONS

In the last few pages we considered how changing the sequence of events can lead to distinctly different results. But what happens when it seems you can reach exactly the same end-position by different routes? Which road do you take?

This is a crucial matter because, as noted earlier, each move order creates its own options for the opponent.

If it seems that your opponent will get those options anyway, you want to place them at the least dangerous point. Usually this means *before* you are fully committed. In other words, give him choices at the beginning, not the end.

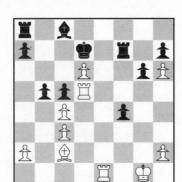

Boey–Filip, European Team Championship 1972
White to play

White has a temporarily dominant position but must act quickly before Black coordinates his forces with 1 . . . Bb7 and a move of his a8-rook. There doesn't appear to be anything significant in 1 Rxc5 Kxd6! 2 Rd5+ Kc7 or in other semi-quiet lines.

As he calculates them, however, White sees that the unused resources in the position are his king and advanced h-pawn. It takes too long to bring the king into significant action. But what about getting the h-pawn moving?

That can be done by 1 Re7+, exchanging rooks, followed by Bxg6. If Black then takes the bishop, White queens. (Do you see how?)

Think about the correct order of moves a minute or two here before reading on.

The right way of doing things is:

1 Bxg6!	hxg6
2 Re7+	Rxe7
3 dxe7+	Kxe7
4 Rd8!!	resigns

The sacrifice of the rook is necessary to queen since 4 h7 fails to 4 . . . Bb7. After **4 Rd8**, however, White will promote (4 . . . Kxd8 5 h7 or 4 . . . Bb7 5 Rxa8 Bxa8 6 h7) and then sweep the board of Black pawns.

But the key to this combination was not the pretty **4 Rd8**; it was the order of the earlier moves. Why did White start with the bishop capture? The reason is that even though it is a sacrifice it is the *least* forcing move in the series. After all, Black could have ignored **1 Bxg6** (1 . . . Rf6 2 Bxh7 Rxh6; 2 Bf5+ Kd8). At least his position would not be a forced loss.

Now consider the consequences of reversing the order; that is, using the rook-trade idea first. After 1 Re7+ Rxe7 2 dxe7+ Kxe7 White would then play 3 Bxg6 and after 3 . . . hxg6? 4 Rd8! we reach the game—the same end-position.

However, in this order Black has plenty of other third moves, such as 3 . . . Be6 followed by . . . Bxd5 or . . . hxg6 or . . . Rg8. Black has more choices in this order. Only **1 Bxg6** produces the optimum result.

The matter of force and sequence becomes even more important in defensive calculation:

Geller–Matulovic, Skopje 1968
White to play

White appears to stand better because of his more advanced knight and better pawns. But **1 . . . d4!**, dissolving the weak d-pawn, should lead to a dead-even game. In fact, because it seizes the initiative—by making a forcing move—it also creates land mines for White to step into.

One of those mines is fairly obvious: 2 Nxd8? is clearly going to be answered by 2 . . . dxe3. Then 3 Nxc6 is the only way to avoid the loss of a piece. Black would then have a choice between the most forceful 3 . . . exf2+ or the equally promising recapture on c6, either of which leave Black with better placed pieces.

White's real choice is between 2 cxd4 and 2 Nxd4. They lead to the same position after 2 cxd4 Nxd4 3 Nxd4 Qxd4 or 2 Nxd4 Nxd4 3 cxd4 Qxd4, with dead equality. So the exact calculator seeks the one that allows his opponent the fewest alternatives. A strong grandmaster, White chose what he thought was the "most forceful." He chose 2 cxd4, perhaps because it retains the threat of 3 Nxd8 and averts such side lines as 2 Nxd4 Rxe3!?.

But **2 cxd4??** allowed another possibility: **2 ... Rxe6! 3 Rxe6 Nxd4!**, after which Black won a piece in all variations (4 Qc4 Nxe6; 4 Rxb6 Nxc2).

One final example to show how difficult defensive calculation can be when your opponent is juggling several ideas:

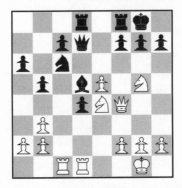

Vinsnes–Krasenkov, Rilton Cup 1990
Black to play

Black appreciated that he was under pressure on both wings with several tactical ideas at work against him. Those ideas include (a) the knight sacrifice Nf6+, (b) the attack on h7 or a knight sacrifice there, and (c) the elimination of a key defensive piece, the Black knight, by way of the exchange sacrifice Rxc6.

With all that in mind, Black examined a few key variations and, finding them harmless, played:

1 ...   **Qe7?**

This attacks the e-pawn, which can only be defended by the humble retreat 2 Nf3. Black understood that he was allowing 2 Qf5 but saw that 2 ... Bxe4! 3 Nxe4 Qxe5! and 3 Qxe4 Qxg5 4 Rxc6 Qh5 was nothing to fear.

He was chiefly concerned, however, with several different move orders employing the ideas mentioned above. The first is 2 Nf6+ gxf6 and now 3 exf6 is easily met by 3 ... Qe5! (4 Qh4 Qf5).

White can prevent that queen centralization by the different sacrificial order 2 Rxc6 Bxc6 3 Nf6+ gxf6—still forced—4 exf6. But then 4 ... Qe2! saves the day. (Note that it was White's first move that created a new opportunity for Black: White's rook is hanging at move five.)

So Black examined yet another sequence: 2 Nf6+ gxf6 and now 3 Nxh7 with the threat of 4 Nxf6+ and the idea of meeting 3 ... Kxh7 with 4 Rd3 and 4 Rh3+. But this can be met by 3 ... Nxe5! and then 4 Nxf6+ Kg7 5 Nh5+ Kg6!.

As much as he shuffled the moves around, Black saw no explicit danger. Unfortunately, he missed the one move order that punishes him:

2 **Rxc6!**	**Bxc6**
3 **Nf6+**	**gxf6**

On 3 ... Kh8 White can choose either 4 Nfxh7 or 4 Qf5 g6 5 Qh3 h5 6 Nxh5!.

        4 Nxh7!!

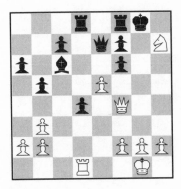

This is the sequence of ideas that eluded Black. Now 4 ...
fxe5 allows 5 Nf6+ Qxf6 6 Qxf6 with a won endgame.

4 ...		Kxh7
5	Qh4+	Kg7
6	Qg4+	Kh8
7	Rd3	Be4

Last hope (8 Qxe4?? Rg8!).

8	Rh3+	Bh7
9	Qf5	resigns

BAILOUT

One of the special tricks of calculation technique is being
aware of escape routes that appear in the tree of analysis. These

enable a player to bail out of a long variation before the end-position. For example:

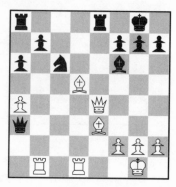

Wirthensohn–Huebner, Swiss Championship 1991
White to play

Black's last move, . . . Rfe8, sets all sort of alarms for White. It is, of course, a forcing move that attacks the White queen. But it invites the question: "What squares lose protection as a result?"

The pertinent answer is f7. Being an aware calculator, White examined **1 Bxf7+! Kxf7** and the natural followups 2 Rxb7+, 2 Qc4+, and 2 Qd5+. He eventually found that **2 Qc4+!** was best, since 2 . . . Kf8 3 Bc5+ is bad for Black and 2 . . . Re6 allows 3 Rxb7+ Ne7 4 Bc5 Qc3 5 Rxe7+! or 3 . . . Be7 4 Bc5.

So White could be fairly certain that after beginning the combination with 1 Bf7+, he would face a position with **2 . . . Kg6!**. Is there anything clear after that? White wasn't sure. He played the bishop sacrifice anyway, because he had spotted a bailout: After 2 . . . Kg6 he could repeat the position with 3 Qg4+ Kf7 (obviously forced) 4 Qc4+! Kg6.

And if he couldn't find anything to be confident about after that, White knew he could just repeat the position again and claim a draw. (In fact, there is a very good continuation—3 Rb3! Qe7 4 Qg4+ with excellent winning chances; e.g., 4 ... Kf7 5 Rd7 or 4 ... Bg5 5 h4 h5 6 Qg3!).

Of course, even with a bailout opportunity you must calculate the consequences of the main line accurately if you decide to go into it. Here is a similar example:

Ljubojevic–Smyslov, Petropolis 1973

1 e4 c6 2 d4 d5 3 exd5 cxd5 4 c4 Nf6 5 Nc3 e6
6 Nf3 Be7 7 Bf4 dxc4 8 Bxc4 0-0 9 0-0 Nc6
10 Rc1 a6 11 a3 b5 12 Ba2 Bb7 13 d5!? exd5
14 Nxd5 Nxd5 15 Bxd5 Rc8 16 Re1 Bf6! 17 Bd6!
Re8

Clearly 17 . . . Qxd6?? 18 Bxf7+ was impossible. White now studied the position at some length and played **18 Bxf7+?!**
Kxf7 19 Qd5+ Kg6.

He has a draw, if he wants it, with 20 Qd3+, since 20 . . . Kh6? 21 Rxe8 Qxe8 22 Qf5! is too hot to handle (22 . . . Ne5 23 Qf4+ Kg6 24 Nxe5+ Bxe5 25 Rxc8).

But White refused the bailout and went in for **20 Rxe8?**
Qxe8 21 Qd3+ Kf7 22 Re1, hoping to bring the rook decisively into play.

However, he was lost soon after **22 . . . Ne7!** (23 Qb3+ Bd5 24 Rxe7+ Qxe7 25 Qxd5+ Qe6, or 23 Bxe7 Bxe7 24 Ne5+ Kg8 25 Qb3+ Kf8 26 Qe6 Rc7, or 23 h4 Qd8).

Bailouts do not always lead to forced draws, of course. Sometimes when you're midway through the tree leading to a major advantage, you realize there's a major flaw in your analysis and you have to bail out with only an equal position. So be it.

Usually, bailouts occur in forcing lines.

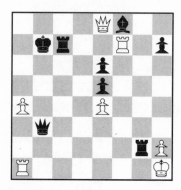

Gipslis–Van Wely, Gausdal 1992
White to play

Here White, with the initiative, has just delivered a rook check at f7 and Black found the only reply, . . . Rc7. What next?

White, an experienced grandmaster, makes a remarkably naive move, **1 Kxg2??**. It lacks any forcing power whatsoever and permits Black a myriad of checks. Black found **1 . . . Qc2+** and suddenly White saw that 2 Kg3 Qd3+ 3 Rf3 allows 3 . . . Rg7+ and wins. The game continued **2 Kh3 Qd3+ 3 Kh4 Qxe4+ 4 Kh3 Qe3+ 5 Kg2 Qd2+! 6 Kg3 Qg5+ 7 Kh3 Qh5+ 8 Kg3 Qg6+!** and **9 . . . Rxf7** won).

What should White have done? He should have examined 1 Rxc7+ Kxc7 2 Qf7+!. He could have seen that 2 . . . Kb6 now allows 3 Kxg2 when 3 ... Qb2+ can be met by 4 Qf2+ and White wins.

But the main reason White should have played the 2 Qf7+ line is that on 2 ... Kc6, the only other reasonable alternative, White could assure himself of at least a perpetual check with 3 Qe8+. With this bailout option he could have guaranteed the same result (a draw) as his best chance after 1 Kxg2??.

In fact, after 2 ... Kc6 White does not have to bail out but can continue the game with 3 Kxg2, after which he has some winning chances following 3 ... Qb2+ 4 Kh3 Qc3+ 5 Kh4 Qxa1 6 Qxf8.

CALCULATING IN STAGES

One of the most widely reprinted gems of calculation in chess history was a combination played by a future world champion, Mikhail Botvinnik, against a past one, José Capablanca.

Botvinnik–Capablanca, A.V.R.O. 1938
White to play

White began a 12-move combination that ran **1 Ba3!**
Qxa3   2 Nh5+! gxh5   3 Qg5+   Kf8   4 Qxf6+   Kg8

5 e7!. In the face of unstoppable mate, Black ran out of checks after 5 ... Qc1+ 6 Kf2 Qc2+ 7 Kg3 Qd3+ 8 Kh4 Qe4+ 9 Kxh5 Qe2+ 10 Kh4 Qe4+ 11 g4! Qe1+ 12 Kh5 resigns.

But it wasn't until more than 40 years later that Botvinnik revealed that he hadn't seen 12 moves ahead.

"I must admit that I could not calculate it right to the end and operated in two stages," he wrote. First he saw as far as 5 e7 and figured out that Black had no more than a perpetual check. That meant he could safely play the first stage—up to 6 Kf2—without risk of losing. Once that position occurred on the board he was able to find the White king's method of escape from checks.

Calculating in stages is a method of breaking down the un-fathomable into bite-size chunks of analysis. A more recent example:

Nunn–Fedorowicz, Wijk aan Zee 1991
White to play

Here White saw the idea of exploiting the long diagonal with Be2 and Rxd5, since . . . exd5 is then illegal and . . . Qxd5 allows Bf3!, skewering Black's queen and rook. But the direct route, 1

Be2 threatening 2 Rxd5, fails to 1 . . . Rc8, forcing White to defend c2.

So White considered, and eventually played, a different order, which allows him a couple of bailouts. The first stage went:

> **1 Rxd5!**   **Qxd5**
>
> **2 Be2**

Now most moves lose quickly to 3 Bf3 or 3 Rd1. For example, 2 . . . Qxd6 3 Rd1 Qe7 4 Qc3! with 5 Qc6+ threatened,
or 3 . . . Qb4 4 Qf3 Rc8 5 Qb7, or 3 . . . Qb8 4 Bf3 Be7 5 Bc6+
Kf8 6 Rd7, etc.

> **2 . . .**   **Qxa2**

At this point, the end of the first stage, White can begin to
calculate again, having foreseen that 3 Qc5 is good enough to
lead to a favorable endgame (3 . . . Qd5 4 Rd1! Bxd6 5 Qxd6).

> **3 Qf3!**

This begins a second stage. Key variations run 3 . . . Rc8 4
d7+! Kxd7 5 Qb7+ and 3 . . . Qd5 4 d7+ Ke7 5 Rd1 Qxf3 6 d8Q+.

> **3 . . .**   **Bxd6!**
>
> **4 Qxa8+**   **Ke7**

White need not have calculated this far, but if he did he
could pause again before starting the third stage. One natural,
but faulty, continuation is 5 Qxh8?? Bxf4+ and mates.

Instead, White found **5 Qb7+ Kf8   6 Bc5** and if 6 . . .
Bxc5 then 7 Qc8+ picks up the bishop with check. The game
actually ended with **6 . . . Qa1+   7 Kd2 Qxh1   8 Qb8+.**

As we've seen in this chapter, there are many intermediary
steps the careful calculator performs before making his move.
Some merely confirm the correctness of his tree of analysis
(the bottom line, is it over?) while others (move order, bailout,
calculating in stages) may simplify the process of calculating.

Six

CHOICE

> "Half the variations which are calculated in a tournament game turn out to be completely superfluous. Unfortunately, no one knows in advance which half."
>
> —Jan Timman

I n an obvious sense, all chess moves are a matter of choice. But there are often critical points in a game in which you must choose between two or more moves that on first examination appear equally good. This is often true even when dealing with relatively simple, forcing positions.

Ljubojevic–Szabo, Hilversum 1973
White to play

One idea stands out here: White should try somehow to get his queen to the mating square b7, probably via a check along the b-file. White pursued this with:

1 Qc3	d5!

Now White saw that his intended 2 Qb4+ was stopped and that the alternative idea 2 Qa5 and 3 Qa6 allows the defense 2 . . . Qf6+ and 3 . . . Qxc6.

2 Rc1

Protecting the c-pawn and renewing the Qa5-b5+ threat.

2 . . .	d4!
3 Qa5	Rd5

And Black has seized the initiative. After the game, White made a great effort to prove he had missed a win—and eventually he succeeded. But even if you know there is a simple win in the diagram, it's not so easy to find. Black claimed that after the game he asked 50 spectators their opinions of the position, and that all agreed 1 Qc3 was best. "Then I understood why Ljubojevic found his move so natural!" he concluded.

Natural, but quite inferior to 1 Qd3!, which mates immediately.

What happened was that White failed to appreciate that he had a choice. This is one of the many problems that arise in a game when we are faced with two or more equally attractive ideas.

More often when we make a bad choice it happens in a position that has CHOICE written all over it in capital letters. Then there is often a right move and a wrong move, or sometimes a good move and a better move. (And, sadly, in some positions only a bad move and a worse move.)

The worst mistake when confronted with a choice is to believe it doesn't make any difference which path is taken.

Hauchard–Shirov, Santiago 1990
White to play

It used to be axiomatic for annotators to criticize that most common of choice errors with the words "Wrong rook!" Here is a typical example.

White should play a rook to d1 so he can return his extra piece and eliminate the two terrible passed pawns when Black plays . . . d3. But which rook?

Not seeing any particular difference, White made the commonsense choice, activating his unused a1-rook and leaving his other rook on its half-open file. Yet that is a blunder.

    1 **Rad1?**   **Qxc5**

    2 **Kh1**

Forced by the threat of 2 . . . d3 with discovered check.

    2 **. . .**   **d3**

    3 **Bxd3**   **exd3**

If White had played 1 Rfd1! he could now continue 4 Rxd3 and have some survival chances. But here 4 Rxd3 loses outright to 4 . . . Qf5!!. There *was* a difference in rook moves in the diagram. (White ended up playing **4 Qc3** and lost after **4 . . . Re3!**.)

Another case in point:

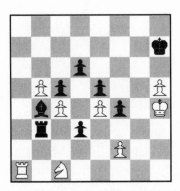

Ljubojevic–Larsen, Las Palmas 1974
Black to play

White has just retreated his knight from e2. Both play-ers have dangerous passed pawns, but Black has to spend a tempo to move his attacked rook before he can push his d-pawn.

Seeing little difference between the various rook-moves, Black continued:

1 ...	Rc3?
2 Nxd3!	Rxd3
3 Kg5	

White takes his time but knows that he is winning, with 4 Ra7+ or 4 b6. The immediate 3 b6 allows 3 . . . Rb3 and 4 . . . B-moves.

3 ...	Ba3
4 b6!	Rb3
5 b7	Rxb7
6 Rxa3	

And White won the rook endgame without further incident. But going back to the diagram we can see that there is a significant choice to be made. And once we see that, we are closer to finding that 1 . . . Ra3! turns a loss into a win (2 Rxa3 d2!).

(White can make it a bit harder with 2 b6! d2 3 b7 d1Q 4 b8Q—but not 4 Rxa3 Kh6!—4 . . . Qh1+ 5 Kg5, but after 5 . . . Qg2+ he must lose.)

The loser in that game, Bent Larsen, once said that when mentally examining a sequence—that is, without looking at a board—you often don't actually "see" a position in your mind until you have to make a choice.

Visualization of a sequence, he added, is not a case of watching a "moving picture" that advances one frame at a time. In most calculating, you make moves quickly in your mind without trying to picture the entire board. "Then, maybe you stop after a few moves in a critical line, since now there's a choice. And then maybe you 'see' the position."

In other words, choice becomes a *stop sign*.

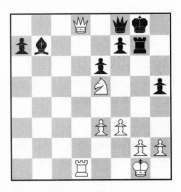

Marshall–Rubinstein, Bad Kissingen 1928
White to play

White is confronted with a broad but pleasant choice. He can offer to play an endgame, or force one (with 1 Rd7 or 1 Qxf8+). Or he can threaten to win with a queen move that prepares 2 Rd8, such as 1 Qa5, 1 Qf6 or 1 Qh4.

The Rd8 idea seems the most natural, but which is the proper queen move? Each seems to have its pluses and minuses. For example, 1 Qa5 has the added benefit of threatening the a-pawn. And with 1 Qh4 White also threatens the h-pawn as well as Nd7-f6+ (e.g., 1 . . . f6 2 Nd7 or 1 . . . Bd5 2 Nd7).

Unaccountably, White chose **1 Qf6?**. It may appear the most menacing, but after **1 . . . Qc5!** his initiative is over (2 Rd8+ Kh7 3 Nxf7? Qxe3+ or, reversing the order, 2 Nxf7 Qxe3+ 3 Kh1 Bd5).

In the game, White continued **2 Qd8+**. But Black avoided the repetition of the position with **2 . . . Kh7! 3 Qd3+ f5** and soon had a winning superiority: **4 Nd7 Qe7 5 e4 fxe4 6 fxe4 Bc6! 7 e5+ Kh8 8 Nf6 Qc5+ 9 Qd4 Rxg2+**, etc.

What goes into making a choice? If we could count on 100 percent accuracy in our calculations, we'd naturally choose the line that leads to the greatest advantage.

But in the real world, we can't rely on such certainty. More often we're faced with situations like this:

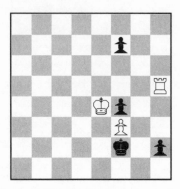

Rogers–Shirov, Groningen 1991
Black to play

Black saw two apparently equivalent methods of clinching the draw. The more elaborate way is 1 . . . Kg3!, a classy waiting move that forces White to remove one of his well-placed pieces. After 2 Rh8, for example, Black has 2 . . . f5+! 3 Kxf5 Kxf3 4 Rxh2 Kg3 and 5 . . . f3, with a certain draw.

But that's a lot of calculating, and it leaves White with considerable options. After the game, Black explained that he wanted something "simpler," something with a shorter tree and a more clear-cut end-position. So, even with plenty of time on his clock he chose:

1 ...	Kg2??
2 Kxf4	h1Q
3 Rxh1	Kxh1
4 Kg3!	

Now it was easier to calculate variations, but unfortunately for Black there was only one. It goes 4 . . . Kg1 5 f4! Kf1 6 Kf3 Ke1 7 f5 Kd2 8 Ke4 and Black, with his king sealed off, cannot avoid the loss of his pawn and the game (8 . . . Kc3 9 Kd5! Kb4 10 f6 and Kd6-e7).

In that example, seeking the "simpler" and faster option did Black in. But in other situations, the temptation to play something more forceful turns out to be fatal.

Chekhov–Azmaiparashvili, U.S.S.R. Team Championship 1984

1 d4 d5   2 c4 e6   3 Nc3 Be7   4 Nf3 Nf6   5 Bf4 0-0
6 e3 c5   7 dxc5 Bxc5   8 Qc2 Nc6   9 Rd1 Qa5
10 a3 Ne4?   11 cxd5 exd5   12 Rxd5 Nxc3   13 bxc3
Qxa3   14 Ng5! g6   15 Bc4 Bf5   16 Rxf5!

This sacrifice can be made quickly by calculating in general terms—if you are confident of your evaluation skills. White can say to himself, "For the price of the exchange I destroy his king position, pick up the pawn at f5, and have a dangerous attack against h7." (Actually, if he calculates more precisely White may become discouraged by realizing that 16 . . . gxf5 17 Qxf5 fails to 17 . . . Qxc3+.)

16 ...	gxf5
17 0-0	Ne7
18 Be5!	Bd6

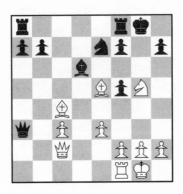

Stop sign. White must choose between retaining his bishop—19 Bd4 and if 19 . . . Bc5 then 20 Bf6—and going for the immediate kill with 19 Qe2 and 20 Qh5. Exchanging on d6 and then 20 Qe2 and 21 Qh5 is not a serious option because Black's queen can then defend the kingside easily.

In light of what happens, it would be easy to explain that White did not examine 19 Bd4 sufficiently. Actually, he saw that it was a winning move, with variations such as 19 Bd4 Qa5 20 Qe2 f4 (necessary, to defend h7) 21 Qh5 Qf5 and now 22 Nxf7! Qxh5 23 Nh6 mate.

     19 Qe2?

But he played this because it was "more convincing."

| 19 ... | Bxe5 |
| 20 Qh5 | Kg7! |

And this was the simple move he overlooked. White's error was in part visual—not seeing that the king could go to a square that in the diagram is covered by a bishop.

After **20 . . . Kg7** the king proved remarkably safe, and after **21 Qxh7+ Kf6** it survived to make a draw in the endgame.

A third criterion, besides the forcefulness and length of a variation, is the clarity of its end-position:

Korchnoi–Udovcic, Leningrad 1967
White to play

Having sacrificed a piece for a brutal attack, White has good reason to look for the knockout blow. But there is nothing to be gained from 1 Rf3+ Kg8.

So White begins to weigh the alternatives, which are 1 Rg3, with Qg6 and Bd2xh6+ in mind, and the immediate 1 Qg6 with Rf3+ or Rg3 coming up. Both have their benefits, and, in fact, both lead to wins. But one is better.

1 Qg6!

This is superior to 1 Rg3 Bxb4! 2 Qg6 Qg5!, after which White has a decisive material edge (3 Rxg5 hxg5 4 Qxh7 Bxb5). But as the winner explained later, "I did not want to play with a queen against three enemy pieces."

After 1 Qg6 the only way to defend against both 2 Qxh7 and 2 Rf3+ is:

1 ...	Rg7
2 Qxh6	Bxb5?
3 Rg3	resigns

Black should have played 2 . . . Kg8 3 Rh3 Kf7 but White still wins by trading off all four bishops and overpowering the king with his heavy pieces (4 Bxd7 Qxd7 5 Bxe7 Qxe7 6 Qh8! Qg5 7 Rf3+ Ke7 8 Qf8+ Kd7 9 Qd6+).

Even though this variation is much longer than the 1 Rg3 alternative, it is much preferable because the final position is so much easier to win.

TACTICAL VS. TECHNICAL VS. POSITIONAL

Sometimes choice is a matter of style. Two paths may lead to end-positions of the same value but one way will be selected by tacticians, another by positionally oriented, or endgame oriented, players.

Aron Nimzovich is remembered today chiefly for his imaginative—and by the standards of his day, bizarre—approach to strategy. But he was also a formidable tactician and calculator and had a fine grasp of pragmatic play. He explained his approach to making choices after his great tournament success at Karlsbad 1929.

Nimzovich–Tartakower, Karlsbad 1929
Black to play

White threatens the win of a piece with h5-h6, as well as the dangerous opening of the h-file. Black responded:

1 ...   gxh5

And Nimzovich began to calculate. He saw quickly that with 2 Bxf6 Bxf6 3 Qh6 his threats of 4 Qxf6+ and 4 Qxh5 and 5 Qxh7 mate would force 3 ... Bg7 4 Qxh5 h6.

Then the natural way of continuing the attack would be 5 g5. He concluded that that would be strong enough to force Black to play 5 ... f5!. And that created a stop sign for Nimzovich.

He realized there would then be a perfectly good positional plan of 6 gxf6 followed by Bh3xd7 and the exploitation of the light squares. Or he could win material and continue the mating attack with 6 gxh6.

"All this is extremely complicated," Nimzovich wrote, "and therefore I played after no longer than five minutes' thought **2 Bxf6 Bxf6   3 Rxh5 Bg7   4 Nh1!**." This required very little calculation and insured a big positional edge once the knight reaches h5.

White's practical approach paid off, as he won soon after
**4 ... f6 5 Qh2 h6 6 Ng3 Kh7 7 Be2 Rg8
8 Kf2** followed by Rg1 and Nh5.

In the next, much more elaborate example, White also believes
he is close to a win and begins to calculate in greater depth:

Dolmatov–Lerner, Tashkent 1983
White to play

1 Nf5+!	gxf5
2 Qg3+!	

The choice between this and 2 Bxf5 Rh8! 3 Qg3+ Kf8 or 2
Qxf5 Rh8 was not difficult to make. Black's next move is
forced, since here 2 ... Kh8 allows 3 Rxf5! and a quick mate.

2 ...	Kh6

Clearly, White must take on f5 now or very soon. But how?
There are two winning lines here, and as White put it afterward, one is for tacticians and the other for pragmatists.

Pragmatists might choose 3 Bxf5 with threats of 4 Rxd5 and
4 Qh3+. Then the defensive try 3 ... Bxa2+ 4 Kxa2 Qc4+ 5

Kb1 Qh4 covers several key kingside squares. But if you visualize that position well, it's not hard to see that White then wins with 6 Rd6+! (6 . . . Bxd6 7 Qxh4).

Therefore, Black has to vary his move order with 3 . . . Qc4, after which 4 Qh3+ Qh4 5 Qxh4+ Bxh4 6 Rxd5 leaves White with a pawn-up endgame. The win then is almost a technical matter but it is fairly certain (6 . . . f6 7 Rd7 or 6 . . . Bf6 7 Rd6 Kg7 8 Be4, etc.).

Bottom line: With best play, 3 Bxf5 leads to a certifiable win that will require several more moves of work.

Tacticians, on the other hand, may prefer a shorter road to victory. It requires a series of forcing moves beginning with 3 Rxf5, which threatens Qh3+-g4+ and Rh5 mate. Black needs a flight square and the best way to make one is 3 . . . Rg8.

Then 4 Rh5+! is the only way to keep the initiative, but with a bit of hard calculating the win can be found: 4 . . . Kxh5 5 Qh3+ Kg5 (not 5 . . . Bh4 6 Qf5+ Bg5 7 g4+ Kh4 8 Qh7+ Kxg4 9 Rg1+, etc.) and now 6 Qf5+ Kh6 7 Qh7+ Kg5.

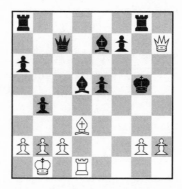

Position after 7 . . . Kg5 (variation)

With the king lured up to the fourth rank, White can close off the escape routes with 8 Rf1!; e.g., 8 . . . Be6 9 h4+ Kg4 10 Qe4+ Kh5 11 g4+! Kxh4 12 Qh1+ and mate in a few moves.

"Unfortunately," White recalled, "there just wasn't enough time to allow the calculation of all this." So he played a third line, which appeared to be an improvement on the first line.

3	Qh3+?!	Kg7
4	Bxf5	

Now 4 . . . Qc4 does nothing to block the kingside threats. However, with a change in move order Black gets a superior version of the pragmatists' line above.

4	. . .	Bxa2+!
5	Kxa2	Qc4+
6	Kb1	Qh4
7	Qe3	Rad8

Black prevents the Rf3-g3 knockout and prolongs the game quite a bit. White managed to find the only winning plan now (**8 Qxe5+ Bf6 9 Qc7 Rxd1+ 10 Rxd1 Qf2 11 Be6!**) and eventually won the endgame. But he had chosen the last and least of the three winning paths.

DEFENSIVE CHOICE

In calculation we have to recognize stop signs both in our own forcing lines and in our opponent's. Failure to recognize such stop signs even occurs in prepared opening analysis, as in this curious case:

Huebner–Korchnoi, Interpolis 1989

1 e4 e5   2 Nf3 Nc6   3 Bb5 a6   4 Ba4 Nf6   5 0-0 Nxe4   6 d4 b5   7 Bb3 d5   8 dxe5 Be6   9 Nbd2

Nc5 10 c3 Be7 11 Bc2 Bg4 12 Re1 Qd7 13 Nf1
Rd8 14 Ne3 Bh5 15 Nf5 0-0 16 Nxe7+ Nxe7
17 b4 Na4

Black examined this opening in some detail before the game and, as one of the world's foremost tacticians, considered the tempting candidate move of a bishop sacrifice on h7.

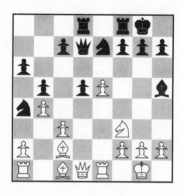

18 Bxh7+!   Kxh7
19 e6

Now when he saw the position appear on the board, Black rechecked his previous analysis. Clearly, 19 . . . fxe6 is bad because of 20 Ng5+ Kg8 21 Qxh5 or 20 . . . Kg6 21 g4, with a winning position in either case.

Black's intention when analyzing the position at home was to insert the zwischenzug 19 . . . Bxf3. Then 20 Qxf3 would allow him to play 20 . . . fxe6 safely, with a fine game.

The crucial line occurs, of course, when White answers 19 . . . Bxf3 with something more forceful, and that's why Korchnoi planned on 20 Qc2+ Be4 21 Rxe4 and now 21 . . . fxe6!. Despite the availability of any number of discovered checks, Black's position is safe and quite sound.

But while studying the position for 50 minutes at the board, Black suddenly realized that White has a *choice* at move 20. He could play 20 Qd3+! instead of 20 Qc2+, with the significant difference that 20 . . . Be4 allows 21 Qh3+, followed by winning the queen. So . . .

19 . . .   **resigns**

It's tempting to head into variations in which your opponent has the least choice. But, as we should know by now, this is a double-edged sword.

Kupreichik–Sveshnikov, Kuibyshev 1986

1 e4 c5   2 Nf3 Nc6   3 Nc3 e5   4 Bc4 Be7   5 d3 Nf6   6 Ng5 0-0   7 f4 exf4   8 Bxf4 d6   9 0-0 h6 10 Nf3 Be6   11 Qd2 d5   12 exd5 Nxd5   13 Bxd5 Bxd5   14 Bxh6!? gxh6   15 Qxh6

White has two pawns for his sacrificed bishop, but no immediate threats. A rook-lift to g3 or h3 would be a dangerous threat, but it is at least three moves away. Black therefore has a broad choice, chiefly centering either on a forceful defense eliminating possible attacking pieces (15 . . . Nd4), or on the slower addition of more defensive pieces (15 . . . Be6 and 16 . . . Bf5).

In fact, in the postmortem analysis, Black was winning most of the variations that continued with 15 . . . Be6; e.g., 16 Ne4 Bf5 17 Nfg5 Bxe4 18 Nxe4 Qd4+ 19 Kh1 Qg7, and so forth.

15 ...	Nd4?
16 Nxd4	Bg5

Black intended this zwischenzug rather than 16 . . . cxd4 17 Nxd5 Qxd5 because then White has time for Rf3-g3+.

17 Qh5	cxd4
18 Nxd5	Qxd5

It never occurred to Black that there would be a significant choice here. After all, he is the one doing the threatening (with 19 . . . Be3+, winning the queen). The quiet 19 Kh1 would allow an easy defense with 19 . . . Kg7 and 20 . . . Rh8.

19 Rf4!!

Now Black is virtually lost. On 19 . . . f6 there follows 20 Qg6+ and Rf3-h3 mate. Against **19 . . . Rae8 20 h4 Re5 21 hxg5 Rxg5 22 Rg4!** (the game continuation) Black collapsed quickly: **22 . . . f6 23 Rf1 Kg7 24 Rxf6! Kxf6 25 Qh6+ Ke7 26 Rxg5 resigns**.

Summing up, we should remember certain basic rules of choice.

(1) Choices exist in every position, and if we don't look for alternatives we're shortchanging ourselves.

(2) There are pluses and minuses to each alternative and it is the calculator's task to recognize and weigh them.

(3) There is no single criterion for making a choice. The criteria may be tactical, practical, technical, or any number of others.

(4) Our opponents get to make choices, too, and we should try to limit them.

Finally, a bit of serendipity: In studying our opponent's options we sometimes develop new ideas for ourselves. But in doing so we also create new options for our opponent:

Mecking–O. Rodriguez, Las Palmas 1975
Black to play

Black has sacrificed a bishop for a kingside attack that has reached its apex. If there is going to be a time for hard calculation, it is now. Unfortunately for him, the direct mating ideas, such as 1 . . . Rxg3+ and 1 . . . R8f5, don't work. (In the latter case White simply answers 1 . . . R8f5 with 2 Qe8+.)

Black therefore studied the only other violent try in the position, 1 . . . Rxf2. He saw that 2 Rxf2 Qxg3+ 3 Kf1 Bh3+ was strong for him (4 Ke2 Re8+ 5 Kd2 Rxe1 6 Kxe1 Qg1+ 7 Ke2 Bg4+).

Therefore, he needed to correctly evaluate the consequences of the defensive queen sacrifice 2 Qxf2! Rxf2 3 Kxf2 Qh2+ 4 Ke3. He saw that 4 . . . Qh6+ was a sure draw and that 4 . . . Qxg3+ 5 Bf3 Bf3! 6 Rxf3 Qe1+ 7 Kf4 h6 followed by advancing the kingside pawns was a winning try.

But as he studied the situation, Black concluded that White could not strengthen his position. For example, Bxf3 allows . . . Bxf3 and mate on g2. So he figured his choice was between 1 . . . Rxf2 and some other move that improves the position for . . . Rxf2 on the following move.

    1 . . .   **h5??**

    2 Bg5!

With this White not only stops 2 . . . h4 but also prepares to seal off the kingside with 3 Bh4. Black now has no choice but to capture on f2. Yet he finds that White's last move has made a major difference.

    2 . . .   **Rxf2**

    3 Qxf2   **Rxf2**

    4 Rxf2!

And White consolidated smoothly since Black, without control of h4, lacks a perpetual check. The game ended with **4 . . . Qxg3+ 5 Rg2 Qe1+ 6 Kh2 Bxd1 7 Rd2! resigns**.

Resignation was a bit premature but the outcome is fairly certain after 7 . . . h4 8 Bf4 g5 9 Be5 g4 10 Raxd1 g3+ 11 Kh3, because White's king is safe and his pieces are ready to overwhelm the queen.

What is striking about this example is that Black failed to see the most significant differences between (a) the immediate 1 . . . Rxf2 and (b) the preparatory 1 . . . h5. Had he done so he would have found (c) 1 . . . h6!, which would have won quickly. By creating luft—while not allowing 2 Bg5—Black creates the powerful threat of 2 . . . R8f5 and 3 . . . Rh5, as well as an improved version of the . . . Rxf2 idea.

Clearly, there are a lot of ways to miscalculate, and in the next two chapters we'll take a closer look at them.

Seven

MONKEY WRENCHES

*"Nothing is more disturbing than the upsetting of
a preconceived idea."*

—Joseph Conrad

W e can think of calculated variations as if they were mechanical devices, with elaborate systems of connect-
ing parts (subvariations), with demands for fuel and energy
(material and force), and with stop-and-start controls and the
like. But any mechanism can be thrown out of kilter by a monkey wrench. This chapter deals with the monkey wrenches.

The most common ones are:

(a) Assumption
(b) Quiet move
(c) Destruction of guard
(d) Zwischenzug (in-between move)
(e) Attack-defense
(f) Desperado

ASSUMPTION

It is impossible to calculate well without making certain assumptions. A master will think to himself, "I go there and he
must reply such-and-such. Then I play the rook check and he

must go to the e-file. Then I play such-and-such and I win a piece." Those "musts" are his assumptions.

When you begin to recheck variations, it is essential to firm up those assumptions, to make sure the "musts" are really "musts," and not just "most likelies."

Here's a fatal "most likely":

Balcerowski–Krantz, Stockholm 1966

1 d4 Nf6   2 c4 g6   3 Nc3 Bg7   4 e4 d6   5 f3 0-0
6 Be3 e5   7 d5 c6   8 Qd2 cxd5   9 cxd5 a6   10 0-0-
0 Re8   11 Kb1 Nbd7   12 Nge2 b5   13 Nc1 Nb6
14 Bd3 Bd7   15 g4 Rb8   16 Bg5 Nc4   17 Bxc4 bxc4
18 h4 Rb7   19 h5 Qc7   20 hxg6 hxg6   21 Bh6

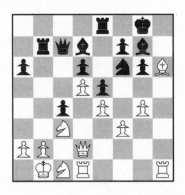

21 ...   Reb8?

Black decides against the cautious 21 . . . Bh8 in favor of a combination. If White captures on g7 now, Black will give up his rooks for the White queen and b-pawn. Black's moves are all checks in this variation until he has time to retake on g7 (22 Bxg7 Rxb2+ 23 Qxb2 Rxb2+ 24 Kxb2 Kxg7), so he has reason to have faith in his assumptions.

22 Bxg7!   Rxb2+
23 Ka1!!

But Black is betrayed by those very assumptions. Now 23 . . . Rxd2 24 Bxf6 sets up a mate on h8 that can be delayed but not avoided. And since 23 . . . Kxg7 24 Qh6+ also leads to mate there, Black vainly played on with **23 . . . Nh5 24 Qh6 f6   25 gxh5** and got mated after all: **25 . . . Be8 26 Qh8+ Kf7   27 Qf8 mate**.

That was a fairly striking, but complex, example with a lot of pieces on the board. Yet very good players can make very bad errors of assumption with only a few legal possibilities to consider:

Duras–Spielmann, Karlsbad 1907
White to play

Rudolph Spielmann, who ranked among the world's best players for three decades, gave this as an example of a "chess accident." The endgame would be drawn at virtually any level of skill. But in this particular encounter of grandmasters, White responded quickly to Black's checking move . . .

1 Rf4??

. . . because he wanted the game over quickly. He saw, of course, that 1 . . . Rxf4+ 2 Kxf4 was a classic example of the opposition—and a book draw. But the game was over *too* quickly:

1 . . .   Kg5!
White resigns

After 1 Rf4, how many Black moves were there for White to consider? Basically, only three: (1) the exchange of rooks, (2) a lateral retreat, such as 1 . . . Ra5, and (c) the winning reply.

It wasn't that Black had misevaluated the forced result of 1 . . . Kg5 (2 Rxf5+ Kxf5). As a master he would have instantly known it was a win for Black. The reason White lost was that he didn't consider 1 . . . Kg5 *at all*.

For a more recent example on a slightly busier board:

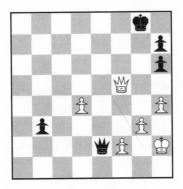

Karpov–Agdestein, Match 1991
White to play

White has an extra pawn but Black has considerable compensation because his b-pawn is farther advanced than White's d-pawn. White can see, quite plainly, that 1 Qd5+ and 2 Qxb3 leads to a hopeless draw (2 . . . Qxf2+ and 3 . . . Qxd4).

The mistake here is astonishing because it was made by the outstanding example in our time of a practical calculator. Knowing that he could force a draw, Anatoly Karpov rushed headlong into a variation that turned out to lose quickly. How did this happen?

1 d5??

It happened because White counted on Black replying 1 . . . b2. "After all," he might have asked himself, "what other useful move does Black have?" There would follow 2 d6 and now 2 . . . Qd1 3 d7 b1Q 4 Qxb1 Qxd7 or 2 . . . b1Q 3 Qxb1 Qxf2+ 4 Kh3 leaves White with good technical chances of scoring a full point.

1 . . .   Qc2!

A relatively simple move, but the simplest of moves are often overlooked when we make false assumptions. Black now wins a tempo to advance his passer. The game ended with:

2 Qf3	b2
3 d6	b1Q
4 d7	Qbd1
5 Qa8+	Kg7
White resigns	

Usually when we make a faulty assumption, it happens because we count on our forcing move being met by an obedient reply (1 ... Rxf4+? in the Spielmann example or 1 ... b2? in the Karpov case). This mental sloppiness occurs quite often when we give checks, the most forcing moves of all.

Hodgson–Wolff, Preston 1989
White to play

White is in serious trouble because of the double attack on his d3-bishop and because of the vulnerability of his a1-rook on an exposed diagonal. He could have searched for a tricky response such as 1 0-0-0! after which anything might happen (although after 1 ... b5! he appears to be lost). However, White saw a forcing line and played it.

> **1 Nxe5?**   **Bxe5**
>
> **2 Qf2+**

Neat: After the exchange of queens, Black's pinned knight hangs with check. Unfortunately . . .

> **2 ...**   **Kg7!**

And resignation was in order because 3 Qxc5 Nxd3+ wins material. White actually played 3 **Bc4** and resigned after 3 **...** **Qxf2+ 4 Kxf2 Nc2**. As Grandmaster Eduard Gufeld once said of one of his own faulty assumptions, "I forgot that chess is not checkers—and captures are not obligatory!"

False assumption is one of the most serious dangers to a calculator because it carries with it more than just a heavy penalty on the board. There is also a *psychological* price to pay.

Once you realize you've made an assumption mistake, you start second-guessing yourself. And when you start doubting your assumptions, you are half-beaten. This doubting may linger into the next game, or for several games. Each time you begin to calculate you may feel yourself questioning your conclusions because you remember that mistaken assumption of the past.

At the board, suddenly realizing that you've made a wrong assumption can absolutely derail your train of thought.

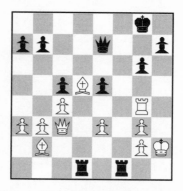

Eliskases–Henneberger, Libverda 1934
Black to play

Here White has a slight material edge but Black's connected rooks threaten mate on h1. White has allowed the rooks to penetrate because he calculated the effect of his last move, **1 Bd5+.**

Wherever the king moves, White can release the mate danger:

(1) 1 . . . Kh8?? 2 Qxe5+ and mates;

(2) 1 . . . Kg7 2 Qxe5+ Qxe5 3 Bxe5+ Kh6 (3 . . . Kf8 4 Rf4+ trades a pair of rooks) 4 Rh4+ Kg5 5 Bf4+ and 6 g4!.

(3) 1 . . . Kf8 2 Rf4+! Rxf4 (2 . . . exf4 3 Qh8 mate) 3 exf4 and 4 Qxe5 must win.

All very neat. White must have been congratulating himself when:

       1 . . .   **Qf7!!**

Stunned, White quickly responded . . .

       2 Bxf7+   **Kf8!**

. . . but now realized that the only way to avoid mate was to resign. In the postmortem he realized that his 2 Bxf7+?? was a blunder. If he had studied the position more fully he would have seen 2 Rxg6+!, which frees a square for his g-pawn (2 . . . hxg6?? 3 Bxf7+ and 4 g4 wins) and forces 2 . . . Kf8 3 g4 Qxg6 4 Qxe5!, after which White's threats are so much greater than Black's that a draw would likely result.

Faulty assumption also occurs frequently with recaptures. As we noted in Chapter Four, captures, particularly of the more valuable pieces, are among the most forcing of moves. But there are severe limits to their power to compel:

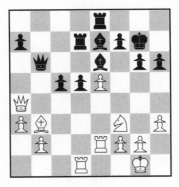

Yusupov–Short, Barcelona 1989
White to play

White's positional idea—the attack on d5—has become a tactical idea because of the pin on Black's d7-rook. With that in mind, White continued:

1 Rxd5??

White is certain to escape with the pawn (or more) after 1 . . . Bxd5 2 Qxd7 or 1 . . . Rxd5 2 Qe8 Qxb3 3 Qxe7. He mistakenly assumes Black must take on d5 immediately.

1 ...   Red8!

But here there was nothing to do but resign since a piece is lost (2 Rxd7 Bxd7 3 Qc4 Be6!).

And while we are usually more careful about wrong assumptions when we are doing the forcing, it is another matter entirely when performing defensive calculation.

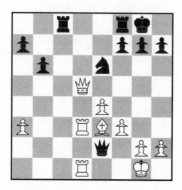

Dreev–Anand, Candidates Match 1991
White to play

Black has just played . . . Qe2, threatening 1 . . . Rc2. White continued:

1 Qd6??

So that the queen can retreat to g3 and defend after 1 . . . Rc2. "Of course, if Black puts a rook on d8 I can play 2 Qxd8 and mate him on the last rank," White probably said to himself. However:

1 ...   Rcd8!
2 Qxd8   Nxd8!

And White soon resigned.

ADVANCED ASSUMPTION

Perhaps the most common assumption error, as we've seen, involves the "I-check-him-and-he-must-go-there" situation. Naturally, there are many versions of this. We often assume that the other player will give us a check, or that he cannot allow us to queen a pawn or somesuch. We come to that mistaken conclusion perhaps because it would be consistent with his previous move or because it just looks natural.

Zsu. Polgar–Belyavsky, Munich 1991

1 d4 f5   2 Bg5 g6   3 Nc3 d5   4 e3 Bg7   5 h4 c6
6 Bd3 Qb6   7 Rb1 Nd7   8 Nf3 Ngf6   9 h5 Ne4
10 hxg6 hxg6   11 Rxh8+ Bxh8   12 Bxe4 fxe4
13 Nh4 Kf7   14 Qg4 Nf8   15 Qg3 Be6

White has been playing for the last four moves with the intention of penetrating on the kingside with her queen. She can do that now with 16 Qf4+ Bf6 17 Bxf6 and 18 Qh6 but decides instead to go after the g6-pawn.

With 16 Bh6 White threatens 17 Bxf8 and 18 Qxg6+ or 18 Nxg6. Of course, Black does not have to recapture on f8 at move 17. But if he doesn't, he'll just be a piece down, right?

16	Bh6?	Bf6
17	Bxf8	g5!!

Surprise: By agreeing to remain temporarily a piece down, Black traps two enemy pieces on the kingside. Even after **18 Bh6 gxh4   19 Qh2** White was lost: **19 ... c5! 20 Ne2 Qa5+   21 Kf1 Qxa2   22 Re1 Qxb2** etc.

Another example, of a mistakenly assumed check:

Dolmatov–Makarichev, Palma de Mallorca 1989

1 e4 e5   2 Nf3 Nf6   3 d4 Nxe4   4 Bd3 d5
5 Nxe5 Nd7   6 Nxd7 Bxd7   7 0-0 Qh4   8 c4 0-0-0
9 c5 g5   10 f3 Nf6   11 Be3 Rg8!?   12 Nc3 g4

Black thought over his last two moves for about an hour, and this had a typical psychological effect on his opponent. White examined the most natural defense (13 Qe1 g3 14 hxg3 Rxg3 15 Ne2). He stopped his calculations when he located the most dangerous variation (15 ... Rxg2+ 16 Kxg2 Qh3+ 17 Kg1 Bd6!) and then found a fine refutation—18 cxd6 Rg8+ 19 Bg5!!, after which the White king escapes by way of the newly cleared f2-e3-d2 route.

Had he examined the position a bit deeper he would have chosen 13 g3! and if 13 . . . Qh3 then 14 f4 Nh5 15 Qe1! with a solid defense.

13 Qe1?   **g3**

White most expected 13 . . . Qh5. Now he rechecked his variations, discovered his error—and also found there were no good bailouts available.

     14 hxg3   **Rxg3**
     15 Qd2

What he saw too late was that 15 Ne2 is met not by the assumed rook sacrifice (15 . . . Rxg2+?) but by the improvement 15 . . . Bd6!, after which 16 Nxg3 Bxg3 threatens the queen as well as mate on h2. After 16 cxd6 Black wins with 16 . . . Rxg2+ 17 Kxg2 Rg8+ 18 Bg5 Rxg5+ 19 Ng3 Bh3+ or 18 Ng3 Qh3+.

     15 . . .   **Bxc5!**
     16 dxc5   **Rdg8**

Now there is no defense to . . . Rxg2+ since 17 Rf2 allows 17 . . . Rh3 and 18 . . . Rh1+. White actually played **17 Rfd1 d4**   **18 c6 dxe3**   **19 cxd7+ Kd8** and resigned in view of 20 Qe2 Rxg2+ 21 Qxg2 Qf2+!.

Often assumption errors go hand in hand with move-order errors:

Tseshkovsky–Gufeld, Vilnius 1975
White to play

White is temporarily a piece behind but he can regain it with 1 Rxe4, and the endgame after 1 . . . Bxd4+ 2 Rxd4 Qxb7 3 Qxb7 Rxb7 4 Rd2 is excellent for him.

But White correctly believed he deserved more than a mere pawn-up ending. The geometry of Black's defenses got him thinking of a mixture of the ideas Bxe5+ and Rf8+. But in which order?

White can win with 1 Rf8+! Rxf8 2 Bxe5+, which forces 2 . . . Rf6, and then the simple 3 Bxb8. Perhaps he saw only 3 Qf7, which appears stronger, but then gave up on the combination when he saw the reply 3 . . . Qb6+ 4 Kh1 Bxg2+! 5 Kxg2 Qf2+ and it is Black who wins.

So he reversed the order:

      1 Bxe5+?   Rxe5
      2 Rf8+?

It was time to bail out with 2 Qc3!, after which White retains an advantage—but no win—following 2 . . . Qb6+ 3 Rf2 Qc5 4 Qxc5 and 5 Rxe4.

2 . . .   **Rxf8**

3 b8Q

And here White looked into Black's eyes as if expecting him to resign (3 . . . Rxb8 4 Qxb8+ and 5 Qxe5+). Instead Black made a move that defends everything and also makes decisive threats.

3 . . .   **Qf6!**

4 Qxa7   **Bd3!**

Even with two queens White cannot defend the trio of squares, e1, f1, and f2.

5 Qd1   **Rxe1+**

And White resigned because 6 . . . Qf1+ forces mate. Situations like this should be a warning to all calculators.

QUIET MOVE

One of the things we assume most often when we calculate is that forcing moves are going to follow forcing moves until the sequence is over. But often it is a nonforcing move, a "quiet" move, that makes a combination work. Or it can be a quiet move that refutes a sequence.

This is particularly dangerous when it is your opponent who is doing the forcing (or nonforcing) and you have to figure out when to stop calculating a sequence.

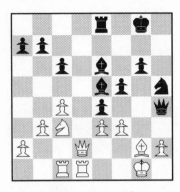

Spacek–Motwani, Luxembourg 1990
White to play

To fend off the attack on the dark squares White played 1 f4, fully aware of the possibility of a sacrifice.

1	f4	Nxf4
2	exf4	Bxf4
3	Qf2	

So far, so calculated. Now on 3 ... Qxh2+ 4 Kf1 Bg3 5 Qxa7, or 4 ... Bxc1 5 Rxc1 (or 3 ... Bxh2+ and 4 ... Bg3), Black has compensation for a sacrificed piece but White also has excellent defensive chances.

3	...	Qh6!

An easy move to miss because it is (a) a retreat and (b) a noncheck in a position rife with more forceful moves. Yet a quick look will show that the threats of 4 ... Be3 and 4 ... Bxc1 are so dangerous that White has only one move.

4	Qe1	Qxh2+
5	Kf1	Bxc1
6	Rxc1	e3

The advance of the e- and f-pawns quickly decided: **7 Ne2 f4 8 Ng1 Bg4 9 Rc2 e2+! 10 Rxe2 Rxe2 11 Nxe2 f3** etc.

Now let's examine how early in the game an error may be made:

Kruppa–Bareev, U.S.S.R. Club Championship 1988

1 e4 e6 2 d4 d5 3 Nc3 Nf6 4 e5 Nfd7 5 f4 c5 6 Nf3 cxd4 7 Nxd4 Qb6 8 Be3

With his last move White not only prepares to discover an attack on the Black queen (e.g., 9 Qd2 Nc6? 10 Nxe6) but also dares his opponent to grab the b2-pawn, which must have been Black's intention when he played 7 . . . Qb6.

After 8 . . . Qxb2 White's knight is hanging on c3, and moving it doesn't seem to generate dangerous compensation (9 Na4 Qb4+ 10 c3 Qa5; or 9 Ncb5 Na6 10 Rb1 Qxa2 11 Ra1 Qb2 12 Rxa6 bxa6 13 Nc7+ Kd8 14 Nxa8 Bb7).

Therefore, the variation to consider most carefully is 8 . . . Qxb2 9 Ndb5!, which threatens both 10 Rb1, trapping the queen, and the check on c7.

Bareev, however, found an adequate defense in 9 . . . Qb4, which extricates the queen from any trap, prepares to defend c7 with 10 . . . Qa5, and maintains an attack on c3, so that 10 Nc7+ Kd8 11 Nxa8? allows a strong counterattack with 11 . . . Qxc3+ 12 Bd2 (12 Kf2 Bc5) Qc5.

Black, who within a few years had become one of the world's best players, looked for other dangerous 10th and 11th

moves in this last, key variation, and then confidently went
ahead:

8 ...	Qxb2?
9 Ndb5!	Qb4
10 Nc7+	Kd8
11 Bd2!	

A devastating "quiet" move, which wins a decisive amount
of material. Black either loses the trapped rook or, as Bareev
chose, drops his queen to 11 ... Kxc7 12 Nb5+ Qxb5 13 Bxb5.
Black missed 11 Bd2 because it seems to be so lacking in force,
merely a defensive move, protecting c3.

Finally, when provoking a combination that leaves your opponent with a myriad of threats, it is very dangerous to overlook a quiet move:

Vaganian–Geller, New York 1990
Black to play

White's last move, 1 Qf4, prepares a knight invasion at c7.
But after examining this in some depth, the veteran grand-

master playing Black calculated this forcing line: 1 . . . a6 2 Nc7 g5!, since 3 Qxf6 Re1+ 4 Rxe1 Qxf6 5 Nxa8 Qxd4+! and 6 . . . Qxd3 gives Black at least equality.

| 1 . . . | a6? |
| 2 Nc7! | |

Any other move renounces any chance for advantage. Now 2 . . . Nh5 allows White to retain the edge with 3 Qh4.

2 . . .	g5
3 Qxf6	Re1+
4 Rxe1	Qxf6
5 Kh1!!	

This is the quiet move Black either underestimated or overlooked entirely. His rook cannot escape (5 . . . Ra7 6 Re8+ Kg7 7 Rxc8! threatening Ne8+). So Black played.

5 . . .	Qxd4
6 Rbd1!	Kg7
7 Nxa8	

And Black resigned after a few moves: **7 . . . Qa7   8 Rc1 Qxa8   9 Re8**. White may have been merely lucky—not seeing 5 Kh1 in the diagram position any more than Black did. But Black made the crucial error by forcing matters into an area he was not certain of.

DESTRUCTION OF THE GUARD

Another common monkey wrench that can upset a careful calculation is the elimination of a crucial piece. Typically, that piece is captured, overworked, or lured elsewhere.

Calculators should be particularly wary about this when they are "stretching" their own pieces, that is, linking several of them together in a fragile, tactical tether.

Adams–Shirov, Biel 1991
White to play

White is a pawn up but he clearly has kingside problems, with 1 . . . Rxg5 and 1 . . . f3 threatened. He decides to solve two problems with one move:

1 Bxf4?

This seems to make sense because each White piece is protected by another one. But in precisely this kind of position there is the danger that one piece will be deflected.

1 ... Bc4!

A very simple move, with an elementary threat to win a piece by 2 . . . Bxe2. White searches and searches for an antidote. But there is none (2 g3 Bxe2 3 Qxe2 Rxf4!), and after **2 Be3 Rxf2 3 Bxf2 Bxe2 White resigned**.

Naturally, when you raise the stakes by initiating a sequence that involves a lot of hanging or sacrificed material, the price of miscalculation rises. So does the amount of material your opponent is willing to give up in order to eliminate the one piece that makes your sequence work.

Case in point:

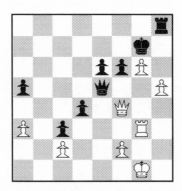

Tal–Korchnoi, U.S.S.R. Championship 1958
White to play

In this early game between future stars, White holds the initiative and Black has an extra pawn. White saw he could draw with 1 Qf3, since Black cannot allow the queen to penetrate at b7 and would have to play 1 . . . Qd5. Then 2 Qf4! (or even 2 Qxd5 with a drawn endgame) Qe5! would repeat the position.

But it also occurred to White that he had a choice here, and he opted for a combination that, since it was forcing, he thought was probably better than 1 Qf3.

1 h6+?	Rxh6
2 Qxh6+?	Kxh6
3 g7	

And the pawn cannot be blocked, so Black must take a perpetual check, White thought. However . . .

3 . . .	Qxg3+!

And with a three-pawn edge (4 . . . Kxg7) Black won easily. White built his combination on the existence of two elements, the rook and g7-pawn. What he overlooked was that if either element was eliminated, even at the cost of Black's queen, White's position would collapse.

A key element, essential to a sequence, may even be the existence of a flight square.

Shishov–Zagoryansky, Riga 1953
White to play

Here we have a disguised version of a last-rank mate. White's queen is attacked. But he also sees that 1 Qxh6 Rxh6 2 Rg8+ and 3 Rd8 is a mate. What can go wrong with such a forcing line?

1 Qxh6?? Rxe2+!

And Black wins because the king can go safely to e6 after 2 Kxe2 Rxh6 3 Rg8+ Kd7 4 Rd8+. White misread the position in the diagram by not recognizing that a vital element of the combination—the unavailability of e6—was only temporary.

ZWISCHENZUG

Zwischenzug is a German word that means "in-between move"—in between the assumed moves of the expected sequence. Like sand in the cogs of a machine, a zwischenzug can interfere, slow down, or completely halt the wheels of the mechanism.

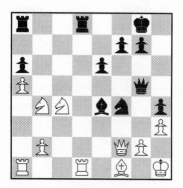

M. Gurevich–Geller, Helsinki 1992
Black to play

Having sacrificed a piece, Black plays the natural followup:

1 ...   Nxh3

2 Qe3

Now 2 . . . Qf5 3 Rd4! offers little. So Black should simply grab some material back with 2 . . . Rxd1 3 Rxd1 Qxe3 4 Nxe3 Nf2+ 5 Kg1 Nxd1 6 Nxd1. In the resulting endgame, White's two minor pieces are only a bit better than Black's rook and two pawns.

2 ...   Qxe3??

But this is just a blunder, overlooking the in-between-move:

3 Rxd8+!   **resigns**

Black does not get to fork the king and rook now and will have only two pawns for a piece in a lost endgame.

Note incidentally that after the correct 2 . . . Rxd1 White can insert his own zwischenzug 3 Qxg5, which is more forcing because the capture of a queen carries greater weight than that of a mere rook. But then Black has an even more forcing reply, 3 . . . Rxf1+!, which leaves him two pawns ahead.

The consequences of missing a zwischenzug are rarely mild. Often they turn a very simple maneuver into a shambles. When you're increasing the tension in a position—that is, when your pieces must coordinate precisely—or when your material is hanging all over the board, or your king is walking the plank, you must make sure there are no surprises.

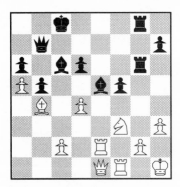

Ljubojevic–Kasparov, Linares 1991
Black to play

White has just played 1 d4, trying to slow down Black's attack. With 1 . . . Qg7, and if 2 Qf2 then 2 . . . Bf4, Black's initiative remains on track. But the world champion thought he saw a more forceful route.

1 ...	Rxg2??
2 Rxg2	Rxg2
3 Kxg2	Qg7+
4 Kh1	

And White, a rook ahead, should have won quickly. (He later blundered.) But what did Black overlook when he sacrificed his rook?

The answer came in the postmortem analysis when Black explained that he had been counting on 2 . . . Bxf3 (not 2 . . . Rxg2). But in rechecking his tree limbs at move two he saw that 2 . . . Bxf3 3 Rxf3 Qxf3 loses to the elegant zwischenzug 4 Qc3+!! Qxc3 5 Rxg8+, followed by 6 Bxc3.

Moral: You can afford to overlook zwischenzugs in quiet positions, but not when you've just sacrificed a rook.

A zwischenzug must meet two criteria: (a) it must be sufficiently forcing to prevent the sequence from continuing normally, and (b) as a result, the sequence cannot achieve its intended objective.

The absence of either criterion renders the zwischenzug harmless. A zwischenzug that can safely be ignored is useless. And a forcing but irrelevant insertion—such as the familiar "spite check" that a player often tries just before resigning—succeeds only in lengthening the game by a move or two. Computers are known to be zwischenzug fanatics, throwing material at their opponent's pieces in a sacrificial orgy to delay being mated.

Niemala–Tal, Riga 1959

1 d4 Nf6   2 c4 c5   3 d5 e6   4 Nc3 exd5   5 cxd6 d6
6 e4 g6   7 f4 Bg7   8 Nf3 0-0   9 Be2 Re8   10 e5
dxe5   11 fxe5 Ng4   12 e6 fxe6   13 0-0 exd5
14 Nxd5 Be6   15 Bc4 Ne5   16 Bg5! Nxf3+   17 Qxf3
Qxg5   18 Rae1 Rf8!

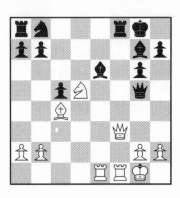

Here White makes a costly decision, all the more so since
he has at least two excellent moves. The first, which requires
little calculation, is 19 Qe4, attacking the e6-bishop and in-
directly threatening b7 and the undeveloped rook at a8 (e.g.,
19 . . . Bf5 20 Ne7+ Kh8 21 Nxf5 gxf5 22 Qxb7 and White
wins back material favorably).

The second alternative, which calls for White to look a bit
further, is the queen sacrifice 19 Qxf8+ Bxf8 20 Rxe6, and now
Black can prevent either 21 Re8 or 21 Nc7 but not both.

The queen sacrifice seems to lead to a bigger advantage
than 19 Qe4. But White chose a third sequence, which starts
out relatively quietly and then picks up force.

19 Rxe6

Now on 19 . . . Rxf3 he inserts a zwischenzug—20 Re8+!—with consequences such as 20 . . . Kf7 21 Nc7+! Kf6 22 Rxf3+, or 20 . . . Bf8 21 Rxf3, winning in either case.

19 . . .	**Bd4+!**

Black gets the first opportunity to play a zwischenzug. It meets the forcing requirement (being a check), and it also makes a difference in White's intended sequence by clearing g7 for Black's king.

20 Kh1	Rxf3
21 Re8+	Kg7
22 Rxf3	Qc1+
23 Bf1	Nc6!

Black could have won through other means but this seizes the initiative and finishes off nicely. The game ended with **24 Rxa8 Ne5   25 Rff8 Ng4** (also winning is 25 . . . Nf7) **26 Rf3 Nf2+   27 Kg1 Ne4+   White resigns**.

A zwischenzug is a double-edged sword. By inserting a surprise move into a forcing sequence you increase the chances of being surprised yourself:

Wheeler–Povah, London 1977

1 c4 e5   2 Nc3 Nf6   3 Nf3 Nc6   4 g3 Bb4   5 Bg2 0-0   6 0-0 e4   7 Ng5 Bxc3   8 dxc3 Re8   9 Nh3 h6 10 Nf4 b6   11 Be3 d6   12 Bd4 Ne5   13 b3 Bb7 14 Qc2 Qd7   15 Rad1 Qf5

16	Nd5	Nxd5
17	Bxe4?	

This zwischenzug deserves a better fate. It is more forcing than 17 Qxe4 Qxe4 18 Bxe4, which also gives White a pin on the d5-knight but leaves Black free to liquidate favorably with 18 . . . Nxc4!.

17 . . .   Qh3!

What did White miss in this game? Perhaps he overlooked the strength of this move, which threatens mate (18 Bxd5 Ng4). Or maybe he saw this far and overlooked that 18 Bxe5 (eliminating a key part of the mating attack) Rxe5 19 Bxd5 allows 19 . . . Rh5.

18 Bg2

Or perhaps he saw all of the above and just counted on this zwischenzug, which appears to drive the queen back (18 . . . Qh5 19 cxd5 Ng4 20 h3).

18 . . .   Qxg2+!

Black can vary the move order with 18 . . . Nf4 (19 Bxh3 Nxh3 mate; 19 gxf4 Qxg2 mate; 19 Bxb7 Ng4). But the text is prettier and at least as fast: 19 Kxg2 Nf4+ 20 Kg1 Nh3 mate.

ATTACK-DEFENSE

Calculation involves a rhythm of thrusts and parries. You threaten his rook, he defends it. You check his king, he moves it. You surround his bishop, he tries to break out of the web. In each case, the player with the initiative is doing the threatening and the opponent is doing the responding. This is what makes counting out easy: the comfortable, reliable rhythm.

But suppose you make a threat and your opponent responds with a move that not only defends against your threat, but makes a threat, or *threats*, of its own. Suddenly, your forcing sequence is halted. Now *he* is doing the forcing.

Khalifman–Speelman, Munich 1992
Black to play

White's last move, 1 Qxd4, offers Black a poor endgame, which he naturally rejects. Nevertheless, Black should have sat on his hands before playing . . .

1 . . .   Qc6??

If this is as good as it looks (threatening mate on g2 as well as the rook on a4), Black is winning outright. But it's a chimera.

2 Qxg7! resigns

Black did not see that the queen defends g2 on this square—as well as threatens 3 Qxh8+—and thereby gains time for 3 Rxb4.

That example was caused by a visualization problem: Black didn't foresee that a piece could attack h8 and at the same time defend g2. In the next case we have a different kind of oversight, an attack-defense move met by an attack-defense move.

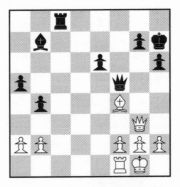

Ivkov–Larsen, Candidates Match 1965
White to play

It's a quiet position in which Black's pieces are more active but a draw seems virtually inevitable because of the bishops of opposite colors. After 1 Be5 and a subsequent Rd1 White should hardly lose.

1 a3??

He decides to eliminate a pair of pawns before playing Be5.

    1 ...   **Rc4!**

White resigns

What did White overlook? He saw 1 . . . Rc4, of course, but assumed that he could just threaten mate with 2 Be5, defending against the threat while threatening mate.

The surprise to him was 2 . . . Rg4!, which meets his attack-defense move with one of Black's own. It not only defends against the threatened mate on g7 but wins through an attack on g2.

The attack-defense problem becomes more common as your tactical ideas get more sophisticated and the sequence takes on more finesse. The possibilities for being surprised multiply.

Lapiken–Reshevsky, U.S. Open 1955, Long Beach

1 e4 c5 2 Nf3 d6 3 d4 cxd4 4 Nxd4 Nf6 5 Nc3 g6 6 Be3 Bg7 7 f3 0-0 8 Qd2 a6? 9 0-0-0 b5 10 a3 Bb7 11 g4 Nc6 12 h4 h5!? 13 gxh5 Nxh5 14 Rg1 Kh7 15 Kb1 Qc8 16 Nd5! Nxd4 17 Bxd4

Black has good prospects in the endgame—if he can reach it—because of the weakness of White's kingside pawns. But we're more interested in what happens as the minor pieces are liquidated.

    17 ...   **Bxd5**

Black visualizes a distant position in which the only minor pieces left are his good knight and White's less-than-wonderful light-squared bishop.

18 Bxg7   Ba2+

The point of this forcing finesse is to bring the queen into a better view of the world on e6. There is also a positional benefit in denying White the opportunity to capture on d5 with a pawn, creating potential pressure against e7 via the e-file.

White gets no time to carry out his own threat, 19 Qh6+ and mate next, because Black's last move is a check, as will be 19 . . . Qe6 after White takes the bishop on a2.

19 Kxa2   Qe6+

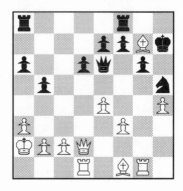

20 Kb1	Kxg7
21 Be2	Rh8
22 Rg5	Qf6
23 Rdg1	e5!

And after 24 . . . Nf4 he was on the road to victory. But he was very lucky, since he was quite lost after 19 . . . Qe6+.

Had White found 20 Bc4!, Black could have quietly resigned. The only way then to protect his queen and also avoid 21 Qh6+ is 20 . . . Qxc4+. But then 21 b3! closes the diagonal for good, and threatens the queen once more.

One further example shows that sometimes a double attack can be met by a double defense.

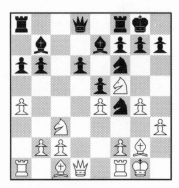

Kholmov–Anikaev, Rostov-on-Don 1976
White to play

Black has just dropped a knight onto f4—and it was a blunder.

    1 **Bxf4**   exf4

    2 **e5!**

A double attack that wins a piece. White threatens 3 exf6 as well as 3 Bxb7.

    2 ...   Bxg2

Black makes the best of a bad deal. White, a veteran grandmaster, can seal the win of material with 3 exf6 since if Black continues desperado-style with 3 . . . Bxf1, he loses more material after 4 fxe7!.

    3 **Nxe7+?**   Qxe7

    4 **exf6**

This appears to be the same thing as 3 exf6 but with extra force, since the queen is threatened, not just a bishop on e7.

4 ...   Qb7!

This is what White overlooked. Black protects both pieces at once. The game later ended as a draw.

DESPERADO

A further complication in a calculated sequence arises when one capture is met by another, setting off a chain reaction. Usually this involves mutual captures and a very short chain reaction: I play queen takes queen. You re-establish material equality by answering rook takes queen. I have no more captures and the chain ends.

But sometimes, even with several protected pieces on the board, we work out longer chains in which pieces that are about to be captured inflict as much damage as possible.

For example, in 1949 a new idea in the Scotch Game was introduced in the game Bogolyubov–Schmid, West German Championship: 1 e4 e5   2 Nf3 Nc6   3 d4 exd4 4 Nxd4 Nf6   5 Nc3 and now 5 ... Nxe4?!

Subsequent analysis showed that White can obtain an edge with 6 Nxe4 Qe7 7 f3 d5 8 Bb5 Bd7 9 0-0. However, in the original game White responded:

6 Nxc6

Black cannot recapture on c6 because then 7 Nxe4 would win a piece. So he had to play:

6 ...   Nxc3

Now if White recaptures on c3, Black will follow suit on c6 and remain a pawn ahead (remember, he took the e-pawn at move 5).

| 7 **Nxd8** (forced) | **Nxd1** (ditto) |
| 8 **Nxf7** | **Nxf2** |

Actually Black can equalize more easily with 8 ... Kxf7, when material is even.

9 Nxh8   Nxh1

There's nothing left to take and the desperado sequence is over. In the game White continued **10 Bd3?** (10 Be3!) **Bc5! 11 Bxh7 Nf2 12 Bf4 d6** and had the worst of it.

In this example, the marauding knights each played the role of desperado, a piece that seems doomed to be captured (even though neither knight actually was). And, being doomed, they were determined to scorch as much earth as possible.

Desperado situations need not last long, and a sequence doesn't always involve captures of the same kinds of material (pawn for pawn, piece for piece). When the captures are unequal, the "winner" of the sequence is usually the player who makes the most damaging capture.

Tiviakov–Ostenstad, Gausdal 1992
White to play

Here's an odd, though hardly unique, example of a double blunder by masters, thanks to desperado tactics. White finds a clever way to win a pawn and avoid the consequences of 1 . . . Qe3+.

      1 Nxd5??

This is based on Black's vulnerable first rank: 1 . . . Rxc2?? allows 2 Rxf8 mate.

1 . . .	**Rxf1+??**
2 Rxf1	**Qd8**

Of course, the exchange on f1 changed little: 2 . . . Rxc2 3 Rf8 mate). The game ended with:

3 Bh4!	**Qd7**
4 Qc5!	**resigns**

But it would have been quite a different story if Black had found 1 . . . Qxc1!, shortcircuiting White's idea in all variations. Black then wins at least a piece.

If the same kinds of pieces are being captured, the player who makes the *final capture* is often the one who wins. This principle accounted for one of the shortest games ever lost in an Olympiad team tournament (it was lost by the artist Marcel Duchamp). The game Müller–Duchamp, The Hague 1928, went   **1 c4 e5   2 Nf3 Nc6   3 Nc3 Nf6 4 d4 exd4   5 Nxd4 Bb4   6 Bg5 h6   7 Bh4**, and now Black entered a faulty desperado sequence with **7 . . . Ne4? 8 Bxd8 Nxc3**. He counted on winning back the queen after 9 bxc3 Bxc3+ or 9 Qd2 Ne4, or on winning gobs of material compensation (9 Qb3? Nxd4).

But he missed **9 Nxc6!**, and after **9 . . . Nxd1+ 10 Nxb4 Black resigned**. His opponent had made the first and last capture.

When invited into a desperado derby by your opponent you need to keep a clear idea of when one of you can stop capturing and head for a tactical exit.

Spassky–Timman, Montpellier 1986
White to play

White played the seductive 1 Bxh6, based on the idea that after 1 . . . gxh6 2 Qxh6 he is attacking both the f6-knight and the h3-bishop and may be able to force a perpetual check if matters become too complicated. For example, if he reaches the position after 2 . . . Bxg2 3 Qxf6 Bh3 and determines that 4 Re4 or 4 Ne4 is unsatisfactory, White can bail out with checks on the g- and h-files.

    1 Bxh6?   **Bxg2!**

Perhaps only now did White see that 2 Qg5 Qg4 3 Kxg2!, which wins a pawn, is not Black's best defense and that instead he can play 2 . . . Ne8 3 Kxg2 Qe6!, winning the bishop. (In the diagram it is very difficult to see how the bishop on h6 can become trapped.)

    2 Bxg7

When in a desperado derby, do as the desperados do. Now 2 . . . Kxg7 3 Qg5+ Kh7 4 Qxf6 is a favorable line for White.

    2 . . .   **Nh7**
    3 Bxf8

It appears that everything has turned out well for White. He's gotten two pawns and a rook for a bishop. The desperado sequence can end now with 3 . . . Bxf8 4 Kxg2 or 3 . . . Bf3 4 Qe3, after which White wins.

| 3 . . . | Qh3! |

But Black exits first and with a major threat (4 . . . Bf3 and 5 . . . Qg2 mate). The queen move not only makes the threat but also protects the g2 bishop. Unless White has a comparable move (defending the f8-bishop while meeting the mate threat), he must lose material; e.g., 4 Qe3 Bxf8 5 Rxb7 Bh6! and 6 . . . Ng5; or 5 f3 b6! and . . . Bc5.

4 Qh6	Bxf8
5 Qxh3	Bxh3
6 Rxb7	Ng5

And although material is roughly equal, Black's pieces work together much better than White's. He won a long endgame.

It is crucial in calculating such sequences to keep two key points in mind:

(a) What is the score (the material balance or imbalance) after each move?
(b) Where does it end? That is, what will it look like at the time of the last capture?

It was a failure to answer the second question correctly that cost humanity a game in one of the first victories by a computer over a grandmaster.

Miles–Deep Thought, Long Beach 1989

1 d4 d5 2 c4 dxc4 3 e4 Nf6 4 Nc3 e5 5 Nf3
exd4 6 Qxd4 Bd6 7 Bxc4 0-0 8 Bg5 Nc6 9 Qd2
h6 10 Bh4 Bg4 11 0-0-0?

Black's last two moves contained a tactical point, allowing
a desperado that White misses:

11 ...	Bxf3
12 gxf3	Nxe4!

As a result, the h4-bishop is en prise and White will not regain the pawn after 13 Nxe4 Qxh4 14 Nxd6 because of 14 . . .
Rad8 (15 Nf5 Qxc4).

White may obtain some counterchances in that line (e.g.,
with 15 Qc3 and a later Rhg1), but he decides he has to go
into the full desperado because at the end of it he sees material equality.

13 Bxd8?	Nxd2
14 Bxc7!	

The move White was counting on. His position will not be
particularly pretty after 14 . . . Nxc4 15 Bxd6 Nxd6 16 Rxd6

or 14 . . . Bxc7 15 Kxd2, but at least the number of pawns will be the same for each player.

14 . . .   Bxh2!!

Wrong again. "I must admit I totally overlooked the decisive counter-desperado," Miles said after the game. By using this order of moves, Black wins a pawn. Clearly 14 . . . Bxc7 15 Kxd2 Bxh2?? loses a piece. But here 14 . . . Bxh2 15 Bxh2 Nxc4 or 15 Rxd2 Bxc7 makes off with a pawn.

White consoled himself with **15 Bxh2 Nxc4   16 Rd7** but after **16 . . . b6** he had scant compensation and lost in 38 moves.

Desperado calculation often seems like a totally new game, something like Loser's Chess, that offshoot of chess in which the players take turns trying to lose material to one another. It requires some of the most stringent calculation technique. You not only have to keep count of the quickly changing material situation, you must also keep an eye out for surprise moves that stop the chain reaction—in your opponent's favor.

A classic example of the last point is:

Bialas–Joppen, West German Championship 1961

1 e4 c5 2 Nf3 Nc6 3 d4 cxd4 4 Nxd4 e5 5 Nb5 a6 6 Nd6+ Bxd6 7 Qxd6 Qf6 8 Qc7 Nge7 9 Nc3 Qe6 10 Bd3 b5 11 0-0? Rb8!

This begins a game not of Loser's Chess but of Trap the Queen. Having failed to insure an escape route (11 Qb6), White is faced with an ominous 12 . . . Rb7.

12 f4!   Rb7
13 Nd5!

A clever defense. Black can't play 13 . . . Rxc7 because 14 Nxc7+ forks king and queen. And he can't capture on d5 because the c8-bishop hangs with check.

Moreover, White has a threat of his own: to trap Black's queen with 14 f5. The immediate 13 f5 leads to a bad endgame after 13 . . . Rxc7 14 fxe6 dxe6, Black having made the first and last capture.

13 . . .   0-0!

Black can make a desperado of his queen here with 13 . . . Qxd5, hoping for 14 exd5 Rxc7 15 dxc6 Nxc6 (or even 14 Qxb7??, when 14 . . . Qc5+! buys out of the chain reaction and gains time for 15 . . . Bxb7).

But White has a better way of surrendering his own trapped queen after 13 . . . Qxd5, and it's 14 Qxc8+ Nxc8 15 exd5, so that on 15 . . . Nb4 16 fxe5 Nxd5 he can take command with 17 Be4 and 18 Rd1.

14 f5

This is the position both sides have been playing for: White because it's the best he can get, Black because it's an easy win. Still, the win is tricky.

It comes from 14 . . . Nxf5!, after which White has nothing better than 15 exf5 and then to resign after 15 . . . Qxd5, since White's queen remains trapped.

A similar, but inferior, version of this is 14 . . . Nxd5, which transposes into the easy win after 15 exd5? Qxd5. The flaw in this thinking is that it leaves the Black queen hanging while White takes over the tactical initiative.

14 . . .	Nxd5?
15 Qxb7??	

Too greedy. White can recoup with 15 Qxc8! because 15 . . . Rxc8 16 fxe6 re-establishes material equality and leaves Black material hanging at d5 and f7.

After 15 Qxc8, Black does better with 15 . . . Qd6! 16 Qxb7 Rb8, trapping the queen again. But by then he will have spent too much time and material to do it, and 17 Qxb8+ and 18 exd5 gives White a winning edge.

15 . . .	Qd6!!

Now this move wins. Black recognizes that it's time to halt the chain reaction of captures. When the music stops, White's queen is still trapped (16 Qa8 Nc7). In the game, he actually played **16 Qxc8 Rxc8   17 exd5 Qxd5   18 Rd1** but saw no point in continuing the struggle after **18 . . . e4! 19 Be2 Qc5+   20 Kh1 Qf2!   21 Bf1 e3**.

Before we leave this wonderful example, let's consider what would have happened on 14 . . . Qxd5 instead of the faulty 14 . . . Nxd5 or the superior 14 . . . Nxf5. Then, faced with the possibility of 15 . . . Qc5+, which ends the chain reaction once and for all, White could not afford any additional captures such as 15 Qxc8 or 15 Qxb7. But he could have survived into the ending with 15 exd5 and 16 dxc6.

The basic dangers of desperado play are:

(a) Overlooking a capture that allows your opponent to come
out materially ahead when the chain reaction stops.

(b) Allowing him to halt the carnage at an embarrassing moment (e.g., 15 . . . Qd6!! above).

Eight

OVERSIGHTS

"No plan survives contact with the enemy."
—*Field Marshal Helmuth von Moltke*

I n the course of calculating you are bound to make oversights. You will simply overlook moves by your opponent
that didn't seem possible when you first charted the course of
the next few moves. Every player makes this kind of mistake
sometimes.

But if you learn how to calculate properly, you can reduce
the frequency and severity of oversights and avert crises before
they occur on the board.

Of course, nobody guesses his opponent's next move 100
percent of the time. In fact, 50 percent is a pretty good figure
to shoot for. The grandmaster who anticipates every move his
opponent plays is a figure of myth.

Only during certain periods of a game—portions of familiar openings, textbook situations in the endgame, and during
forcing combinations—can a player be reasonably certain of
what will happen next.

The difference between winning and losing, however, is the
nature of these very natural surprises. You may overlook a good
knight maneuver or a timely defensive retreat. Those oversights usually won't cost you much. But you *don't* want to overlook knight-takes-queen-double-check.

Larsen–Petrosian, Santa Monica 1966
Black to play

A classic example of a major oversight occurs in this game. Black, then the world champion, is being pressed but is still several moves away from a crisis. He sees that he can beat off the attack with 1 . . . e6, and also appreciates that the endgame that follows 2 Qxd8 Rfxd8 3 Rxe5 dxe5 4 Bxc5 is not at all clear because Black's pawns are well centralized and mobile. But he plays:

<table>
<tr><td>1 . . .</td><td>Ne6?</td></tr>
<tr><td>2 Rf3</td><td></td></tr>
</table>

Now the threat of 3 Rh3 and 4 Qh6 is so dangerous that Black must calculate very carefully. He has a choice between:

(a) kicking the enemy queen with 2 . . . Bf6 (e.g., 3 Qh6 Bg7 4 Qh4 Bf6), and
(b) taking the big risk with 2 . . . f5 3 Rh3 Kg7!?.

From a practical point of view, it is much more comfortable to pick (a). The variations are easier to count out and you run less chance of mate. But, and this is the main point, even in

(a) you have to make sure you aren't overlooking something big.

2 ...	**Bf6?**
3 Qh6	**Bg7**

And by "big" we mean a capture, a check or, in this case, a dangerous move that allows the queen to remain in mating proximity.

4 Qxg6!

Larsen saw this move when he played 2 Rf3, since otherwise he would have had to concede his plan was wrong and retreat the queen to h3 or h4. But Petrosian clearly had no idea this was in the air when he was choosing between 2 ... f5 and 2 ... Bf6.

The move 4 Qxg6 is one of the most famous in chess history, but, as both players readily acknowledged, its main lines were fairly simple to calculate. The rest of the game went **4 ... Nf4   5 Rxf4 fxg6   6 Be6+**. Now 6 ... Kh7 7 Rh4+ Bh6 8 Bxh6 leads to mate, so Black played **6 ... Rf7 7 Rxf7 Kh8   8 Rg5 b5   9 Rg3** and **resigned** before the decisive rook check.

Once we become trained at chess tactics—when we readily recognize pins, skewers, last-rank mates, and the like—the number of our oversights will decline sharply. But they will never disappear completely. There are simply too many causes, especially psychological ones, to plague us. To reduce our oversights further we have to recognize these causes.

Here's an instructive but typical example of a grandmaster overlooking a winning move of his own. He didn't find it because for once his instinct told him not to examine it.

Christiansen–Shirov, Biel 1991
White to play

White, materially behind, has queen checks available at h7 and f8 but they don't seem to lead anywhere. His g1-bishop is pinned and useless. And he is faced with . . . Nf2 mate.

Yet White has a simple winning move that threatens a mate in two and that Black can only delay by sacrificing his pieces randomly.

1 h3?	Rf6!

Black drew in a few moves when White was forced to take perpetual check. The winning move, found days later by Shirov, is 1 g3!!, threatening 2 Qf8+ Kg5 3 h4 mate. But, as Black was the first to point out, it is an extraordinarily hard move to find.

Why? Because 1 g3 seems to invite danger. It opens a very dangerous diagonal leading to White's king. Without the bishop on e4, Black mates with 1 . . . Qe4+. Psychologically, 1 g3 is the kind of move we would consider only after exhausting virtually every alternative.

SIMPLE VISUAL OVERSIGHTS

The most elementary—and most embarrassing—oversights are the one-movers, the strong moves that are so obviously good that we could not have dreamt of allowing them. But somehow we do: We allow an enemy piece to advance deep into our side of the board. Or we miss a strong retreat. Or we just have a blind spot.

Kupreichik–Polugayevsky, U.S.S.R. Championship 1974

1 e4 c5   2 Nf3 d6   3 d4 cxd4   4 Nxd4 Nf6   5 Nc3 a6   6 Be2 e5   7 Nb3 Be7   8 f4 0-0   9 a4 Nbd7 10 g4 d5   11 Nxd5 Nxe4   12 0-0 Ndc5   13 c4 Nxb3 14 Qxb3 Bc5+

For various reasons White is reluctant to move his king. But his tactical antennae should be going up all around the White side of the board after a check like this. Yet . . .

      15 Be3??   **Nd2!**

This was a case of White believing that on his side of the board he was relatively secure. Less explainable is the following, with pieces so close to one another.

Popovic–Ljubojevic, Manila 1990
White to play

Black has no convenient way out of the discovered check if he tries to win. So he tries . . .

   1 . . .   **Qc4**

White immediately notices that 2 Ne3+ fails to 2 . . . Qe6. He then examines other discovered checks, rejecting each one when he sees they achieve nothing after the same 2 . . . Qe6, or in the case of 2 Nd4+, a king move.

So he settles on the one discovery that actually accomplishes something:

   2 Nxd6+??

This at least wins a pawn. However . . .

   2 . . .   **Kxd6!**
   White resigns

Donald Byrne, a strong American amateur and coach of the 1950s and '60s, recommended that players always think about their positions mentally when away from the board. In this way you often "see" a move that your mind blocked out when you last examined the position with your eyes.

But when seated at the board, it pays to recheck every significant change in the position—every capture, sacrifice —by examining as many enemy responses as you feel comfortable with. I've known masters who, when considering a move that would likely force resignation, will consider every legal reply.

In this way few accidents like the following are likely to happen:

Yermolinsky–Braude, New York 1992
White to play

White, with a growing edge, has been attacking on the kingside for the last 20 moves, and for the last 15 Black's queen has been sitting passively at g8. But perhaps not as passively as you might think, because here White forgets about it and plays:

    1 Rxe6??

He can win with a move like 1 b6 but was counting on the exchange sacrifice followed by 2 Qxf5+ as being a clearer win.

    1 ...   **Qxe6!**

White simply did not remember that the queen was still on the board. He played on a few moves and resigned.

RETREATS

Psychologists have said that the kind of strong moves most likely to be overlooked are retreats.

Part of the momentum of calculation leads us to believe that "I advance there and he must advance there, or else I've improved my position." But when your opponent can take a well-developed piece and move it backward, we often blot that out of our consciousness and don't even try to evaluate it. We've trained our force-oriented calculating minds to look mainly for counterattacks and counterthreats.

A notorious example:

Fischer–Larsen, Santa Monica 1966
White to play

White has been working up an attack against the vulnerable dark squares but here avoids 1 Bh6 in favor of . . .

    1 b3?   **b4!**

Now 2 cxb4 d4! would give Black the better chances. White thought briefly about the new situation and replied:

2 Qh3?	bxc3!
3 Qh6	Ne6

White resigns

What did Fischer overlook? It certainly wasn't 3 . . . Ne6. No, according to his opponent, White had counted on the game ending with 3 Bf6 Ne6 4 Qxh7+ Kxh7 5 Rh3+ "and 6 Rh8 mate."

But this fails miserably to 5 . . . Qh6!, a retreat that ends all threats. Once Fischer saw this he went through the motions of 3 Qh6 but resigned when he realized how hopeless was his attack and how destroyed was his queenside.

An even simpler retreat cost Black an embarrassing defeat in the following:

Kasparov–Anand, Dortmund 1992

1 Nf3 d5	2 c4 c6	3 d4 Nf6	4 Nc3 dxc4	5 a4 Bf5
6 e3 e6	7 Bxc4 Bb4	8 0-0 0-0	9 Qe2 Nbd7	
10 Ne5 Re8	11 Rd1 Qc7	12 Nxd7 Qxd7	13 f3	
Nd5	14 Na2 Bf8	15 e4 Bg6	16 Qe1 f5??	

17 exd5! resigns

What happened? Black didn't appreciate his opponent's last move and assumed that he could now play 17 . . . exd5, simultaneously attacking the queen and the c4-bishop. When he realized that 18 Be2! was legal, he resigned.

Even a short-range retreat, particularly to the side of the board by a centralized piece, is often overlooked. The following, coming in the middle of a close world championship match, was called "the blunder of the century."

Karpov–Kasparov, World Championship 1987
Black to play

Hyperbole aside, it is a perfectly natural occurrence. White, with a slight advantage, used his previous two moves to shift his rook from c2 to f6.

1 ...	Bb6
2 Rc6??	Na5!

Winning the exchange and ultimately the game.

White was victimized by several psychological factors. First, he saw he was making progress with his last few moves and disliked the prospect of having to play 2 Bxb6 axb6! 3 Rf2.

Second, a5 had been occupied the previous move, so Black's moving a piece to that square did not readily occur to White. And, perhaps crucially, Black's key move withdrew his best-placed piece backward and to the side of the board.

Related to retreats is the problem of "short moves." When his rivals complained that they could never guess Anatoly Karpov's moves it was often because they generally involved shifts of a piece one or two squares away.

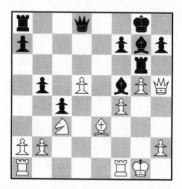

Korchnoi–Salov, Amsterdam 1991
White to play

1 Nxb5??

And White resigned immediately when he saw Black's "short" reply.

1 ...   Qe8!

This kind of oversight occurs most often with the most valuable pieces. Because the queen has such great mobility, we assume that our opponents will sweep it across the board.

LINE BLOCKS

Another minefield for calculators lies in positions in which a key diagonal or file can be forcefully cut by a surprise move. We call these line blocks.

In the following example, the White knights might be a match for the enemy bishops if they could be anchored by some supporting pieces or pawns. To avoid retreating the attacked d5-knight White tries to calculate a way out. The idea that occurs to him involves Black's vulnerable first rank.

Tseshkovsky–Miles, Palma de Mallorca 1989
White to play

There is a good idea here, but White does not find it. It is 1 Rxd4 exd4 and then 2 Qf5, threatening mate, which gains time for 3 Nc7. Instead, White finds the attractive . . .

    1 Rc1   **Bxd5**

    2 Qc8

This looks better. In fact, isn't White winning? What can Black do about the threat of 3 Qxa8 followed by 4 Rc8?

    2 . . .   **Rc4!!**

That's what. By cutting the c-file communication, Black insures he will remain a piece ahead (3 Qxa8 Rxc1+ and 4 . . . Bxa8; 3 Nxc4 Qxc8; 3 Rxc4 dxc4).

The winner in the last example had a similar experience with the White pieces. This time, in an even more perilous position, he found a way to cut communication on a diagonal.

Miles–Pritchett, London 1982
Black to play

Despite White's domination of the d-file and pressure on f7, it is Black's attack that arrives first. He can win directly with the simple 1 ... Qc2 2 Rb1 Re1; e.g., 3 Qxf7+ Kh8 4 Rdd1 Bxc3!.

But Black saw the idea of the bishop capture in another scheme . . .

| 1 ... | Bxc3 |

. . . which seems to win even faster, as . . . Bxb2+ cannot be averted. However:

| 2 Qxf7+ | Kh8 |
| 3 Be5!! | resigns |

An incredible final move and an easy one to overlook. Actually, it is quite logical, since it's the only way to defend b2. It works by cutting communication along the e-file and the

long diagonal, since otherwise 3 . . . R2xe5 4 Qxg7 mate and
3 . . . Bxe5 4 Qxe8+ and mates.

What made White's third move so hard to visualize is the
chess blindness that occurs on heavily fortified squares. Your
mind tells you that such a move as 3 Be5 is not worth a second's consideration in any subvariation because the square is
defended by three Black pieces.

To reinforce how common this kind of error is, here's an example that occurred in a tournament game by a future world
champion—and also in the home analysis of a past champion.
The latter's analysis was reprinted many times before someone
spotted the error.

Kasparov–Roizman, Minsk 1978
White to play

1 Bg5

Mikhail Botvinnik awarded this move an exclamation
point and much praise for his former pupil. Botvinnik's notes
go on to say that 1 . . . Rxg5 is not possible because of 2 Nxf6
"and Black's position is torn asunder."

But let's remember what we've been saying about pieces going to "impossible squares."

| 1 ... | **Rxg5!** |
| 2 **Nxf6** | **Bf3!!** |

The f-file is now safely blocked (3 Qxf3 Qxf3 4 Rxf3 Bxf6 or 3 g3? Bxf6 or even 3 Rxe7+ Kxf6! 4 Qxf3+ Qxf3 5 Rxf3+ Kxe7 and Black wins).

In fact, White must meet 2 . . . Bf3 with 3 Nxd5 Rxg2+ 4 Qxg2 when Black has a perpetual check with 4 . . . Rxg2+ 5 Kh1 Rf2+.

UNVEILED ATTACKS

A corollary to the sudden closing of lines is the instant opening of others. The human eye and mind can get just as used to certain diagonals and files being closed as they can to their being open. And that leads to surprises in situations like this:

Kuijpers–Jongsma, Amsterdam 1968
White to play

White was lost within two moves. How is that possible?

The position looks like a typical Sicilian Defense middle-game in which White gains the upper hand by way of a standard sacrifice: He puts one of his knights on b5 and after it's captured he retakes with the other knight, followed, after a Black queen retreat, by Nxd6+ or Qxd6. Materially, he may get only two pawns for the piece but experience has shown that it is very difficult for Black to extricate himself. What can be wrong with that?

1 Ndb5?	axb5
2 Nxb5	Nb3+!
White resigns	

The opening of the queenside files (3 axb3 Ra1 mate) doesn't seem possible in the diagram. But it happened.

Seirawan–Kudrin, U.S. Championship 1981

1 c4 Nf6 2 Nc3 e6 3 e4 c5 4 e5 Ng8 5 d4 cxd4
6 Qxd4 Nc6 7 Qe4 d6 8 Nf3 dxe5 9 Nxe5 Bd7
10 Nxd7 Qxd7 11 Bg5 Nf6 12 Qe3 h6 13 Rd1
Qc7 14 Bf4 Qa5 15 Be2 e5? 16 Bf3 Rc8 17 0-0
Bb4 18 Nd5 Bc5 19 Qe2 Kf8 20 Bd2 Qxa2??

Black had a bad game but this removes all doubts. What he has overlooked is the sudden opening of . . .

21 Nxf6 gxf6
22 b4!

. . . the second rank. Now 23 Bxh6+ and 24 Qxa2 is the main threat, and Black had to choose between allowing that and 23 bxc5, e.g., 22 . . . Nxb4 23 Bxb4.

A more elaborate example befell White in this promising position.

Lane–Velikov, Toulouse 1990
White to play

White has a dangerous attack directed at h7, and with 1 Bg5 the threat of 2 Bxf6 and 3 Qxh7 mate virtually forces 1 ... Rfe8. Then 2 Rae1 leaves White with a substantial initiative.

But White thought he had a more immediate trick, based on the same idea of capturing on f6.

1 Rxf6

This looks decisive. All the reasonable Black replies seem to lose:

(a) 1 ... Qxf6 2 Bg5, hitting the queen and threatening 3 Qh7 mate;
(b) 1 ... gxf6 2 Bf4, ditto;
(c) 1 ... Bxa1 2 Bxg7!, threatening mate on both h7 and h8.

But Black has a stunning reply.

    1 ...   **Bf2!**

By unveiling the threat of 2 ... Qxa1+ as well as attacking the queen, Black effectively ends the contest. White didn't bother to play out 2 Qxf2 Qxa1+ 3 Qf1 Qxf6 or 3 ... Qxf1+ 4 Rxf1 gxh6.

THE RETAINED IMAGE

Nikolai Krogius, a Russian grandmaster and psychologist, analyzed in some detail another kind of mental trick that we calculators play on ourselves. Krogius called it the retained image—the retention of certain incorrect, out-of-date information about a position during the course of a calculated sequence.

In some cases our minds will simply not allow us to "see" what is evident.

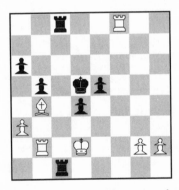

Gallagher–Maier, Swiss Championship 1991
Black to play

Black has some drawing chances if he can eliminate a few more White pawns. With that in mind he tries:

    1 ...   **Rg1??**

And was embarrassed into resignation after:

    2 Rxc8

We can understand the confusion in Black's mind. In the diagram the c1-square is controlled by one Black rook and occupied by another. It is a square White can only dream of occupying some day. So 1 . . . Rg1 threatens not just to win a pawn but to win the b2-rook with 2 . . . Rxg2+.

It never occurred to Black that 2 Rxc8 Rxg2+ 3 Kc1! was possible. He retained the image of a piece still occupying that square.

In the following game White could have resigned after the 14th move because he failed to visualize the sudden appearance of an enemy rook on e2.

Christiansen–Epishin, New York 1990

1 c4 e5   2 Nc3 Nf6   3 g3 Bb4   4 Bg2 0-0 5 e4 Bxc3 6 bxc3 Re8 7 Ne2 c6 8 Qb3 b6 9 0-0 Bb7 10 f4 exf4 11 d3 d5 12 Bxf4 Nbd7 13 exd5?? Rxe2 14 Bf3 Qe7 15 Qd1 Re3 16 dxc6 Rxf3 17 Qxf3 Qc5+

White soon resigned. What did he overlook at move 13? He counted on regaining his sacrificed piece favorably with 14 dxc6—not seeing 14 . . . Rxg2+! until it was too late. In his mind, the rook was still on e8.

Let's move on to an example involving two former world champions:

Spassky–Karpov, Belfort 1988
White to play

White has reason to believe he is close to a win and correctly begins his search for the winning combination. Equally correctly, he comes up with the idea that Black is most vulnerable at g6. He concludes he can mate by sacrificing on that square.

1	Reg4	Re1+
2	Kh2	Rxc1

And here White resigned. He had seen this far, of course. But he was counting on playing 3 Rxg6+ fxg6 4 Qxg6+ Kf8 5 Bxh6+ Rxh6 6 Qg8 mate.

Only when the position after 2 . . . Rxc1 appeared on the board did White realize that 5 Bxh6+ would involve a piece that no longer existed.

Once White played 1 Reg4? in the last example there was no backing out. But more often a player can correct a faulty analysis by rechecking his variations along the way. Black's failure to spot a retained image in the following game cost him dearly.

Ehlvest–Andersson, Brussels 1988

1 e4 c5 2 Nf3 e6 3 d4 cxd4 4 Nxd4 Nc6 5 Nc3
a6 6 Be3 Qc7 7 f4 Nxd4 8 Qxd4 b5 9 Be2 Bb7
10 0-0-0 Rc8 11 Rd2 Nf6 12 Bf3 Be7 13 Rhd1
0-0 14 e5

Here Black thought for a long time trying to choose between two move-orders. He did not intend to retreat the
knight in either case. As an experienced Sicilian Defense
player, Black knew that he should meet e4-e5 with . . . b5-b4.

14 . . .   Bxf3?

The first mistake. If Black plays the correct 14 . . . b4, the
desperado line 15 exf6 bxc3 16 fxe7 cxd2+ 17 Rxd2 Rfe8 offers White nothing (18 Bxb7 Qxb7 19 f5 f6! or 19 Qxd7 Rxe7
20 Qd8+ Re8).

In fact, White's best answer to 14 . . . b4 is 15 Na4, after
which 15 . . . Bxf3 and 16 . . . Nd5 is excellent for Black.

15 gxf3   b4?

This compounds the error. Now was the time for Black to
recheck his previous analysis based on the new position after
15 gxf3. He would likely have noticed that the g-file is now
partly open. And he would have cut his losses by way of 15 . . .
Ne8! 16 Qxd7 Bb4.

16 exf6   bxc3
17 Rg2!

After retreats by bishop (and queen), the easiest move to
overlook is the lateral shift of a rook or queen. Black could have
resigned here (17 . . . Bxf6 18 Qxf6) but continued until . . .

17 . . .   Qb7
18 Rxg7+   Kh8
19 Rg8+!   resigns

White can now capture on e7 with discovered check (19

... Kxg8 20 Rg1+ Kh8 21 fxe7+ or 19 ... Rxg8 20 fxe7+
Rg7 21 Rg1! Qxb2+ 22 Kd1 Qb1+ 23 Bc1 Rg8 24 Rxg7
and wins).

OPTICAL ILLUSIONS

The most humiliating oversights are those, similar to retained
images, that involve surprises such as this:

Zapata–M. Gurevich, Manila 1990
White to play

In time pressure, White saw the idea of a fork on f6 in connection with a capture on d5. So on the final move of the time
control he could have played 1 Nf6+, after which Black would
probably have resigned in view of 2 Nxd5.

But it was White who ended up resigning: He played **1
Qxd5??** first, only then realizing that the knight was pinned
after 1 ... Qxd5. With more time on the clock White would
have rechecked his variation more thoroughly.

Too often we make oversights because we think too logically.
Logic can be a powerful ally in the generation of ideas, the

inspiration stage of calculation. But in the counting out stage and particularly in the rechecking process, it can't be relied on.

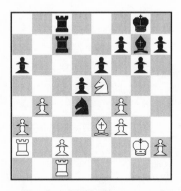

Sherwin–Benko, U.S. Championship 1966
Blacks to play

Black has a better position on the kingside, queenside, and center. He can win easily with 1 . . . Rxc2+, for example (2 Rcxc2 Rxc2+ 3 Rxc2 Nxc2 4 Bc1 Bxe5! 5 fxe5 Ne1+ and 6 . . . Nd3 is a won endgame).

But Black decided that he could shorten the game quite a bit with:

    1 . . .   **Ne2**

Makes excellent sense. Now after the attacked rook moves, Black can capture on c2, he thinks. Isn't it better for Black to have a rook on the seventh rank and threaten all sorts of discovered checks than (as after 1 . . . Rxc2+) to trade off all the rooks?

    2 Re1   **Rxc2??**

Failure to recheck! With 2 . . . Nc3 and 3 . . . Na4 Black is still winning.

    3 Rxe2!

Of course. It was all a mirage, and Black must lose a piece.

IT'S A BIG BOARD

As we mentioned in Chapter Two, players tend to calculate by focusing their attention on grids, that is, on chunks of 16 to 20 squares, rather than the entire board. Usually this is sufficient to understand the key elements of a position. But there are costly exceptions.

Even the greatest players overlook the simplest moves because they don't look at the other side of the board.

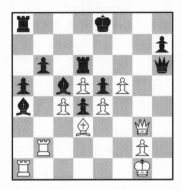

Kasparov–Petrosian, Moscow 1981
White to play

    1 Rxa4??   **Qc1+!**

The future world champion explained that Black's winning move, crossing from one side of the board to the other, "simply escaped my field of vision." He resigned shortly after 2 Kf2 Qxb2+.

Mentally we tend to divide the board into two wings and to assume that matters on one wing cannot normally affect the other. This is what hurt White in the following:

Malaniuk–Hector, Politiken Cup 1992

1 d4 d5   2 c4 c6   3 Nf3 Nf6   4 e3 Bf5   5 cxd5 cxd5   6 Qb3 Qc7   7 Nc3 e6   8 Bd2 Nc6   9 Rc1 a6 10 Ne5 Bd6   11 Nxc6 bxc6

White now saw a forcing four-move combination that seemed to win at least a pawn.

12 Bxa6?	Rxa6!
13 Nb5	Qb8
14 Nxd6+	Qxd6
15 Qb7	

This is the point. The attacked rook cannot retreat or be protected by the nearby queen. But here's what White overlooked at move 12:

15 ...	Bd3!

So simple. White went through the middlegame motions with **16 Qc8+ Qd8   17 Rxc6 0-0** but was already quite lost.

There is no simple remedy for this malady except to remind yourself periodically that there are (at least) two wings on the board. In the last example, White lost "mental sight" of the f5-bishop because of his concentration on the queenside.

A comparable error is to forget that your own pieces can swing from one side to the other.

Short–Piket, Wijk aan Zee 1990
White to play

Black has just captured on a2 in what is shaping up as a traditional battle of wing attacks. Who will break through faster? White on the kingside or Black on the queenside?

The answer should be "White on the queenside!" White played the logical and consistent 1 **Rxh7??** and only drew after 1 **... Bc6 2 Qe2 Rxb3!**.

Afterward, a grandmaster-spectator asked why he didn't play 1 g6. White replied that he rejected the move because the Black knight covers the h6 square and therefore 1 ... hxg6 2 Rh8+ Kg7 was perfectly playable (3 Qh6+?? Nxh6).

No, no, the spectator said. The main point of 1 g6 is to threaten 2 Ra5!, trapping the queen. (Black is, in fact, lost after 1 g6 even after 1 ... Ba4 2 Qd4 or 1 ... Rxb3 2 Qd4).

Summing up, we've found there are several factors that lead us to miss good moves: discounting the strength of retreats, focusing on only part of the board, retaining images of a position that no longer exists, and so on. Aside from being aware of these dangers, there is no simple way of avoiding oversights except this: Recheck *everything*.

Nine

RECHECKING

> *"Mistrust is the most necessary characteristic of the chessplayer."*
>
> —*Siegbert Tarrasch*

E ven after you've worked out the general features of a calculated line, whether two moves deep or 10, and you're certain of the evaluation and move order, you're still not done. In a game of speed chess or a coffee-house game, you might stop there and make your move. But in a more serious situation, such as a tournament game, you should check over your analysis.

There are several methods of verifying your work. The checklist of questions to ask yourself includes:

(1) Am I somehow making a crass error, like mentally making two moves in a row? Or moving a piece illegally?

(2) Am I certain of what the final position looks like? Where are the pieces? Did I make a mistake in visualization? For example, am I still seeing that bishop on b3 in the final position when I've sacrificed it on my second move?

(3) Is there, in fact, a better way of using the basic ideas? Can I improve matters with the insertion of an intermediary move?

(4) In looking for my opponent's weak spot have I over-
    looked my own Achilles' heel, something that will
    short-circuit my intended sequence?

The benefits of rechecking variations should be obvious.
Yet it is shocking how often a player will plunge into a high-
risk variation, even with plenty of time on his clock, after only
a cursory inspection of the main lines, a once-over for the entire tree.

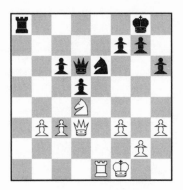

Bernstein–Lasker, St. Petersburg 1914
Black to play

Here is one of the most famous examples of bad rechecking. In what was arguably the greatest tournament held up to
that time, world champion Emanuel Lasker nearly failed to
qualify for the finals because of this game.

With an advantage as Black, he seeks a way to exploit
White's kingside, either with 1 . . . Qh2 or 1 . . . Qg3, followed
in either case by 2 . . . Nf4 or even 2 . . . Qxg2+.

The two queen moves are similar, but not exactly alike. After either one White will probably capture on e6. But 1 . . .
Qg3 2 Nxe6 fxe6 3 Rxe6 Ra1+ would win for Black, and so

would the improved version with the zwischenzug 2 . . . Ra2!.
(White could play 2 Ne2, of course, but then 2 . . . Qh2 is very
strong.)

| 1 . . . | Qh2? |
| 2 Nxe6 | Ra2 |

This threatens mate on g2 and h1. Clearly White has one
reply and clearly Black must have counted on it when he considered the position of the diagram.

| 3 Re2 | Ra1+ |
| 4 Kf2 | |

This move was obvious. Yet Lasker completely missed it.
According to an eyewitness, Siegbert Tarrasch, the world
champion said afterward that he believed somehow White
would now be mated on e1. But there is no mate, and after
4 . . . fxe6   5 Qg6! he had to play the ending a pawn down,
and eventually lost.

WALK-THROUGH

Whether beginning a combination or simply defending a difficult position, before playing a move that requires serious calculation it always pays to walk through the variation mentally
one more time *slowly*. The mind can play all sorts of tricks on
the calculator who rushes.

Mikhail Tal liked to recall how in his first serious match he
rejected a simple defensive idea that would have left him a
rook ahead, and began to analyze instead "a fantastically beau-
tiful" combination. He decided to play it. But after several
moves had been made he "discovered the whole point of my
combination lay in the move Bf8-g5 (!!!).

"And since bishops don't move that way, I had to resign."

Something similar happened to David Bronstein in his most important event when after lengthy thought he came up with "a wonderful combination." But he then passed up both a chance to walk through his analysis—and paid the price. It began when, as Black, he initiated an early queen-side attack:

Botvinnik–Bronstein, World Championship Match 1951

1 d4 e6   2 c4 f5   3 g3 Nf6   4 Bg2 Be7   5 Nc3 0-0
6 d5 Bb4   7 Bd2 e5   8 e3 d6   9 Nge2 a6   10 Qc2 Qe8   11 f3 b5!

This looks like a blunder because of . . .

      12 Qb3!   **Bc5**

Black forges on. He can bail out with 12 . . . Bxc3 13 Nxc3 bxc4 14 Qxc4 Qf7 with a fine game positionally.

      13 cxb5

Now with 13 . . . axb5 14 Nxb5 Qf7!, attacking the d-pawn, Black can obtain a solid initiative for his sacrificed pawn: 15 e4 fxe4 16 fxe4 Ng4 or 15 Nbc3 c6.

But, as Bronstein explained many years later, he had intended a much more elaborate continuation of the sequence he began at move 11. His idea was to allow White to queen a pawn in such a way that the new queen would become trapped and would lead to a Black material edge.

However, once the sequence began Bronstein was afraid to recheck his variations because he might be frightened off by some nonexistent refutation. "How many times has precisely that happened with me!" he added.

13 ...   Bd7?

Black saw that 14 bxa6 Nxa6 was risky; e.g., 15 0-0 f4 16 gxf4 exf4 17 Nxf4 Bxe3+!, winning a piece. So he guessed White's next move.

14 Na4!   Ba7

Black can also cut his losses here with 14 ... axb5 15 Nxc5 dxc5.

15 b6   Bxa4

Black is consistent: On 15 ... cxb6 16 Nxb6 Bxb6 17 Qxb6 Nxd5 18 Qxd6 his situation would be worse than what happens.

16 b7!   Bxb3

A remarkable position. Here Bronstein turned pale and his "head began to spin," he recalled. In his calculations back at the diagram position he had counted on playing . . . Bb6 here, and after White plays bxa8Q, he wins the queen back with . . . Bxd5.

White would then have to give up his second queen and emerge from the complications with only a rook for it. But . . .

17 bxa8Q

. . . it was not Black's turn to play, but White's. Bronstein had blundered into a bad line by mentally making two moves in a row. Play continued:

17 . . .	Bb6
18 axb3	Qb5

And having lost the exchange, Black was in serious trouble. (But he later drew).

A more contemporary example reveals an even stranger aberration.

Hjartarson–Salov, Barcelona 1989
White to play

Black has just played the blunder . . . Rc5, and White knows why it is a blunder. He quickly calculated the winning reply. But then decided on **1 Be2?** instead, realizing his error only when he pushed his clock.

Where is the win? It starts with 1 Bxe5 dxe5, which removes the pawn support for the c5-rook. Then 2 b4! axb4 3 axb4 traps the rook in the middle of the board.

Why did White reject that? Because he convinced himself that the variation failed to 3 . . . cxb3 (that is, en passant) 4 Qxc5 Qa5 with a mating attack. Of course, a thorough review of the variation would have shown him that the en passant capture is not legal.

The reason we make such errors is that often when we calculate we add and subtract moves to the trees very quickly in order to consider the maximum number of candidates. Inevitably, a few things are overlooked. So before choosing a final move, we should take an extra minute to re-examine those trees. Among the questions we should ask are:

WHERE ARE THE PIECES?

Spectators are often surprised by the moves of the greatest players. But virtually everyone, amateur or grandmaster, who watched the eighth game of the 1990 world championship match unfold were struck dumb by this:

Karpov–Kasparov, World Championship 1990
White to play

Anatoly Karpov, with an excellent position—even with mating chances along the h-file—and with thirteen minutes to play nine moves, took three minutes before selecting:

1 Bd2??

When the move appeared on a huge electronic demonstration board, Valery Salov, among others, was sure there had been a mechanical error. "Here I am, a well-known grandmaster, and I couldn't explain to the spectators what White intended to do in answer to 1 . . . Rxd5," he recalled.

There was no answer. Karpov later explained that he had calculated 1 Bf4, with its threat of 2 Be5! and 3 Rh1 mate. He concluded that 1 . . . Bd6 was forced, and then 2 Bd2! would win material (2 . . . Nb7 3 Rxa7; 2 . . . Bc7? 3 Bc3).

Since that might have been a winning position, good calculating technique required White to walk through his line once more and ask about the end-positions: "Where are the pieces?" Had Karpov done this he would have seen **1 . . . Rxd5**, which, luckily for him, led only to a draw, and might have found the improved idea, 1 Bc1! (1 . . . Bf8 2 Bb2 Bg7 3 Bf6!), which might have won.

It's not just bad positions that arise because of costly unchecked mental variations. It's also good positions that *don't* arise because we dismiss them prematurely. When Mikhail Botvinnik was world champion he once overlooked a win that, as one observer put it, "every patzer in the room noticed."

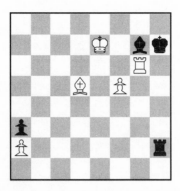

Botvinnik–Gligoric, Hastings 1961-62
White to play

Black has just retreated his bishop from c3. White looked at two natural moves, 1 Kf7 and 1 Rxg7+. The latter looks good because of 1 ... Kxg7 2 f6+ Kg6 3 f7 and the pawn promotes (3 ... Re2+ 4 Be6).

But White studied and studied the position and then played **1 Kf7?** Didn't he see the combination, he was asked later? Yes, he replied, "but in visualizing the position I made a mistake and mentally placed the Black king on g7 instead of g6."

It's embarrassing when you lose sight of pieces in the course of a game. It's humiliating when you do it in print:

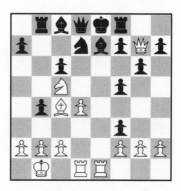

Pkhakadze–Fridinsky, U.S.S.R. 1972
Black to play

This comes from a game analyzed in a Soviet magazine by Black, a master, and also by grandmaster Eduard Gufeld. Their comment at this point was: "If 15 . . . Nxc5 16 dxc5 Qc7, then 17 Rd6! White's initiative is sufficient for a draw.

"For example, 17 . . . fxg2 18 Qxh7 g1Q 19 Bxf7+ Rxf7 20 Qg8+ Rf8 21 Qxg6+ with perpetual check."

That's a long variation, but it's worth trying to visualize it out to the end. Do this in your head and try to think of where all the pieces are. Then play the position out on a board, and you'll see what the annotators missed: There's a Black queen on g1 that can move backward and simply capture that White queen on g6!

That was a long and difficult variation to walk through. But even in short variations—as short as two moves in length—it's wise to take time before initiating a line of play by mentally picturing what the board looks like at the end of your calculations.

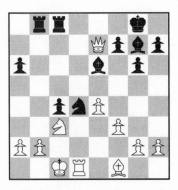

Saidy–Marovic, Malaga 1969
Black to play

Black has sacrificed his queen for rook and bishop, and a bit of an attack. With 1 . . . Nb5, for example, he can obtain considerable long-term counterplay against the king (2 Na4 c3!; 2 Nxb5 axb5 3 a3 Bf8 followed by 4 . . . b4).

But Black's position also suggests he may have something quicker. The tactical idea that has caught his eye is to catch the White king in the corner at a1, where something like a smothered mate can occur after . . . Nc2+.

How to get there? Well, 1 . . . Bh6+ 2 Kb1 Rxb2+ is a start. After 3 Kxb2 Rb8+ 4 Ka1 Nc2 we have the mate. White can avoid this with 4 Ka3 or even with 4 Nb5. But the knight move is too risky because of 4 . . . Bg7! (better than 4 . . . Nxb5 5 Rd8+ or 4 . . . Rxb5+ 5 Kc3!).

Therefore the main line seems to be 1 . . . Bh6+ 2 Kb1 Rxb2+ 3 Kxb2 Rb8+ 4 Ka3. Now there is no . . . Nc2 mate. But Black's tactical eye has spotted the possibility of winning back the queen with . . . Bf8. The immediate 4 . . . Bf8 fails to

5 Qxf8+ and 6 Rxd4, after which Black is a piece down and has nothing left to fuel his attack.

So Black takes one last look. And there it is: After 4 Ka3 he can play 4 . . . Nc6, attacking the enemy queen and removing the knight from capture with a gain of time. Then, regardless of where the queen moves, Black will play 5 . . . Bf8+! and emerge with at least material equality.

1 . . .	Bh6+?!
2 Kb1	Rxb2+?
3 Kxb2	Rb8+
4 Ka3	Nc6
5 Qc5!	Bf8
6 Rd6	

Black completely missed this defense. He missed it because he failed to ask himself where the pieces were after 4 . . . Nc6. Had he asked, he would have seen that the rook was available for blocking the bishop's diagonal

6 . . .	Ne5

Black tries to use tricks to make up for what he failed to do with solid calculation. White avoided 7 Qxe5?? Rb6! and won with **7 f4! Nd3   8 Bxd3 cxd3   9 Qd4 Rc8   10 Kb2 resigns**.

One further example illustrates faulty calculation by both players, but only one is punished. White fails to visualize where his rook and king will be after three moves and allows what should have been a winning fork. But it all works out well in the end.

Beni–Schwarzbach, Vienna 1969
Black to play

Black played **1 . . . Bf6,** not so much to attack the rook as to defend g7. The move also leaves the d-pawn hanging and it must have occurred to White that a trap was being set.

What happens on 2 Rxd6? he asked himself. Black can play 2 . . . Bxc3 3 bxc3 and then what? On 3 . . . Qxc3 Black seems to be both attacking and defending. But he's given up his dark-square bishop, and that suggests some kind of trick such as 4 Bd4! (attacking the queen and g7) Qxf3 5 Rxg7+.

So White continued:

| 2 Rxd6!?! | Bxc3 |
| 3 bxc3 | Qa3+ |

This is what White overlooked. He didn't see that his rook was unprotected at d6, that White's b-pawn was now on b2, and that this now-possible check was a fork.

4 Kb1   Qxd6

End of sad story? No, because even though it was not intended, White has a winning position after all. Black, who almost certainly saw the 4 . . . Qxd6 position when he played 1 . . . Bf6, has made another of our rechecking errors. He stopped too short.

5 Bd4!!

Now g7 can be defended by 5 . . . g6 but then 6 Qh5! is a killer (6 . . . Ne5 7 fxg6 Nxg6 8 Qh6 for example). And 5 . . . Ne5 6 Qg3 or 6 Qg2 is fairly deadly.

Black actually played **5 . . . Qh6** and allowed the wonderful windmill combination **6 Qh3! Qxh3 7 Rxg7+ Kh8 8 Rxf7+ Kg8 9 Rg7+ Kh8 10 Rxd7+** and mate next. (Yes, he overlooked the immediate 10 Rg8 mate).

REMEMBER TO REMEMBER

There's a story about Richard Reti and the day in 1925 he set a new world record in Sao Paolo by playing 29 blindfold games simultaneously. On his way out of the playing site an Argentine fan rushed over to Reti to bring him his beloved portfolio.

"Thank you very much," Reti replied. "I always forget it. I have a terrible memory."

Our ability as players to visualize incredibly complex and lengthy variations—and then forget something relatively simple—is something we have to live with. Often you'll hear this refrain in postmortem: "I saw the combination, but then I forgot what move makes it work."

Sometimes what we overlook isn't even a two-mover.

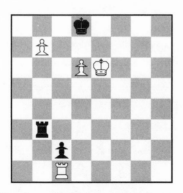

Gunsberg–Tchigorin, Match 1890
Black to play

These two players were world championship challengers, but you wouldn't guess it from the way Black plays here. He sees why 1 . . . Rxb7 can't be played. (Do you?) And the game continued:

1 . . .	Re3+!
2 Kd5	Rb3
3 Kc6	Rc3+!
4 Kb6	Rb3+
5 Kc6	Rc3+
6 Kd5	Rb3
7 Ke6	

And now with *exactly* the same position as in the diagram, Black forgot what he was thinking a few minutes before and plays . . .

7 . . .	Rxb7??
8 Rh1!	

And Black had to resign or be mated.

A more modern example proved just as costly:

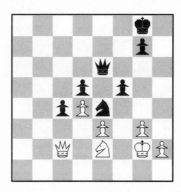

Yusupov–Timman, Candidates Match 1992
Black to play

Here Black found the winning plan 1 . . . Nf6 followed by
2 . . . Ng4—even if White plays 2 Nf4. There followed:

| 1 . . . | Nf6! |
| 2 Nf4 | Qe4+? |

Played after 15 minutes' thought. Black saw that 2 . . . Ng4!
3 Nxe6 Nxe3+ 4 Kf3 Nxc2 is a win (5 Kf4 c3) but simply forgot about it.

You can often forget your original intention when you see an
appealing alternative line, particularly one that seems to win.

3 Qxe4	dxe4
4 Kf2!	Ng4+
5 Ke2	Nxh2
6 Ng6	

But it doesn't win, and after **6 ... c3   7 Ne7+ Kf7
8 Nxf5 Nf1   9 Kd1 Kf6   10 g4 g6** a draw was agreed.

Ideally, we could prevent forgetfulness the way postal players do, by recording our analysis on a sheet of paper. Unfortunately, that is quite illegal in over-the-board play.

A good, *legal* alternative remedy for this and similar calculating maladies is to stop before making the first move of a calculated sequence and explain your train of thought to yourself as if to a stranger. Black, for example, would have said back at the diagram: "Okay, first I'm going to play 1 . . . Nf6, after which 2 . . . Ng4, winning the e-pawn, cannot be prevented. In fact, I can even meet 2 Nf4 with 2 . . . Ng4!"

With this device, it becomes much harder to forget what must be remembered.

GHOSTS

That procedure would also help deal with ghosts, another of the common pitfalls that befall calculators. These are flashbacks to ideas, variations, or other bits of analysis that occurred in the calculator's mind earlier in the game.

Rather than recheck his thoughts, the calculator often relies on past work. In the Tchigorin rook endgame, this would have saved Black. But that's because the position was precisely the same in the diagram as six moves later. In most games positions don't repeat exactly:

Larsen–Smyslov, Hastings 1988-89
White to play

This was the kind of position in which we say White can calculate "without an opponent." He has been slowly improving his position for many moves and decides the time is right for:

| 1 | f5! | exf5 |
| 2 | Qb7?? | Kf7! |

And White can no longer win (3 Qb1 Ke6 4 Qf1 Ra8, etc.).

Afterward White wondered how he could have missed the winning 2 e6!, the necessary prelude to 3 Qb7, which then wins.

He answered the question himself: White had earlier calculated a similar variation with the White queen on c7. Then . . . Kf7 was no defense because the pawn advances to e6 with check. This bit of information remained in his consciousness in a misleading form and he mistakenly believed that Qb7 would be a winning move as soon as Black played . . . exf5.

Here's a more elaborate example.

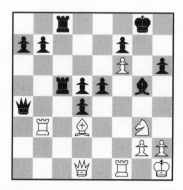

Silman–Root, Los Angeles 1990
White to play

In this complex, sacrificial position, White played:
    1 h4!
. . . which was based on 1 . . . Bxh4 2 Qg4+ Kf8 3 Qg7+ Ke8
4 Rxb7 and wins.

What happens if Black blocks with 2 . . . Bg5, you may wonder? Then White counted on penetrating to h7 with 3 Qf5 e4
4 Nxe4!. For example, 4 . . . dxe4 5 Qxe4 Kf8 6 Qh7 Bxf6 7
Rxb7! and wins (7 . . . Qe8 8 Rxf6 Rc1+ 9 Bf1).

But, as Silman commented later, this last variation "actually contributed to my defeat since I soon tried to reconstruct
it in a completely different situation." Amid deepening time
pressure, play continued:

1 ...	Rc1
2 Qf3	e4

And now the relatively simple 3 Qg4 and 4 hxg5 must win, as White intended when he played 2 Qf3. But as Silman recalled in *Inside Chess*:

"After Black played . . . e4 I stared at the clock and saw that I had a couple of minutes left. I looked at the board and my brain went dead. . . . Panic! . . . Then I remembered . . ."

3 Nxe4??

White recalled only the key idea in the 1 h4 Bxh4 variation. This "ghost" cost him the game:

3 . . .	dxe4
4 Qxe4	Rxf1+
5 Kh2	Bf4+

White resigned as soon as the time control was reached: **6 Kh3 Qd7+ 7 g4 Rh1+! 8 Qxh1 Qe6 9 Rxb7 Qe3+.**

Throughout this book you've been confronted with diagrams showing complicated positions, and it probably took you a good deal of time to recognize the key elements in each new position. But if you had been playing the game in question, you could have reached certain conclusions much faster.

That is because you would have visualized the diagram position, or an approximation of it, earlier in the game and made certain assumptions about it. For example, you might have concluded previously that such a position is very favorable to you, that you should try to trade queens if given the opportunity, that your first positional priority is creating a passed c-pawn, and so on.

Those assumptions stay with you and may become unwelcome ghosts. So when making a major decision in a game it always pays to question your assumptions. Let's see how:

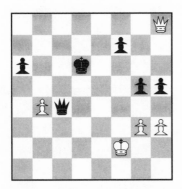

Alekhine–Kashdan, Bled 1931
Black to play

Facing the world champion, a young American master (Black) used his extra pawn brilliantly:

       1 ...   g4!!

The point was revealed after . . .

       2 Qxh5   Qd4+

Now White sees that after 3 Kg2 Black can exchange queens and win: 3 . . . Qd2+ 4 Kg1 Qe3+ 5 Kh2 Qf2+ 6 Kh1 Qf1+ 7 Kh2 Qxh3+! 8 Qxh3 gxh3 9 Kxh3 and now 9 . . . Kd5 10 Kg4 Kc4 11 Kg5 Kxb4 12 Kf6 a5 13 Kxf7 a4 14 g4 a3 15 g5 a2 and queens.

Play continued:

3 Ke2 Qe4+   4 Kd1 Qd3+   5 Kc1 Qf1+   6 Kd2 Qg2+   7 Kd1 Qf1+   8 Kd2 gxh3   9 Qc5+ Ke6 10 Qc8+ Kf6   11 Ke3 Qe1+   12 Kf3 Qe6   13 Qc3+ Kg6   14 g4

Black can nurse his passed pawn home with careful but simple play: 14 . . . Qd5+ 15 Kg3 Qg2+ 16 Kh4 h2 and there is no perpetual check (17 Qd3+ Kg7 18 Qc3+ f6! 19 Qc7+ Kg6).

298 / THE INNER GAME OF CHESS

But Black now suffers a delusion. He believes he can get the same kind of king-and-pawn endgame that would have won for him in the 3 Kg2 variation mentioned above. After all, 14 ... Qf6+ forces queens off the board and brings the Black king closer to the queenside, whereas White's king will have to spend time winning the h-pawn before it can go after the f-pawn.

14 ...	**Qf6+?**
15 Qxf6+	**Kxf6**

What he should have done at move 14 is visualize this position and ask himself: "Does my a-pawn still win the race against the g-pawn?"

The answer would have been: "No! I'm two tempi behind the other variation."

16 Kg3	**Ke5**
17 Kxh3	**Kd4**
18 Kh4	

And here Black saw nothing better than to accept White's draw offer. He had become yet another victim of a ghost.

LASKER'S LAW

One of the easiest ways to improve your tournament results is to learn to sit on your hands.

Kharitonov–Dautov, Kaliningrad 1986
Black to play

White has sacrificed a piece to develop a virulent attack along the g-file (Rag1 and Rxg7+). Defensive measures such as 1 . . . Bf6 2 exf6 offer little hope of salvation. Black tries a different tactic: confusion.

       1 . . .   **g5!?**

Clearly hoping for something like 2 fxg5?? Ng6, clogging the attacking lanes. But there can't be anything wrong with 2 Qxh4, can there?

       2 Qxh4?

What's wrong with this seemingly obvious move is that there was a much better one.

       2 . . .   **g4!**
       3 f3   **Qh7**
       4 Qxh7+?!   **Kxh7**

And after **5 fxg4 fxg4 6 Rxg4 Nf5** Black had survived the worst and had real drawing chances.

But after 1 . . . g5 the game would likely have ended within five moves, not 20, if White had continued 2 Rag1!. For ex-

ample, 2 . . . g4 3 Rxg4+! fxg4 4 Rxg4+ or 2 . . . Ng6 3 Rxg5!
Bxg5 4 Rxg5, winning the queen in either case.

White failed to heed Emanuel Lasker's sage advice: When
you see a good move, don't make it immediately. Look for a
better one.

There's a logical basis for this. Winning moves do not come
about because of the brilliance of the players but because of
the soundness of their position. A powerful position can generate more than one tactical idea. And often that idea can be
improved a bit.

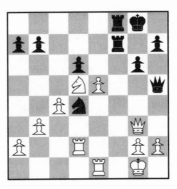

Panno–Bravo, Fortaleza 1975
Black to play

It's Black's move and he surely must see 1 . . . Ne2+. The
fork of king and queen forces 2 Rdxe2 after which 2 . . . Qxe2!
appears to win the exchange (3 Rxe2?? Rf1 mate).

But there are two things wrong with this picture. Laszlo
Szabo, the Hungarian grandmaster, recalled that he began to
improve his calculation when he reminded himself of this
motto: After you're finished calculating, calculate one move
further.

Following Szabo's advice, we look at the position after 2 . . . Qxe2. Since Black is threatening 3 . . . Rf1+, we should be looking for something forceful by White. That suggests a check: 3 Ne7+ works if Black takes the knight (3 . . . Rxe7?? 4 Rxe2) but not if he finds 3 . . . Kh8!. On the other hand, there is 3 Nf6+!, which forces 3 . . . Rxf6 4 exf6 when Black has lost his material and positional advantages.

But if we apply Lasker's Law, we succeed in finding a better move: It's **1 . . . Qe2!**, which forced immediate resignation. Black threatens 2 . . . Qxd2 as well as 2 . . . Rf1+ or 2 . . . Qf1+. And 2 Rdxe2 Nxe2+ 3 Rxe2 Rf1 is mate, or 2 Rdd1 Qxd1 3 Rxd1 Ne2+, etc., while 3 Kh1 Nxg3+ 4 hxg3 loses the exchange.

The superior move you should look for need not be the first one of a sequence but may come two or three moves later. For instance, in the following diagram the potential tactical idea should occur readily: It's the last rank.

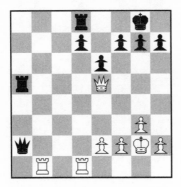

Crouch–Speelman, Hastings 1992-93
White to play

Once White sees that idea, several candidate moves occur to him, including 1 Rxd7, 1 Qc7, 1 Rb8, and even 1 Qb8 (1 ... Rxb8?? 2 Rxb8 mate). They all appear to be easily met by 1 ... Raa8. So, White, who is a pawn behind, regained his material with **1 Rxd7** and then drew after **1 ... Rf8!** and **2 Rb2 Rxe5**.

But there is a win, and the method is 1 Rb8 Raa8 and now 2 Ra1!!, since 2 ... Qxa1 3 Rxd8+ Rxd8 4 Qxa1 costs a queen, as does 2 ... Rdxb8 3 Rxa2 (3 ... Rxa2?? 4 Qxb8 mate).

In the next example the move to find is actually a spectacular third move in the sequence. At first, White sees that with 1 Ne6+ Bxe6 2 Qxd3 he can trade off Black's pesky knight and get closer to an ending. But in that ending his exchange may be no better than Black's pawns.

Portisch–Forintos, Hungarian Championship 1971
White to play

A further look shows him that 1 Qxd3(!) Bxd3 2 Ne6+ and 3 Nxc5 reaches another endgame but one that doesn't seem nearly as good. Before abandoning this position, White employs Lasker's Law at the third move.

1 Qxd3!	Bxd3
2 Ne6+	Kh6

Forced, since other king moves permit 3 Rf8 mate.

3 g4!!

A terrific finesse. By creating the threat of 4 Rh3 mate White forces . . .

3 . . .	g5
4 Rf6+	Bg6
5 Nxc5!	

Now we have a much superior endgame to the ones considered back at the diagram. After **5 . . . dxc5 6 Rxb5** Black has only a pawn for the exchange, and he eventually lost.

A graphic example of grasped—and missed—opportunities like this was the following. Set this one up on a board and consider all the calculating mistakes:

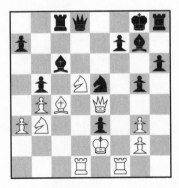

Bronstein–Shcherbakov, London 1992
White to play

White has sacrificed two pawns to place his rooks and two
minor pieces on superior squares. Black's last move (. . . b5)
appears to refute the attack, but White finds:

    1 Nd4   **bxc4**

    2 Nf5!

White's original intention was likely 2 Nxc6 Rxc6 3 Nf6+,
but it would not have taken him long to see that 2 . . . Qxf6 3
Rxf6 Bxf6 is a winning material edge for Black.

But after 2 Nf5 White threatens two good knight checks on
e7, and the Black queen has no easy escape (2 . . . Qe8 3 Nd6
and then 3 . . . Qe6 4 Nxc8 Bxd5 5 Rxd5 Qxc8 6 Rxe5 with
unclear results).

    2 . . .   **Bxd5**

    3 Rxd5   **Qc7??**

In time trouble, Black misses his chance to transpose into
the last note with 3 . . . Qe8 4 Nd6 Qe6, and should now lose.

    4 Rc5!   **Qd7!**

    5 Rxc8+?

This wins a rook (5 . . . Qxc8 6 Ne7+) but it is not the best. By following Lasker's Law White would have found the superior interpolation 5 Rd1!, after which 5 . . . Qe8 6 Rxc8 Qxc8 7 Ne7+ or 5 . . . Qe6 6 Rxc8+ Bf8 7 Rxf8+! Kxf8 8 Rd8+ wins easily.

| 5 ... | Bf8! |

Now, with a material edge but a far from clear position, White's best is 6 Rxf8+! Kxf8 7 Qa8+! Qe8 8 Qxa7 and 9 Qc5+ with a nearly winning position. But again White played a good-looking, second-best move.

6 Rxf8+!	Kxf8
7 Qxe5??	Qd3+!
8 Kf3	Qxf1+

And now White should have conceded a draw, which was still available via 9 Ke4! Qd3+ 10 Kf3 because 10 . . . e2+ 11 Kg4 h5+ 12 Kh3 wins for White(!).

But he actually played **9 Kg4??** and was lost after **9 . . . Qd1+ 10 Kh3 Qh5+ 11 Nh4 g4+!** and **12 . . . Qxe5**.

IMPROVING THE BREED

Often a sequence can be improved by the insertion of an intermediary move at its very start. An illustration is this opening trap: 1 e4 c5 2 Nf3 d6 3 d4 cxd4 4 Nxd4 Nf6 5 Nc3 g6 6 f4 Bg7 7 e5 dxe5 8 fxe5 Nd5? 9 Bb5+! Kf8 10 0-0 Bxe5.

A Soviet opening manual several years ago claimed that White wins with 11 Nxd5 Qxd5 12 Nf5 with the idea 12 . . . Qxd1 13 Bh6+ Bg7 14 Raxd1 and a winning attack.

However, after 12 . . . Qc5+ 13 Be3 Qc7 14 Nh6 Black can defend with 14 . . . Be6!.

Russian amateurs then tried to save the analysis by examining 14 Bh6+ (instead of 14 Nh6) Kg8 15 Nxe7+ Qxe7 16 Rxf7!? with immense complications.

But, as so often happens, the easiest way to improve a sequence lies at the beginning, not at the end. Here it is quite simple: White plays 11 Bh6+! first. Black cannot interpose (11 . . . Bg7 12 Bxg7+ Kxg7 13 Nxd5 Qxd5? 14 Nf5+). Therefore 11 . . . Kg8 follows, and then White can begin his sequence in improved form: 12 Nxd5 Qxd5 13 Nf5! Qc5+ (forced) 14 Be3 Qc7.

We now have the same position as in the opening manual but with one significant difference: The Black king is on g8 instead of f8. White exploits this difference with 15 Nh6, which is now a decisive check.

Or you can improve a variation with a tempo-gaining move that pushes your opponent's pieces onto bad squares:

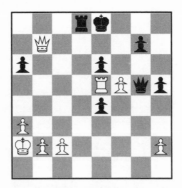

Kasparov–Kamsky, Linares 1993
White to play

At first it seems that White's choice is between 1 Rxe6+ and 1 fxe6. The former is the most forcing, but after 1 . . . Kf8 the only reasonable followup—2 f6, threatening 3 Qe7+—allows 2 . . . Qd5+ and a trade of queens.

The pawn capture also has a major point, since 1 fxe6 Qxe5?? allows mate on f7. Clearly, White stands well after 1 . . . Qe7 2 Qc6+ and 3 Rxh5. But does he have better?

He does with one minor addition:

    1 h4!

Black could have resigned here since the queen now has no way of watching both e7 and d5. The game ended with:

1 . . .	**Qxh4**
2 Rxe6+	**Kf8**
3 f6	**resigns**

Because 4 Qxg7 mate as well as 4 Qe7+ are threatened.

So far we've examined forcing moves inserted at the beginning or middle of a sequence. But often the move that improves a sequence is exceptionally quiet:

Serper–Predzhikh, European Junior Championship 1990

1 c4 g6　2 Nc3 c5　3 g3 Bg7　4 Bg2 Nc6　5 a3 a6
6 Rb1 Rb8　7 b4 cxb4　8 axb4 b5　9 cxb5 axb5
10 Nf3 e5　11 d4!? exd4　12 Nd5 Nge7　13 Bg5 Bb7

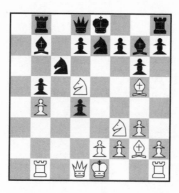

Here White went into a long think about what he called the "natural" combination 14 Nxd4 Bxd4 15 Qxd4! Nxd4 16 Nf6+ Kf8 17 Bh6 mate! (It's natural because it works in a lot of similar opening traps.)

On further inspection, though, he questioned his assumption that Black must play 14 . . . Bxd4. What, he wondered, do I do on 14 . . . Nxd4! and then 15 Bxe7 Qxe7! 16 Nxe7 Bxg2 17 Rg1 Be4. The knight on e7 is lost and the rook on b1 has nowhere to go (18 Rb2 Kxe7? 19 Rd2 but 18 . . . Ne6 19 Rd2 Bc3).

So White decided that the best combination in the position was none of the above.

> **14 0-0!**

Whatever Black does now will result in a White edge.

> **14 . . .**   0-0
> **15 Nxd4!**   f6

Or 15 . . . Bxd4 16 Nxe7+ Nxe7 17 Qxd4 with a positionally won game. As the game proceeded, White's edge was clear following **16 Bf4 Ne5   17 Nxb5 Nxd5   18 Bxd5+** and he won in seven more moves.

The slight but decisive improvement of a sequence was a prime feature in one of the finest combinations played in the early twentieth century:

Breyer–Esser, Budapest 1917

1 d4 d5 2 c4 c6 3 e3 Nf6 4 Nc3 e6 5 Bd3 Bd6
6 f4 0-0 7 Nf3 dxc4 8 Bb1?! b5 9 e4 Be7
10 Ng5 h6 11 h4!? g6 12 e5 hxg5 13 hxg5 Nd5

White has a strong attack for his sacked knight. The natural followup is to get the queen to the h-file (at h8 or h7) as soon as possible. Gyula Breyer, one of Hungary's greatest chess talents, saw that 14 Qg4 virtually forces 14 . . . Kg7 (with the idea of 15 . . . Rh8).

Then White can begin a long but forcing sequence: 15 Rh7+! Kxh7 16 Qh5+ Kg7 17 Qh6+ Kg8 18 Bxg6! fxg6 19 Qxg6+ Kh8 20 Qh6+ Kg8 21 g6 looks very strong. In checking over his sequences, however, Breyer noticed the flaw. At the very end, Black has the defense 21 . . . Bh4+ and 22 . . . Qe7!, covering the h7 mating square.

But before giving up on this wonderful sequence, White began to appreciate how bound up Black is. Black's only defensive idea is 14 . . . Kg7 (and 15 . . . Rh8). And that can be met by 15 Rh7+ Kxh7 16 Qh5+, transposing into the line given above. So, he looked for an improvement on 14 Qg4.

14 Kf1!!

An amazing move. The threat is 15 Qg4, as we'll see.

14 . . .   Nxc3

As brilliant as White's play is from move 16 on, he can win more quickly with 15 Qg4 and then 15 . . . Qxd4 16 bxc3 Qxc3 17 Ke2! followed by Qh4. But Breyer remains true to his original idea.

15 bxc3   Bb7?

Hopeless, in retrospect. Black should start giving material back with 15 . . . f5! 16 gxf6 Bxf6.

16 Qg4   Kg7
17 Rh7+!

Now the sequence works because of White's 14th move. Play continued 17 . . . Kxh7 (17 . . . Kg8 18 Qh4) 18 Qh5+ Kg8 19 Bxg6 fxg6 (19 . . . Re8 20 Qh7+ and mates) 20 Qxg6+ Kh8 21 Qh6+ Kg8 22 g6.

Now since there is no saving . . . Bh4+, Black has to accept the consequences of 22 . . . Rf7 23 gxf7+ Kxf7 24 Qh5+ Kg7 25 f5!. He lost after 25 . . . exf5 26 Bh6+ Kh7 27 Bg5+ Kg8 28 Qg6+ , but even faster would have been 27 e6!.

In endgame such gains of time are often not significant. In fact, many endgame positions can be improved by the loss, rather than the gain, of a tempo. For example:

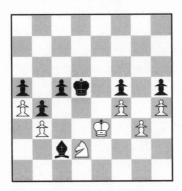

Karpov–Anand, Linares 1991
Black to play

Clearly Black has a big advantage, close to decisive. But he needs a passed pawn or an entry for his king to win. Obvious moves yield nothing here so Black must try to work with the ideas in the position.

What are they? Well, one is the mock sacrifice . . . c5-c4. The other is the serious sacrifice . . . Bxb3. Black probably considered the pawn sack first, with a main line such as 1 . . . c4 2 Nxc4 (2 bxc4+? Kc5 and 3 . . . Bxa4) Bxb3 3 Nxa5 Bxa4 and Black has excellent winning chances.

He probably also examined the flashy 1 . . . Bxb3?! 2 Nxb3 c5 3 Nxa5 b3 before rejecting it as either unsound or unclear.

But then he found the best move, a tiny but very significant improvement on both ideas:

$$1 \ldots \qquad \text{Bd1!!}$$

White can resign here. He clearly cannot move the knight, since 2 Nc4 Bxb3 3 Nxa5 Bxa4 gives Black a pawn more than in the 1 . . . c4 tree.

And king moves are terrible. On 2 Kf2 Kd4 and 3 . . . Kc3, Black wins as he pleases. What is more important is that 2 Kd3 now loses—thanks to White's loss of tempo—to 2 . . . Bxb3! and 3 Nxb3 c4+. Black's little finesse saved him a lot of work.

Once you learn to sit on your hands you'll realize how often you used to play second-best moves that looked fine at the time. Or, as in the following, even third-best.

Lautier–Christiansen, Biel 1991
Black to play

Despite the material equality, Black is in very poor shape and would be close to losing after, say, 1 . . . Bf6 2 Re8. So Black goes in for . . .

1 ...   **Bxg3!?**

White no doubt considered the natural 2 fxg3 Rxg3+ 3 Kf1 Qh1+ 4 Ke2 and may have concluded that he had good chances.

2 Re8

Good enough. Black got a few checks—**2 ... Qh2+ 3 Kf1 Qh1+ 4 Ke2**—and resigned a short time after **4 ... Rxe8 5 Qxe8+ Kg7 6 Bd4+ Kh6 7 Qe6+**.

But if White saw enough to realize that 2 ... Qh2+ was not a serious threat, he should have looked further and found 2 Bg5!, which would have ended the game almost immediately (2 ... Qxg5 3 Qxh7 mate; 2 ... Qh2+ 3 Kf1 Qh3+ 4 Ke2 Qg4+ 5 f3).

One final example, a full game in which White repeatedly passes up one candidate move for a slightly improved one:

Shirov–Hauchard, Paris 1990

1 d4 Nf6   2 c4 c5   3 d5 b5   4 cxb5 a6   5 b6 d6 6 Nc3 Nbd7   7 a4 Qxb6   8 a5 Qc7   9 e4 g6   10 f4 Bg7   11 Bc4 0-0   12 Nf3 Re8   13 0-0 e5   14 dxe6 fxe6   15 Ng5 Nf8   16 f5 h6

White can safely offer a piece here with 17 fxg6 hxg5 18 Bxg5 threatening 19 Bxf6. Then 18 ... N8d7 19 Nd5 (or the more adventurous 19 Qf3) is more than enough compensation for White.

But in rechecking 17 fxg6 White probably saw 17 ... Nxg6! and if 18 e5 then 18 ... Nxe5 with no problems for Black. So ...

17 e5!	dxe5

On 17 . . . hxg5 White has 18 exf6 Bxf6 19 Nd5!, and if 19 . . . exd5 20 Bxd5+ forks king and rook.

18 fxg6!	hxg5

Now we see the improvement provided by his 17th move. If Black tries the 18 . . . Nxg6 idea now, he finds it fails to 19 Rxf6! Bxf6 20 Qh5 and a Ne4 move (20 . . . Qg7 21 Nge4 Bg5 22 Nxg5 hxg5 23 Bd3! and White wins).

As the game goes, White again can win material (20 Nd5) but plays for more.

19 Bxg5	N8d7
20 Qf3!?	Ra7
21 Rad1	Qb7
22 Qh3	Qc6

Now White sees another opportunity employing the same Nd5 idea that has been in the position since move 17. He would like to play 23 Nd5 exd5 24 Bxd5+ Qxd5 25 Rxd5 "and wins."

But this is a false end-position. The real one is 25 . . . Nb6!, after which it is not at all clear that White is winning. So White improves again on a sequence.

| 23 Nd5! | exd5 |
| 24 Rxd5! | |

This is based on 24 . . . Nb6 25 Rd7+! and now 25 . . . Nfd5
26 Qh7 is mate. The most complex line is 25 . . . Nxc4 26
Rxf6! Qxf6! 27 Qh7+ Kf8 28 Rxa7!! (better than 28 Bxf6
Rxd7) and White wins.

| 24 . . . | Kf8 |
| 25 Qh7 | Re6! |

Otherwise 26 Rxd7! or 26 Bh6! wins quickly.

26 Bh6	Ke8
27 Qxg7	Nxd5
28 Qh8+	Ke7

One more finesse. White would love to finish with 29 g7
and queen next move. But 29 . . . Rxh6 30 g8Q Rxh8 is unclear enough for White to ask if he has yet another improvement on an idea.

| 29 g7 | Rxh6 |
| 30 Rf7+! | |

And by finding a forcing method White convinced Black
to give up after **30 . . . Kxf7   31 g8Q+ Ke7   32 Qd8+**
because it is mate next move.

ACHILLES' HEEL

Even when you have rechecked a variation using all of the previous procedures there are times when one final precaution is
useful. If you are considering a forcing line in which you hold
the initiative, stop: Stop calculating in terms of moves and
think in general terms about your own vulnerability.

If you had to put it into words, what is the worst thing you
could say about your position tactically?

Popovych–Kavalek, U.S. Championship 1972
White to play

White has sacrificed the exchange to establish the dangerous pawn at f6 and the Qh6-g7 mating idea. He wants to play
1 Qh6 but that allows 1 . . . Qxf6.

1 Nh4??

With 1 Nd2 White accomplishes pretty much the same
thing (uncovering rook protection of f6, safeguarding g2)
and enables himself to play Ne4 in key lines such as 1 . . .
Kh8 2 Qh6 Rg8 3 Ne4 Qa8 and now the quiet move 4 h3!
prepares Rf3 followed by Ng5 and mates (e.g., 4 . . . Qf8 5
Ng5!!).

But White is too optimistic. He doesn't want to allow 1 Nd2
Rxd2 with equal material.

1 . . .   Rfa8!

Only now does White realize that his first rank is just as vulnerable as his g2-square. On 2 Qh6 Black has 2 . . . Qxf6! 3
Rxf6 Ra1+ and mates. With the knight on d2 White would
have been able to play 4 Rf1.

2 Qxe5   Rf2!

Again exploiting the weakness White failed to appreciate. Now 3 Rxf2 Ra1+ again mates. White played **3 Kg1 Rxf1+ 4 Kxf1** but the handwriting (4 ... Re8 5 Qb2 Qd6) was on the wall.

One of the psychological causes of this kind of mistake is that we recognize only the ways in which our position will improve as a result of our intended move and blot out the ways in which it may be compromised.

Ubilava–Serper, Manila 1992
White to play

White appreciates that he has at least a slight edge, but to prove this he must either break the blockade on squares such as f5 or find a way to use his own outpost at e5 effectively. He finds the correct way to begin:

1 g4!   **hxg4**

Here 2 Nxg4! would be strong; e.g., 2 ... Rfe6 3 Be5+ Kf7 4 Nh6+ or 3 ... Kh7 4 Nf6+ (or 2 ... Rxe1+ 3 Rxe1 Rf7 4 Be5+ Kf8 5 Qf4 and Nh6).

But White sees something more appealing. After 2 hxg4 Black appears to be completely lost, because 3 Bh6+ meets any knight move.

    2 hxg4??   **Rh8!**

It probably never occurred to White when considering the position in the diagram that he could be mated on h1, because at that point his king was shielded by pawns at g2, h3, and h5.

    3 Nf3   **Rh3!**
    4 Nh2   **Ng3**

White was so shaken by his oversight that he missed his best defensive chances (5 Qxg3! Rxg3+ 6 Bxg3) and fell apart immediately with **5 Qf3? Rxf4!**. He resigned after **6 Re7+ Rf7 7 Rxf7+ Qxf7 8 Qg2 Ne2+! 9 Qxe2 Rg3+**.

As a rule of thumb, when a candidate move appears as decisive as 2 hxg4, it calls for the utmost rechecking. That's the hallmark of the practical calculator, as we'll see in the final chapter.

Ten

THE PRACTICAL CALCULATOR

> "He was a pitiful sight to behold. Over and over
> he calculated and recalculated the variations, and
> couldn't understand how I could save myself. Of
> course he couldn't—he was looking for something
> that wasn't there."
>
> —Anatoly Karpov on a Candidates Match game he man-
> aged to draw from a lost position against Lev Polugayevsky

Among the crucial questions you face in every game is how much you must calculate. Or, rather, *when* you must calculate, and when it's simply not worth it.

There are two distinctly different points of view here. The perfectionists believe you should always try to find the best move because otherwise you settle for too many second-rate choices that let superior positions slip into draws and even positions deteriorate into losses.

The pragmatists, on the other hand, believe that the search for the best move is worthwhile only a few times a game because only then is there a *significant* difference between best and second best. And even when there is an objectively "best" move, sometimes it takes too much effort to find it.

Neither side is completely right. Let's see what happens in a classic struggle between a perfectionist and a pragmatist:

Karpov–Korchnoi, Candidates Match 1974

1 e4 e5   2 Nf3 Nf6   3 Nxe5 d6   4 Nf3 Nxe4   5 d4
d5   6 Bd3 Be7   7 0-0 Nc6   8 Re1 Bg4   9 c3 f5
10 Qb3 0-0   11 Nbd2 Kh8   12 h3 Bh5   13 Qxb7
Rf6   14 Qb3

Viktor Korchnoi had already spent 39 minutes on his 11th
move and now went off on another enormous—and to spectator Alexander Kotov "incomprehensible"—thinking binge.
By the time he had decided on his next move Black had only
10 minutes of his original two and a half hours left, and shortly
after that only seconds to reach the time control at move 40.

"What is the reason for Korchnoi's record irrational ex-
penditure of time?," Kotov asked. "Obviously the first impres-
sion is the desire of the creative mind to work out the details
of the position.

"However, in this particular case, this is the decisive error.
It should be noticed that the variations that arise are so numerous that this task is out of the question."

Remember, these words are coming from an outspoken ad-
vocate of deep calculation. But here Kotov was quite right.
The game continued 14 ... Rg6   15 Be2 Bh4?   16 Rf1
Bxf3   17 Nxf3 Bxf2+?   18 Rxf2 Nxf2   19 Kxf2 Qd6
20 Ng5! (a move Black either overlooked or vastly underestimated) Rf8   21 Qa3. When he forfeited on time at move
31 Black had been lost for several moves.

One obvious conclusion to draw from this is that it's wrong
to spend a lot of time and then make bad moves. But it can
also be wrong to invest time lavishly on the *best* moves. Here's
a corollary game, Kavalek–Toth, Haifa 1976:

It followed the same moves as Karpov–Korchnoi until White varied with **9 c4.** There followed **9 ... Nf6   10 cxd5 Qxd5!?   11 Nc3 Bxf3   12 Nxd5 Bxd1**.

Here White sank into thought. He quickly saw there were only two candidates to consider seriously, 13 Nxe7 and 13 Nxc7+. The only other move to avoid losing a piece, 13 Nxf6+, leaves Black a safe pawn ahead after 13 ... gxf6 14 Rxd1 Nxd4 15 Bc4 Ne6 or 15 Be4 0-0-0!.

White first looked at the natural 13 Nxe7 Nxe7 14 Rxd1 and concluded that after 14 ... Nfd5 15 Bc4 he had a small edge because of his two bishops. Looking a bit further, he could see no clear plan after 15 Bc4. So he turned to his second candidate. Let's trace his thoughts:

>**13 Nxc7+!**   **Kd7**
>**14 Bf4**

To decide on his 13th move, White needed to calculate 14 ... Nh5 in great depth because if the bishop retreats, he remains way behind materially.

Anticipating 14 . . . Nh5, he considered the candidates 15 d5 and 15 Bf5+. He gave up on the former because of 15 . . . Nd4 16 Be5 and now 16 . . . Bc2!, saving the bishop.

But White found that 15 Bf5+ Kd8 16 Be5 was good (16 . . . f6 17 Nxa8 fxe5 18 Raxd1 exd4 19 Be4 Bf6 and now 20 b4!). This was one of many points that had to go into the decision to play 13 Nxc7+.

14 . . .	Bg4
15 d5	Nd4
16 Nxa8	Rxa8

White also invested some time back at the diagram considering what would happen on 16 . . . Bd6!?. He concluded he could take advantage of Black's centralized knight with 17 Be3! Bf5 18 Bf1 and then 18 . . . Nc2 19 Bb5+ and Bxa7, returning the exchange but holding a material edge.

17 Be5	Bf5
18 Bf1!	

After finding this fine move in his analysis at move 13, White was confident of gaining the advantage (18 . . . Bc5 19 Rad1 Nc2 20 Bb5+ Ke7 21 d6+ Kf8 22 Re2, for example).

Black actually played **18 . . . Nc2** and more material was whisked off the board: **19 Bb5+ Kd8 20 d6 Nxe1 21 Rxe1! Be6** (21 . . . Bf8?? 22 Bxf6+ and 23 Re8 mate) **22 dxe7+ Kxe7 23 Bd4**.

This is one of the many end-positions White examined at move 13. Other end-positions in his mind went at least 10(!) moves further. White has the two bishops and so Black's queenside pawns will remain vulnerable for some time.

But that's not the entire story. To calculate this morass of tree limbs White spent 90 minutes in selecting his 13th move. He felt exhausted but confident that his analysis was absolutely correct when he chose 13 Nxc7+. And he was correct in his analysis.

But the decision to work it out to the end-position was disastrous. White quickly found himself in severe time trouble, began to make second-best moves, and soon lost control: **23 ... b6   24 a4   g6   25 a5   bxa5   26 Ra1   a6 27 Be2   Rd8   28 Bc3   Nd5   29 Bd4   Nb4   30 Bc5+ Ke8   31 Bd1   Rd2!   32 Ba4+   Bd7   33 Re1+   Kd8 34 Bb6+   Kc8   35 Rc1+   Kb7   36 Bxd7   Kxb6!.**

White resigned on the 52nd move.

What should White have done on move 13? The practical calculator would have seen quickly that neither 13 Nxc7+ nor 13 Nxe7 leads to a decisive advantage. So he would have to choose between two moves that lead at best to modest edges. This would have forced him to budget his time.

White would start with the quieter and easier line: Once he had concluded that 13 Nxe7 leads to a small but certain edge he would know that no matter what he found in 13 Nxc7+ he would have a very playable fallback. At that point he would have allowed himself a reasonable amount of time to gauge 13 Nxc7+.

But once White saw that 14 . . . Nh5 and 16 . . . Bd6 had to be calculated out to a safe degree of certainty, he would have to come to a decision. Either he would give up on 13 Nxc7+ at that point—because sufficient certainty would be almost impossible to achieve. (We saw Aron Nimzovich reason this way in his game with Tartakower in Chapter Six.) Or as Mikhail Tal often did, he would get the gist of several possibilities and play 13 Nxc7+, taking the risk that his intuition about his resources in the later tree limbs would pan out.

"Enough wasted time!" Nimzovich once commented after spending 25 minutes calculating a subvariation that never occurred. "The game of chess is a struggle. Not a mathematical exercise," he said.

And just because you can control your impulse to calculate doesn't mean you won't win a pretty game nevertheless.

Szabo–Böök, Saltsjobaden 1948

1 Nf3 d5   2 g3 Nf6   3 Bg2 e6   4 0-0 Be7   5 c4 0-0
6 d4 c6   7 Nc3 b6?   8 Ne5 Ba6   9 cxd5 cxd5
10 Bf4 Nfd7?

White had reason to believe that Black had erred at least once so far, and this encouraged him to consider a sacrifice on d5. He saw that 11 Nxd5 exd5 needed a better followup than 12 Bxd5 Nxe5. So he searched and found 12 Nxf7!? Rxf7 13 Bxd5, after which 13 . . . Nc6 14 Bxc6 looks good.

But then he saw that 14 . . . Rxf4 or 14 . . . Nf6 15 Bxa8 Qxa8 had to be carefully rechecked. (Are the evaluations correct? Are these true end-positions? Are there zwischenzugs?)

White concluded it would take just too much calculation to be certain. Instead, he played the routine **11 Rc1**. But this did not deny him the chance for brilliancy.

In fact, he won with an even prettier combination: **11 . . . Nxe5   12 Bxe5 b5 13 e4! b4 14 Ne2 Qa5   15 exd5 exd5   16 Nf4! Bxf1**. Here he rejected the two candidate captures on d5 in favor of **17 Qg4! g6   18 Bxd5** and, with the threat of 19 Nxg6 hxg6 20 Qxg6 mate, won in a few moves.

The practical calculator knows that once an idea arises in a game, particularly one with a blocked center, it is likely to remain for several moves. He doesn't have to leap into complications by using the idea the first time he notices it:

Short–Ljubojevic, Amsterdam 1991
White to play

After several moves of preparation on opposite wings, both players have by now noticed a key idea here: the possibility of a White breakthrough along the h-file with Nh7!?, which threatens Nf6 or Bh6+.

White examined the immediate 1 Nh7 here with the continuation 1 . . . Rxh7 2 Rxh7+ Kxh7 3 Rh1+ Kg8 4 Bg5. This looked strong; only 4 . . . f6 held out defensive hope. Furthermore, he saw that 5 exf6 Bf8 and now 6 Qe3 followed by Rh4 and Qh3 was very dangerous. But he also saw that after 6 . . . Rb7! the sacrifice begun by 1 Nh7 was far from clear.

1 Bf4!?

So he makes the practical choice. The Nh7 idea isn't going away.

1 . . .	Rbf8
2 Qe3	Qd8
3 Nh7!	

Now is the time to pull the trigger. Black threatened to solidify the kingside with 3 . . . Rxh1 4 Rxh1 Rh8.

3 . . .	Rxh7
4 Rxh7+	Kxh7
5 Rh1+	Kg8
6 Qh3	Bh4
7 Bh6!	

Better than 7 g5 Kg7! and Black defends with 8 . . . Rh8. The text threatens 8 f4 and 9 Bg5, and after **7 . . . g5 8 f4** White soon had a winning position.

WHEN YOU MUST CALCULATE

There are, of course, occasions when you *must* calculate, when the price of not examining variations in detail is just prohibitive. The trick is recognizing these occasions.

The simplest rule here may seem obvious: You must calculate when you suspect there is a move available that forces a concrete result. (As opposed to the solid but relatively small advantage White obtained in Kavalek–Toth.)

You must think twice when these concrete opportunities arise because you may not get a second chance. Naturally, there are three kinds of concrete results, a win, a draw, and a loss. The one we should be most pleased to calculate should be a win:

Shirov–Kir. Georgiev, Manila 1992
White to play

White has more material and the safer king, and here he decides to go for the knockout. His last move was Qb4 and it isn't hard to see that 1 Qf8 contains numerous threats and bears all the appearances of a winning move.

1 Qf8??   Rxe5!

If it were as good as it looked, it would have ended the game in a few moves. When you have a move that looks that strong, take the natural precaution of spending a little extra time to make sure. Avoid a lot of extra, unnecessary calculation that will get you into time pressure. If 1 Qf8 really was a knockout, there would have been no further time pressure.

As it turned out, White, already short on time, blundered again (3 Kh1 would have drawn) and lost with:

2	dxe5	Qd4+
3	Kh2??	Qxe5
4	g3	Qb2+
5	Kg1	Qxc1+

White resigns

The same rule applies to drawable positions, such as when you are offered a draw or when you can deliver perpetual check or exchange queens down to a dead-drawn endgame. When you have a forced draw, that is precisely the moment to take as much time as necessary to recheck.

Yusupov–Ljubojevic, Bugojno 1986
Black to play

1 ...	g4!
2 Bxg4	Qh1+
3 Ng1	Qg2+
4 Ke2	Qe4+

Here White sees that his king cannot escape via 5 Kd2 because of 5 . . . Bg5+ 6 f4 Qe3+ 7 Kc2 Be4+. So . . .

| 5 Kf1 | Qg2+ |

If Black had any winning hopes he would play 5 . . . Qxg4. Now the onus is on White. But is it an onus? He sees that 6 Ke2 virtually forces 5 . . . Qe4+ with an almost certain draw by repetition.

6 Ke1??

A particularly impractical decision. White had only two minutes for more than 10 moves to reach the time control, and this is precisely the type of position that you don't want to play with so little time. And if you can't calculate with accuracy and thereby find something *better* than a draw, you must play 6 Ke2.

6 ...	Qxg1+
7 Ke2	d3+!

This is probably what White overlooked (counting instead on 7 . . . Qg2? 8 Rxd4!). The game ended with **8 Kxd3 Qxf2 9 Rc7 Qxb2 10 Rd2 Qb6 11 Rxb7 Qxb7 12 Qb4 Qc6 13 Ke2 Bc3** and **White resigned**.

And, of course, there is a third possible result in a game: a loss. When you see your hand about to make a move that you know is going to lose, you must search for alternatives.

You say, "Nobody makes moves they *know* will lose"? But experienced players will tell you it happens. In fact, they will tell you it has happened to them.

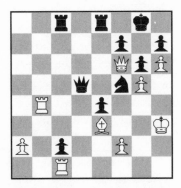

Suba–Conquest, London 1991
White to play

In mutual time pressure, White found:
  1 Bd4
And a paralyzed Black responded:

1 ...	Qxd4??
2 Rxd4	Rc3+
3 Kg2	Rd3
4 Rc4	e3
5 R1xc2	resigns

Now that the time control has been reached, Black has the first opportunity in some moves to recognize how lost he is. But it must have been obvious at the diagram that 1 . . . Qxd4?? was a losing move. In situations like this the practical calculator must look for an alternative. If it doesn't exist—and you forfeit on time—then it won't cost you anything.

But if defense does exist (such as 1 . . . Kf8! 2 Qh8+ Ke7 3 Qf6+ Kf8 here) then your search will have paid off. In fact, if White had then repeated the position (4 Qh8+) Black would have good reason to play for a win (4 . . . Ke7 5 Qf6+ Kd7!?).

GETTING FANCY

These last three examples present extreme, though hardly unique, situations. They occur in almost every game: You see an apparently decisive move and have no time to decide whether to play it or not.

But compare that with the following:

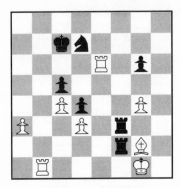

Benko–Dominguez, Las Palmas 1972
White to play

White has an extra pawn and can add the exchange with 1 Bxf3. He was not in time trouble. But he begins to wonder how difficult it would be to win the ending after 1 Bxf3 Rxf3 (2 Kg2 Rxd3 3 a4? Ra3 or 3 Ra1 Rc3).

So he searches for something better. And he finds:

    1 Rb7+??   **Kxb7**

    2 Re2

Very cute. Now 2 . . . Rxe2 3 Bxf3+ leads to a won bishop-vs.-knight endgame because Black is forced to tie a piece down to halt the a-pawn. But instead Black finds:

    2 . . .   **Rxg2+!**

And White, having made what he called "my traditional Rook-oversight," resigned.

White's blunder was understandable. There is a natural human desire to polish off a well-played game with some sparkling move or dramatic gesture. But it's better to make sure of the full point by calculating accurately.

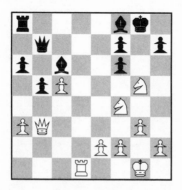

Yusupov–Ljubojevic, Linares 1990
White to play

This position is the result of a fine combination begun four moves before when White sacrificed a knight for a pawn on e6. Now White continued:

1 Nf3

A simple move that deserves no comment and that led to other simple moves and victory in less than 10 moves: **1 ...
Bxc5   2 Nh5   Bxf3   3 exf3   Qc6   4 Kg2   Bxf2
5 Qb2!**.

But White admitted afterward that he was strongly tempted to finish in the style of his previous play, with 1 Nge6. But after examining 1 . . . fxe6 2 Qxe6+ Kh8 3 Qxf6+ Kg8! he didn't see anything for White. Rather than search further for a thematic continuation, White opted for the less pretty—as he put it, "definitely saner"—retreat.

BEWARE UNDERSTANDABLE MOVES

When you were beginning to play chess you learned that you should try to figure out the point of your opponent's last move: Did he threaten something? Did he anticipate a threat of yours?

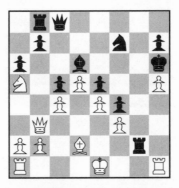

Anand–Timman, Linares 1991
White to play

You still perform this task today—at least you should—although it is by now so routine that you may not do it consciously.

Here, out of a sharp opening, the position has clarified a bit and both sides have good practical chances. White now played:

>1 Qc3

With plenty of time on his clock and some quite reasonable candidates (1 . . . Qd8, 1 . . . Qh8), Black responded:

>1 . . .   Qd7??

. . . which cost him the game. He hadn't performed the elementary beginner's task of asking himself what was the point of his opponent's last move. Had he done so he would instantly have seen:

>2 Bxf4+   resigns

Sometimes a move by your opponent may be so subtle it doesn't seem worth considering.

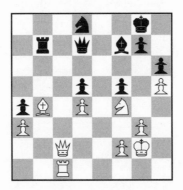

Vasiukov–Popovic, Vrsac 1989
White to play

1 Kg1!

Black apparently misread this move as a useless "pass." In fact, he himself should now pass with something like 1 . . . Ra7, maintaining control of his second rank.

1 . . .   Ne6?

2 Qxf5

Were the king still on g2, Black could respond 2 . . . Nxf4 (with check) 3 Qxf4 Bxh5.

2 . . .   Nxf4

3 Rc8+!

This was the second thing Black overlooked. After **3 . . . Be8   4 Qxd7 Rxd7   5 Rxe8+** he resigned since he will be a piece down.

There is a trap we create for ourselves when we incorrectly guess the reason for an opponent's last move. We think it contains the positional threats A and B, when in fact the main threat, C, is a mate in one.

"One should be wary of easily understandable moves," warned Richard Reti.

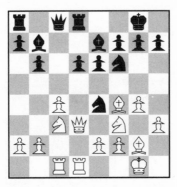

Bareev–Karpov, Tilburg 1991
Black to play

White's pieces are clearly more actively placed. Black chose:

    1 ...   **Nxc3**

White may have thought to himself: "This makes sense. He's probably afraid of 2 g5 and then if 2 . . . Nxc3 I have 3 gxf6 Nxd1 4 fxe7, winning material. He also captures on c3 so he can gain time, such as with 2 Qxc3 Ne4. So I'll play a bit differently, with 2 Rxc3, and if 2 . . . Ne4, then 3 Rc2 so I can later double rooks."

All very logical. However:

    2 Rxc3?   **e5!**

The point of Black's first move was not so obvious. He now wins a piece because of the coming pawn fork on e4. The pin 3 Qe3 exf4 4 Qxe7 fails to 4 . . . Rd7!, trapping the queen. And **3 g5 Nh5   4 Bc1 e4**, as the game went, was hopeless.

And one should also be wary of obviously bad moves:

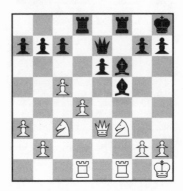

Fridjonsson–McKay, Stockholm 1969
Black to play

      1 ...   **Bc2**

This is the type of time-loser that beginners play. It attacks a rook that can go to a useful square, d2, and later White will be able to double rooks. But White should know that in a world junior championship, which is what this event was, there are no beginners.

      2 Rd2?   **Bg5!**
      resigns

White evidently had so little faith in his opponent's skill he assumed he would play such a move as bad-looking as 1 . . . Bc2. The flip side of this error is . . .

BELIEVING HIM

Players have to have trust in chess: They must believe in their own calculations. Korchnoi once said that another veteran grandmaster, Yefim Geller, was a good attacker "but he calculates variations badly." Geller, he said, "wastes a lot of time, and often does not believe himself."

You know players like Geller: They check and recheck their variations, and then play something entirely different because they don't trust their own analysis. But in competitive chess there is another question: Should you trust your *opponent?*

This matter received widespread attention after a game in the 1965 Candidates Match between Mikhail Tal and Bent Larsen. With the score tied, it began **1 e4 Nf6   2 e5 Nd5 3 d4 d6   4 Nf3 dxe5   5 Nxe5** and now the Dane played **5 ... Nd7!?**.

This was apparently a new move, and it was sufficiently rare to intrigue Tal. His instinct instantly led him to a tactical idea. He later wrote that had it been a simultaneous exhibition, he would have played 6 Nxf7 Kxf7 7 Qh5+, after which Black's king must step into a dangerous center to protect the knight.

But then Tal began to wonder why such a worthy opponent as Larsen, in an opening he had obviously prepared, would allow such a dangerous idea. At this point it was his natural intuition ("The sacrifice must be sound!") fighting his competitive doubt ("He couldn't have overlooked this, could he?").

Tal decided to resolve the matter by calculating everything out to mate if possible. After spending 50 minutes he concluded it wasn't possible and played **6 Bc4**, after which **6 ... e6** led to a balanced, double-edged game and an eventual draw.

Tal's decision provoked years of second-guessing by annotators who tried to show that the sacrifice would have won and that he had been the victim of a psychological trick: He trusted his opponent, and his opponent was bluffing.

Here is the opposite side of the coin.

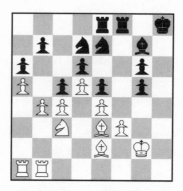

Karpov–Spassky, Candidates Match 1974
Black to play

In this difficult position Black tried:

   1 ...   Nf5!

With 11 moves to go before the time control, White examined 2 exf5 and saw that the most likely candidate reply was 2 ... e4. Was it a sound knight sacrifice?

Karpov took the practical approach: It might be sound or it might not be, but in the time remaining it would be difficult, if not impossible, to reach a definite conclusion. Also, he probably reasoned, a definite conclusion is not necessary because I have a perfectly good alternative that I can clearly see leads to an advantage. Since 2 exf5 e4 fails the test of leading to a concrete result, the pragmatic Karpov responded:

   2 Bxg5!

Played after only four minutes' thought. Now 2 ... Bh6 runs into 3 exf5 Bxg5 4 Ne4, with a large edge.

2 . . .	Nd4
3 bxc5	Nxc5
4 Rb6	

And White won without risk.

This is the dilemma of believing your opponent: If you insist on calling your opponent's bluff you had better calculate everything correctly. If you take his word, your alternative had better be good.

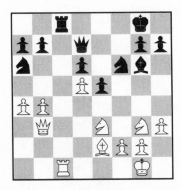

Kasparov–Larsen, Bugojno 1982
White to play

The dangers of bluff-calling are illustrated by the following:
     1 Rc6!
A splendid move—for psychological reasons. It contains a threat to win a pawn (2 Bxa6) and also the minor positional threat of 2 Bg4 Nxg4 3 Rxc8+ and 4 hxg4 reaching an endgame with superior minor pieces.

But the greatest effect of 1 Rc6 is to drive Black, a player known for his stubbornness, into using up 20 of his remaining

25 minutes. Instead of the quiet retreat of the knight to c7 or b8 he plays:

1 . . .	bxc6?
2 dxc6+	Qf7
3 Bc4	

This much Black had to expect. Now the calculations of both players were realized on the board:

3 . . .	d5
4 Nxd5	Kh8
5 Nb6!	Qc7
6 Nxc8	Qxc8

Black saw this far and assumed that 7 Bxa6 Qxa6 would follow.

7 b5!	Nc5
8 Qa3	

The knight must move and the c-pawn will advance after 8 . . . Qf8 9 c7 Nfd7 10 Be6 or 8 . . . Nce4 9 Qe7 Nxg3 and now 10 fxg3, winning in either case. The game was shortened a bit when Black's flag soon fell.

Toward the end of a time control, major decisions like Black's 1 . . . bxc6 are made. One of the psychological traps you can set for yourself is to say, "Well, I've already spent 15 minutes on this and I haven't come to any firm conclusion. But if I decline the sacrifice, then what have I got to show for those 15 minutes?"

The same trap often occurs when you're offered a draw in time trouble and, after lengthy thought, feel compelled to accept because you've taken so much time that continuing the game would be too risky. On the other hand, you can calculate a lot and decline the risks—and still make a losing move:

Dolmatov–Speelman, Hastings 1989-90

1 e4 c6   2 d4 d5   3 exd5 cxd5   4 c4 Nf6   5 Nc3 e6
6 Nf3 Bb4   7 Bd3 dxc4   8 Bxc4 0-0   9 0-0 Nbd7
10 Bg5 Bxc3   11 bxc3 Qc7   12 Bd3 Qxc3   13 Rc1
Qa5   14 Ne5 Nxe5   15 Rc5 Qa3   16 dxe5! Qxc5
17 Bxf6

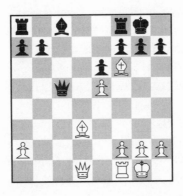

Black has enough extra material—and also enough king-side dangers—to believe that his next move will determine whether the game ends in a win, a draw, or a loss. He must also deal with the immediate threat of 18 Bxh7+ Kxh7 19 Qh5+ Kg8 20 Qg5 g6 21 Qh6 and mates.

After considerable thought he decides to clear a square for his queen to defend g7.

| 17 ... | Re8? |

Black made two mistakes here.

The first is concluding that the bishop can't be taken. The natural line is: 17 . . . gxf6 18 Qg4+ Kh8 19 exf6? Rg8 20 Qh4.

While Black was thinking about his 17th move White rechecked his intended sequence (20 . . . Rg6 21 Bxg6 fxg6 22

Qh6) and suddenly realized that Black can improve substantially with 20 . . . h5! and probably win.

White, in fact, had decided that if the sacrifice was accepted he would continue 18 Qg4+ Kh8 19 Qh4! f5 20 Qf6+ Kg8 and then draw by perpetual checks on g5 and f6.

Black, in his calculations back at the diagram, saw the possibility of a draw but also felt that the position after 20 . . . Kg8 left him too passive. If White could improve at move 21 he might very well win, he felt. For example, Black saw the idea of 21 Re1 followed by 22 Re3 and 23 Rg3+.

Actually, Black is probably quite secure after giving back material with 21 . . . b6 22 Re3 Qxe3! 23 fxe3 Bb7 since White has no way of adding fuel to his attack.

18 Bxh7+!

This is Black's other mistake. The attack is much stronger now (18 . . . Kf8 19 Qg4 gxf6 20 exf6 and mates).

18 . . .   Kxh7
19 Qh5+

This was good enough to win after **19 . . . Kg8   20 Qg5 Qf8   21 Rd1 b6   22 Rd4 Ba6   23 Rg4** and Black kept matters going with **23 . . .   Be2! 24 Bxg7 Bxg4 25 Bxf8+ Kxf8**. Black conceded on move 68.

But White failed to apply Lasker's Law: With 19 Qd3+! Kg8 20 Qg3 Qf8 (not 20 . . . g6 21 Qh3 and mates) 21 Rd1 we get the same kind of position as in the game but it's a bit better after 21 . . . b6 22 Rd4 Ba6 23 Rg4 and Rxg7+ (or 23 . . . g6 24 Rxg6+) with mate following.

SUMMING UP

As we've seen, a chess game can go wrong in many ways. But it can also go right in many ways. There are, in fact, many different—and equally successful—methods of calculating.

Some calculators scan a wide range of candidate moves, while others intuitively examine only one and usually end up playing it. Some players decide on sacrifices only after examining 10-move, multi-branched trees while others develop a sense that allows them to be confident about a sacrifice's success after considering only a few variations. Some try to reach a clear judgment about every tree. Others avoid lengthy, perfectionist searches and rechecking of variations, believing that quick, second-best moves are more practical than time-consuming, optimum moves.

The goal of every calculator should be to find the method most comfortable—and successful—for them. Calculation should be the key that unlocks the inner game of chess, and each person's key is different.

Index